EAGLES' FUN

EAGLES' FUN

A Fun collection of Wild and Wacky Short
Stories Featuring the Eagles Cribbers

Pup

authorHOUSE®

AuthorHouse™
1663 Liberty Drive
Bloomington, IN 47403
www.authorhouse.com
Phone: 1-800-839-8640

First published by AuthorHouse   11/23/2011

ISBN: 978-1-4685-0864-2 (sc)
ISBN: 978-1-4685-0865-9 (ebk)

Printed in the United States of America

Any people depicted in stock imagery provided by Thinkstock are models, and such images are being used for illustrative purposes only.
Certain stock imagery © Thinkstock.

This book is printed on acid-free paper.

Contents

HOSPITAL FUN

CHAPTER I

In the1930s, very few small towns in rural America could boast of having a hospital. Getting to a hospital could mean a trip of several hundred miles or so on two-lane, sometime unpaved roads. Time consuming, and very expensive for people in a country that was emerging from a great depression. This story will take place in a small town with a new hospital, and a rather large one for the size of the town. At this point in time, life expectancy for American men was 59 years, and an American woman could look forward to about 61 years.

Case's Hospital in Eagletown had been in operation for a few years now. Eagletown had three physicians, all working from and in the hospital. House calls were the norm in those days, simply because people who were sick waited in hopes of healing instead of going to the Doctor. Many rural doctors were up all hours of the night attending the sick. One such was Dr. Tammy, an obstetrician, who had spanked almost every young bottom in the Eagletown area, most birthed in their own homes.

Dr, Bill was an internist, and had practiced in Eagletown for many years. It was largely through his perseverance (and a bit of luck) that Eagletown had this nice spacious hospital. Bill was a very skilled surgeon, and almost ten years ago, in his office, on a primitive operating table, he had performed a perfect emergency operation on a ruptured appendix belonging to a very wealthy patient. Mr. Case was a pioneer industrialist in farm equipment and had largely financed the hospital.

Dr. Chrissie was new to Eagletown. Two years out of internship. she had opted for the rural life, and had, through correspondence with Dr. Tammy, established residence here. Chrissie hardly ever left the hospital during the daylight hours. Chrissie was a capable physician, and ruled the hospital with an iron hand. Dr. Chrissie was a little "short" on tact, and had a complete lack of "bedside manner". If you came to her dying, she would just pick up the phone and call Chris, the local mortician for you.

In the chain of command, so to speak, Head Nurses Ros and Monica ruled the two floors during the daytime and Head Nurse Karen had the entire operation at night Their off days were filled by Head Nurse Lilly, who usually worked the night shift.

It was the hot midsummer of 1934. Case's Hospital owned three automobiles All three were black 4-door Ford Model A's. Dependable vehicles, and roomy enough to "sub" for an ambulance in those days. Dr. Bill was in his office removing the cast from the well-mended leg of a local farmer named Marc. Dr. Chrissie was at the nurse's station with Monica, the head nurse on the lower floor. She was mad at Pup, the orderly, over something, and she told him to go outside and water the lawn and shrubs. Chrissie was kind of bossy, and it bothered her that she got very ittle respect from Monica. Monica was a good nurse, though, and she knew and performed her job well. Monica politely said it was almost lunch time, and she needed Pup to wheel the food to the patients. Dr, Chrissy glared and went to the second floor.

Head Nurse Ros was a beauty. By her own assertion, she was the most beautiful woman in Eagletown, and after four drinks, in the world. Chrissie found her tending to Mike, who owned the saloon in Eagletown. Mike had a bad case of gout, and had been admitted by Dr. Tammy, after having been diagnosed with high uric acid retention. He had been on a diet of water, strawberries and watermelon for three days. Mike was hot, he was cranky, his right lower leg and foot were killing him, and he wanted a steak and beer. The second floor orderly, Bonnie, was holding his foot in a tub of warm salt water and Ros was spoon-feeding him some strawberries. Vitamin C and its many benefits had been newly discovered, and it seemed beneficial for gout patients. Dr. Chrissie assisted with getting Mike settled, Ros administered two Anacin tablets, and they went to the nurse's station.

There were two other patients on the second floor. Gaet, who operated the Eagletown stable and blacksmith shop had an intestinal disorder of some kind. Bill had ran some tests under the microscope and isolated some bacteria. They were waiting for the results from the university on those, and a bland diet and rest was all that Gaet was prescribed at this time. Bill wanted him to remain hospitalized because of the possibility of contagion.

The third patient on the second floor was Deni. Dr. Tammy's patient, she had a terrible case of tonsilitis, and Tammy was treating the swelling, trying to get it down so Bill could remove them. Deni was one of the town's biggest gossips. She knew everything there was to know about everyone, and her revelations about the townspeople were starting to get on everyone's nerves.

Dr. Chrissie went over the patient's charts on the second floor and then went to her office downstairs. Everything seemed in order. Pup was wheeling the dirty food trays to the kitchen, and Bill had left on a house call. Case's had eighteen beds and had never been full, With a low patient load, they just put everyone in a private room.

The first floor had four patients, one to be released later in the day. Doo, who played the piano and sang at the saloon, was in 101 with the worst case of painful laryngitis Dr. Chrissy had ever seen. Doo couldn't even make a good croak, and it was chronic. It just wouldn't go away.

Lisa, an attractive, loquacious young lady who worked for Anneke at the bank was in room 107, She had had a severe case of summer flu, and would probably be released tomorrow. Monica was counting the hours for that. Lisa was ambulatory, and never shut up. She was all over the ward, and would go in and pester Doo with incessant chatter, knowing that Doo couldn't answer her, and it infuriated Doo.

Marianne was in room 104, and she was a blonde goddess. (not as pretty as Ros, of course). She worked for Lena at the mercantile store, and had an urinary problem. Sulfa drugs were very new to medicine but Case's had been able to acquire some, and Marianne had responded well to them. Bill was to release her later today. Monica would miss Marianne, a model patient, and Pup adored the ground she walked on.

Room 105 was next to the nursing station, where they placed patients who required a lot of care. Dawn, in room 105 was really a psychiatric case. She had fallen, taken a nasty whack on the head, and was a bit slow in getting "it' back. Physically, she was healthy as a horse, and that was the problem. She was hard to handle, and she wanted out of the hospital, or thought she did. It was about 4pm and Dawn was raising hell for some tea. It was the same thing almost every day. She would become a different personality. Well-educated, and with a brilliant mind, she had many personalities to draw from. Dawn never even drank tea. Today she thought she was a British lady, or somethng, and had to have tea. Yesterday she had been a pirate and was all over the hospital trying to get everyone to "walk the plank". Medicine wasn't ready for Dawn yet.

Marianne had left the hospital that evening just about the time Lilly came on duty. Karen had the night off, and would probably found at at the saloon. She was a two-fisted drinker, a two-fisted fighter, and the best pool player around. Around 11pm, all was quiet in the wards, and the phone rang. It was Dr. Tammie telling her a patient was enroute to the hospital, and she (Tammie) would be there to assist admitting him. Dan, who worked for the city at the cemetery and Chris at the mortuary, had gotten into a swarm of bees, and was in pretty bad shape. Lilly had her night orderly, Paul, ready room 104, vacated earlier and near her station. The bees had hit Dan pretty hard. His vital signs were good, though, and Tammy had given him a morphine injection. They got his bites painted with iodine, worked some unguentine into them, and he was fairly comfortable.

Lisa, ever curious, had gotten up and was giving a lot of advice. Dawn had also awakened and was trying to brush her hair, using her rather large hand-held round brush. The brush apparently set her off. She was suddenly everywhere using the brush as a magnifying glass, checking everyone for "clues", and making professional sounding remarks to an imaginary "Dr. Watson".

CHAPTER II

The five-member hospital board consisted of the three physicians, Lena, a merchant, and Rose, a city council member They were meeting to finalize the hiring of three badly needed nurses-aides. Eagletown was growing, as were neighboring towns, and the hospital was getting to be too much for the existing personnel. they had agreed to hire Nece, an attractive young woman who had no formal training but had scored exceptionally well on the aptitude tests The next applicant approved was Mariska, a, pretty peppy young lady with some formal training in medicine. The third hiree was Georgia, an older very capable woman with previous experience in a large city hospital.

All three wanted to work with Ros, of course, and through a drawn-out process, the Board decided to rotate the three at this time. Their vacancies (days off, vacations, etc.) would go unfilled until they felt they could hire a fourth aide. Nece was assigned to Monica as the first floor was usually the busiest, and she would gain valuable experience sooner. Mariska went to Ros, and the more experienced Georgia's first three-months would be with Karen at night.

Dr. Chrissie probably had the most medical expertise of the three physicians as she had gone to medical school much later, and simply had had more to learn. Bill and Tammy had had to keep up as best they could through medical journals. Dr. Chrissie had "pushed' for an X-Ray machine, which had been ordered and should arrive soon.

Dr. Chrissie had been particularly interested in Dawn's case. She felt Dawn had a form of recurrent amnesia, and little was known about it at this time. Physically, Dawn was fine, and was herself usually until in the afternoons when something would cause her to assume another personality. When Dr. Tammy told her about the hair brush and the ensuing Sherlock Holmes caper, something rang a bell.

Doo had miraculously regained her vocal powers, and was busy catching up on lost talk as she was discharged. Lisa was back at the bank, Dan was still recovering from his bites, and Gaet's lab results should be in today. Deni was scheduled for surgery tomorrow morning, and Mike still wasn't responding well. Ros thought maybe someone was sneaking him hamburgers, but she could find no evidence of it.

Pup had just finished dumping and cleaning the bedpans when they admitted his friend, Nina.

Her back had gone out on her and she was in extreme pain, unable to even walk unassisted. Nina was placed in a wheelchair and taken to the second floor. Dr. Chrissie and Ros gave her some Anacin and got her in bed and as comfortable as possible. Nina owned and operated Eagletown's only clothes—cleaning establishment. In those days there was a lot of dry-cleaning to be done. Mariska brought her in a pitcher of ice water, and they chatted for a few moments.

Downstairs, Monica was frantic. Dawn was missing. She had both Pup and Nece looking for her, and she was nowhere to be found. There was the sudden sound of a siren, and Don, the police chief, pulled into the emergency entrance with Dawn, who was fine. He had found her in the intersection of Pogo and Main with a whistle, directing traffic. She was a traffic cop today, Monica called off the hunt and gave Dawn a shrimp cocktail. Dawn loved shrimp.

The business office was on the main floor, rear, behind Monica's station. A roomy, pleasant office, good view of the grounds, and occupied by Doug, an accountant. Doug was a sort of handsome, well-liked, friendly fellow, and in those days, he got what he could from the patients. The entire country was in dire straits for money yet, and Doug was good enough to keep the hospital in the black. Payday was every Friday. Doug usually had the paychecks handed out by noon, and Anneke and Lisa at the bank usually had them cashed two hours later. Doug always had Pup pick him up a large cherry-coke at Katie's soda fountain on the way back from the bank, as he loved them. A nice quiet routine, really.

Dr. Tammy had been at the hospital almost all day. She and Dr. Chrissie had devised a brace for Nina to wear, and it seemed to help. Dr. Chrissie prescribed something for sleep at night until further notice, and requested warm packs to the affected area every 4 hours or so.

Dr. Bill pulled into the emergency area about 7pm that night and he and Karen and Georgia admitted Ken, who was doubled up with abdominal pain. Bill had Karen administer morphine immediately, as he was sure Ken had a dislodged stone. Ken had moved to Eagletown some years ago and had opened Eagletown Lanes, their 6-lane bowling establishment. They placed Ken in room 101 and settled him for the night. Bill hoped the morphine would cause the stone to pass.

The following afternoon Bonnie was finishing up a few chores and noticed Dawn out on the lawn. Pup or Nece was usually with her, but she seemed alone. She had a waste basket upside down over her head, one arm across her chest, and seemed to be giving orders with the other arm. Pup got to her first, and she told him, "The British are coming. The British are coming." She was either George Washington or Paul Revere all afternoon, fighting the British.

The hospital was unusually busy today, Deni's tonsils and adenoids had been successfully removed, her temperature was normal, and she would be released in a few days. She was detained mostly for post—operative pain. Gaet was going to be fine. He had a slight droop in the left eyelid where a bee had apparently severed a nerve. Ken's stone had passed and he'd be released tomorrow. Mike was finally responding to his diet, and was happily sitting up in his room, enjoying a cigar.

The hospital was filling up, patients coming and going. Despite the activity, When Dr. Chrissie heard of the "Revolutionary War" fought by Dawn she decided to put her plan into action the following day. Discussing it with Monica, they agreed it was a logical solution, and just might work.

That afternoon, Mariska proudly had the Nurse's station all by herself for the first time. Ros had entered a beauty pageant (which she eventually won, of course) and had taken several days off. Mariska was at her desk going over charts and she had decided to check on a few patients and take some temperature readings when she heard a loud tapping on the counter above her head. She looked up, seeing it was Dawn. Looking very serious, Dawn told Mariska, "Quoth the raven, nevermore". Mariska sighed, and taking Dawn by the arm took her downstairs, turning her over to Monica. Dawn was now muttering something about "the lost Lenore" and "dark and dreary". Monica gave Edgar Allen a sedative and put her in bed.

The next morning Dr. Chrissie and Moni had their plans laid, and all hospital personnel were put on alert to notify a nurse's station at the first sign of Dawn being something other than Dawn. Monica had sent Pup to the Eagletown Emporium, Lena's store, to pick up an item for her. It was about 2:30 pm when Bonnie was approached by Dawn. Dawn had a large paper bag, and was reaching in to give Bonnie something. "Ho! Ho! Ho!", Dawn cried, and gave Bonnie a napkin she'd swiped from the cafeteria. Bonnie and Mariska grabbed her and steered her to the first floor station where "Santa" was soon "Ho Ho Ho"-ing and passing out napkins. Dr. Chrissie came over and gave "Santa" a nice gift. It was a very large and pretty hand mirror, and she held it right to Dawn's face. Dawn looked into the mirror, and in a matter of seconds was no longer Santa. She was herself, Dawn!

It had worked! Whatever triggered Dawn's subconscious mind had usually been in the afternoons. The Doctor had figured that Dawn was always fine for several hours after arising because she saw her own image in the large mirror in the bathroom every morning. It would wear off in several hours and Dawn would see or find something that would trigger her subconscious, and she would change entities. The mirror had brought her back to normal.

Dawn was pronounced medically cured and released four days later. Nina was fine in a few days. Her problem had been partially muscular.

No permanent spinal problems were found. Ken had been discharged as his stone has passed. Mike was healed and had gone home. The hospital was averaging around ten patients contantly now, and the staff was busy. Ros had gone to the state capitol to the State Beauty finals (which she won, of course), and was on a month's leave. Mariska was in charge of the second floor for the interim. The X-ray machine was up and running.

Four peaceful months had gone by. Ros was in California in the Miss America pageant (which she, of course, won), and Mariska was filling in admirably.

Monica was tired—long shifts in the hospital, and it was 5pm. One more hour and Karen would relieve her. She left the station for a few minutes, and when she returned, Dawn was there. Dawn had bumped her head again and wanted Monica to look at it. Monica seated her in the emergency room and parted Dawn's hair with her fingers. Monica wore a rather large nurse's type wrist watch, and Dawn noticed it. Suddenly, Dawn stiffened, looked at her open hand, and said, "I'm late! I'm late!" Monica was almost spellbound as Dawn glared fiercely, and said, "Off with their heads! Off with their heads!" Monica sighed, sedated the Queen of Hearts, and put her back in room 105.

THE END

REST HOME FUN

CHAPTER I

The ShadyGrove rest home sat on an attractive, well-manicured block near downtown Eagletown. Wide walkways, comfortable benches, brilliant shrubs, and flower gardens dotted the lush, green lawns surrounding the large two-storied dormitory-type building. Shady Grove contained a large recreation room, an excellent dining room, a large kitchen, a small library, a gymnasium, and had an excellent staff.

In this story you will meet some of the staff and elderly "inmates" of this magnificent rest home. The year is 1975. The facility was built and opened in 1960.

It was Bingo night at Shady Grove, and the big tables were filling up fast. The luckiest Bingo player was usually Jojo, but she wouldn't be playing tonight, as she had gotten sick during dinner, thrown up all over herself, and was sedated and in bed. The 81-year old would just get too excited sometimes and "lose it". Pup and Bonnie, the orderlies, had cleaned up the mess, and dinner had resumed. Jojo shared a room with Debz, who was only 74, and in pretty good shape. Debz, who loved to play cards, would help the older Jojo get dressed and "prettied" up some mornings.

Nece figured she'd win big tonight with Jojo sidelined as she was pretty darn lucky herself. At 71, Nece was one of the younger residents at the rest home, and she was a pretty sharp cookie. Didn't use a walker nor a cane and dressed all by herself. Her roommate was Tammy, who, at 77, was older and getting a bit frail. Nece would never help Tammy, but would call Bonnie or someone if Tammy needed anything or had a "bad spell".

All of the rooms were on the second floor, and the lower floor was mostly facilities with a large office and a nursing-type station. The 5 living areas on the ground floor were roomy one-room apartments, and were really an "assisted living" arrangement. One of these was occupied by Mike and Vickie, a married couple. Another was occupied by Bob and Georgia, also a married elderly couple. Mike, 80, used a walker but still fell a lot. Vickie, 76, was a small, rather wiry woman, and when Mike fell, she would start screaming until someone got him back on his feet. Georgia, 79, and Bob, 81, were still active and ambulatory (albeit a bit slow), and they were a bit standoffish in that they selected their friends. It was quite an honor for some of the other residents to get to dine with this couple on occasion.

The second youngest resident was Scott, who was only 51. Robust and healthy, he was a handsome physical specimen, but he had a cerebral problem. In other words, Scott was crazy. He had been a scientist with the Defense Department, and suffered a nervous breakdown, losing his mind. He had brief, lucid moments, but his medication just wasn't working. Well—liked and harmless, Scott was probably the happiest person in Shady Grove. Scott's biggest problem was that he didn't look like a resident—he looked like staff. Visitors would on occasion spot him, and ask him directions or something. Scott, being a helpful type of person, would try to help, and all hell might break loose. He roomed with Bill, who was almost as big and healthy as he was, but much older. Bill was 79 years old, and ambulatory with a cane—which he would constantly lose. It seemed as though people were always looking for Bill's cane.

Dawn and Ros both had Alzheimer's Disease, and they were roommates. This worked out well, as both repeated the same things day after day, and they could communicate without knowing it was the same thing every day. Dawn was 80, and Ros was78. Both could dress themselves, and neither needed an aid to walk. Dawn was a very prim old lady. Very friendly, she could sit and talk for hours even if there was no one to talk to. Ros was quite a bit more reserved. She was a problem to the staff only when she reverted back to the beauty queen she once was and would try to leave her room wearing only her underclothes. Almost every night Dawn and Ros would anxiously wait to see "Lonesome Dove" on television, as they had always wanted to see it.

Monica was part—owner, a licensed nurse, and a director at Shady Grove. She was passing out Bingo cards, telling all the players to take no more than 6. Scott was helping Bill get seated (he'd lost his cane again). Scott wanted to play and took 1 card, which would still be difficult for him. Chrissie (6 cards) and Karen (6 cards) shared a room and got along well. Chrissie, 75, was in good health, took very little medication, and no bull at all. Stoutly built, no one crossed Chrissie twice. Karen was only 47, the youngest of the residents. Karen had simply just "burned the candle at both ends" for too many years. Karen, who weighed 98 pounds, knew she always had Chrissie on her side, and if Chrissie was around, Karen could get more than a little obnoxious.

Monica always called the balls slowly, giving the slower players a chance to get help with their cards. Bill (6 cards) was helping Scott, and Dawn (2 cards) and Ros (3 cards) were just spotting their cards at random, as they would sometimes forget the number called before they could spot it. Lilly (6 cards) won the first game and got fifteen dollars. Lilly was 75 and shared a room with Tricia, who was 80. They got along well. Tricia was a bit (ahem) overly outgoing and a bit impatient. She lived for the moment and if she saw something she wanted, she wanted it this moment. Lilly liked Tricia, though, and "mothered" her a lot.

Paul was hollering BINGO and jumping up and down. This was the big blackout, and the last game. Monica checked his card and gave him twenty-five dollars. The other players were all grumbling and cussing, looking at their cards, and glaring at Paul. Paul, almost 82, and Dan,82, amicably shared a room. Paul was a good dancer, and the ladies loved him, especially on dance nights. Dan was a great card player and everyone always wanted to be his partner in Spades or Cribbage.

Debbie, the night nurse, was passing out medication for the night, and "tucking" everyone in. Almost finished, she was helping Gaet, 77, get into his bed. Gaet had severe arthritis and movement was sometimes difficult for him. He took a lot of medication, mostly for the pain. With his walker, he got around well, though, and was well liked by everyone. His roommate, Ed, was already asleep. Ed was 79, one of the more active residents, and helped the others a lot. He was a boon to the staff, really. Ed only took one medication, and that was to lower his blood pressure.

Debbie saved the worst two rooms for the last because they were like little kids, wanting to "stay up". At Shady Grove it was lights out at midnight, except for the assisted living units. Lena, 81, and Doo, 78, shared a room. Both had taught high school for years, and both were very "set in their ways". Both were avid readers, and both were very pedantic. They argued and fought constantly, but every time the directors tried to move one or the other out, they would hug each other and cry how they would each "just die" without the other

Debbie sighed—one more room. Lisa and Elaine, both in their mid-seventies, were just the opposite of Doo and Lena. They were huggers and loved up on people every chance thay had. Debbie braced herself, went through the door, and was instantly grabbed and hugged almost to the point of strangulation. When they finally let her so, she medicated them and got them settled for the night. Lisa was a wealthy retired banker and a big spender. Elaine had been a deputy in a large state agency and was still a bit "bossy".

CHAPTER II

Thursday was a beautiful, clear day. Pup and Bonnie had the smaller bus loaded now, and Pup pulled out, heading for Wal-Mart. They would take their eight charges to Wal-Mart for a brief outing and a bit of shopping, They would have lunch at McDonald's inside the store and then return home. Everyone was so excited. Wal-Mart was an adventure to these people.

As the bus pulled into traffic, Bonnie finally got Lisa seated and buckled in. Lisa was complaining that she "hadn't hugged everyone yet". Chrissie, ever protective of Karen, had given her the window seat. Dawn, always methodical, had her "shopping list" clutched in her gnarled old hand, and was animatedly telling her seatmate, Scott, that she was going to get a "Lonesome Dove" tape, as she had always wanted to see it. Scott was having a few lucid moments, and he was rapidly jotting down formulae and equations on the small pad he always carried. A courier from the Defense Department would come to the rest home every other day or so, pick up Scott's formulae, and leave a fresh identical pad for Scott.

The Wal-Mart greeter was swamped with long, happy hugs from and Elaine and Lisa, and they excitedly entered the big store. Bonnie took Lilly. Dawn, Tricia, and Elaine with her. They were going to try to find the tape Dawn wanted, and Lilly wanted to look at the shoes. Elaine was told not to hug any strangers, and they left.

Pup's charges were Scott, Lisa, Chrissy, and Karen. Lisa was told not to hug anyone she didn't know, and they set out for the pet department to watch the colorful goldfish for a while. Karen's mind would wander a bit at times, and she wanted to go to the "bar".

The store had placed some large bags of potato chips on the main aisle, and Tricia just grabbed one, ripped it open, and was sharing with the others. Bonnie even had some, as they would pay on the way out. Lilly finally found some shoes she just loved, and Bonnie made sure Lilly had enough in her purse to pay for them. Dawn was a problem in that she wanted a "Lonesome Dove" tape, and she already had several. Bonnie finally talked her into getting a "Clockwork Orange" tape, telling her how good it was. Elaine made a few small purchases, Tricia was passing around a bottle of delicious, purloined eggnog, and they were hungrily headed to the McDonalds up front.

Pup wasn't that lucky. Karen got bumped and she fell. She got up and started cussing, making a scene. By the time Pup got her and Chrissie settled down, Scott had disappeared. Pup sent Lisa to the front of the store to stop Scott if he tried to leave the store, and told her they would be right there. With Chrissie and Karen in tow, Pup arrived at the entrance. It was jammed with people who seemed to be enthralled by the greeter. It was Scott! Apparently he had seen the greeter coming in, and had been fascinated. Scott was putting on quite a show, and Lisa was hugging him all over the place. Pup got them out of there and into McDonald's, where they had a nice lunch and then went home.

CHAPTER III

You never knew when Mike was going to fall from his walker because he never stumbled. He would just sort of suddenly collapse at the knees and end up on the floor on his butt. Then Vickie would come unglued and start screaming. Unless Scott got him up, it was a two-person task, as he was very heavy. Vickie could scream like a banshee, but as soon as he was on his feet, she was her usual quiet, aloof self.

Shady Grove was having a special dinner. Lisa, the big spender, had ordered T-bone steaks for everyone, followed by cake and ice cream because it was her birthday, and she wanted it celebrated properly. Pup and Bonnie had even put out linens for this one. Getting seated was always the hard part. Each dining table seated four people, and everyone seemed to want to dine with someone other than with whom they were already seated. Everyone was pretty much seated to their satisfaction when Mike, Vickie, Bob, and Georgia made their "grand entrance".

They had almost made it to their table when Mike dropped like a stone. Vickie unleashed her big lungs, and people were pulling hearing aids out of their ears like crazy. Pup and Bonnie got him on his feet and seated, Vickie now acting as though nothing had happened. With everyone now safely seated, Bonnie led them through a big, long "Happy Birthday" to Lisa, who beamed, blushed, and had to be restrained from hugging everyone some more.

The steaks, potatoes, gravy and a vegetable were simply devoured, and Pup and Bonnie were bringing out the ice cream carts. The immense slices of Lisa's birthday cake had been placed on the tables, and everyone was anxiously awaiting their ice cream. Each big ice cream cart had three flavors—vanilla, strawberry, and chocolate. This way each diner could select scoops of their favorite.

Ros and Dawn had a problem in that they couldn't remember their favorite, so Bonnie gave each a large scoop of everything. Pup was serving Lena and Doo, Both were holding their forks, watching greedily as he scooped the ice cream onto their plates of cake. Pup had momentarily forgotten how spastic Doo was with advanced Parkinson's, and before he could grab her arm, she had slammed a huge load of ice cream and cake right smack into the middle of her spectacles. Ice cream covered almost her entire face and was running off her nose and chin. Monica cleaned her up and spoon-fed her some of the delicious dessert.

After dessert, Lisa opened her presents, hugged everyone, and then they all went to the rec room to have a cribbage tournament. On tournament nights Monica would draw names to assign partners because of the bigger prizes. If you drew Scott, Ros, Doo, or Dawn, you were probably doomed at the outset. On the other hand, if any combination of Dan, Nece, Jojo, or Debz happened to pair up, they would probably win. This particular night Jojo and Debz were already partners, and definitely the team to beat. Mike and Lilly, both good card players paired up. Dan, probably the best player of all, drew Doo. Doo had been a good player for years, but now she couldn't hold her cards still long enough to know what she really had, and she dropped them a lot. Nece, a good player, drew Karen, and sighed. Karen was a sort of lucky card player, but she had a short attention span, she didn't see well. and she never knew what the "count" was. Refusing to wear eyeglasses, she had a problem reading her cards.

Georgia was a good card player, and had Elaine for a partner. Elaine happily hugged her for about a small eternity and then sat down opposite her at the table. Lisa, the birthday girl, drew Gaet, another good player, and was happily hugging him around his poor old arthritic neck. wishing him good luck. Bob drew Dawn for a partner, and tried to excuse himself from playing, but Monica told him he was in, and that was that. Ros and Tricia were partners, and old stubborn Ros, who almost always staggered around in heels, tottered over to the table and plopped down with a huge sigh of relief, removing her shoes.

No others wanted to play and Monica had 8 teams, so the tournament began. Nece got a break in that Chrissie, who wasn't playing, helped Karen play her cards, and they got good cards, eliminating Dan and Doo. Getting Dan out was a big uplift to the remaining players. Jojo and Debz won, eliminating Elaine and Georgia.

Dawn had been a super card player in her day, but her memory was so short it was an effort for her to even play, really. Before she would play, she had to ask what the count was "out there'. She was dealt three 5s twice, however, and she and Bob eliminated Lisa and Gaet by only two points.

The fourth table was on fourth street playing their last hand. Mike and Lilly had a good lead over Ros and Tricia, and Tricia was starting to get a bit nasty. The last card played, and, for about the 75th time, Ros asked what the score was. Tricia had a 16-point hand and counted first, Ros still needing 6 to go out. Mike counted, leaving Lilly only needing 2, and she also had the crib. Poor old Ros only had 4 and they were eliminated. Jojo and Debz ultimately won the tournament, and Monica gave them each twenty-five dollars.

It was a beautiful morning and Scott, Dan, and Paul were sitting on a bench near the street enjoying the warm, bright sunshine. Across the walkway Dawn and Ros had occupied a bench, and had been joined by Jojo, who was all prettied up today. Sometimes Debz helped Jojo put bows in her silver-blue hair and used some makeup on her, and Jojo would be so proud of herself. This always upset Ros because Jojo would get more compliments sometimes than she herself did, heels and tight skirts notwithstanding. Ros was a "knockout" for her age. Every inch of her body had been lifted, shaped, or otherwise redone many times, and she looked many years younger than she actually was. Sitting in the sun and people passing by gave ample opportunity to be admired, and she resented Jojo sharing it. Jojo, on the other hand, had no vanity whatsoever. She just enjoyed being "pretty" once in a while. Dawn, of course, was unaware of all this, and just chatted, She excitedly asked Jojo if she'd ever seen "Lonesome Dove", as it was a really good movie, and she had finally gotten the tape.

Mke and Vickie came strolling down the wide walkway, and joined the others. Mike exchanged high-fives with the other guys and sat. The always gracious, but distant Vickie told Jojo how "nice and pretty" she looked this morning, and received a glare from Ros. Dawn moved a bit so Vickie could sit, and told Vickie it was "sure a nice day".

Ed loved working in the grounds and he was helping Pup water and trim a few shrubs. They stopped at the benches to visit for a few minutes. The ladies liked both Pup and Ed as they were always very complimentary. Even old Dawn would bat her eyes a little and preen. Dawn was a very erect lady. She walked very straight and sat the same way.

Doo and Tammy joined the group just as a snow-cone truck came slowly down the street towards them. blaring music. Mike let out a whoop. He really loved snow-cones. Pup signalled the driver to stop and took orders. Just then, Bonnie joined the group with Lilly, Nece, Gaet, and Georgia. The four benches were filling fast, and orders were taken for the snow-cones. Gaet walked very slowly and painfully, and with a cane today. He was seated now, both hands on his cane between his knees, and ordered orange. All orders were taken and Pup and Bonnie were passing out the treats when Lisa appeared, hugged everyone, ordered grape, and insisted all this was her treat. Pup and Bonnie had two left, an orange and a grape, and Dawn and Ros were still waiting. Neither could remember what they'd ordered, so Pup just held both out to Dawn and she took the orange one. This upset Ros because Dawn got first choice, and she said she'd ordered orange. Bonnie took the orange from Dawn and gave her the grape, and Dawn, a bit bewildered, sat down and happily enjoyed her treat. Doo already had hers all over her face and clothing. Lilly was trying to help her and she was getting some to her mouth, making Doo very happy. Nece and Jojo were very good friends and were sharing their cones with each other. The wind picked up a bit after they finished their treats so they went inside and took a nap.

Today was the day they'd all been waiting for. The famous movie star, Kimpike, would be at Shady Grove for lunch, and would meet everyone. Kim was the favorite of the national tabloids, and she simply loved older people. Beautiful, famous, wealthy, and married to a Congressman, she would visit homes for the elderly on occasion (always with an entourage of Paparazzi). Great fodder for the tabloids, and some of the Shady Grove residents were sure to be in the spotlight with the famous star.

Never had the residents of Shady Grove looked so fine. The men all wore suits and ties, and the ladies were all dolled up, made up, and perfumed. Pup and Bonnie were even dressier than usual. Pup was wearing a pale blue turtle-neck that looked expensive, and Bonnie wore a colorful blouse and a neat skirt. Monica had donned a print dress and wore heels. Needless to say, Ros was decked out like a treenager, and Debz had done almost a complete makeover on herself and Jojo. Lisa was stunning in her new outfit. She had bought an entire wardrobe for the occasion, and had loaned or given a lot of her older fine clothes to some of the other ladies.

The big white limo parked and the famous star entered the rec room, followed by group of people carrying cameras. Lisa and Elaine, who looked sharp in a new gown with a lot of jewelry, immediately grabbed and hugged her until she was able to escape. The gracious Kim wanted to meet everyone. Being introduced to Dawn, Dawn told Kim she was pleased to make her acquaintance, she was sorry she had forgotten her name, and had she ever seen Lonesome Dove? Shaking hands with Gaet, Kim relaxed her grip as she could see pain in the old gentleman's eyes. She helped him to sit back down, hugged his arthritic neck, and kissed his forehead. Bob and Georgia were always formal. Georgia gave Kim a light hug, and Bob bowed, took and kissed her hand. Mike jumped to his feet, his knees buckled, and he fell on his butt at the star's feet, Vickie was screaming her head off and hearing aids were coming out of ears. Scott got Mike on his feet, Vickie shut up instantly, and they were introduced to Kim. The two former teachers, Lena and Doo, shook hands with the famous star, Lena holding Doo's hand steady so Kim could clasp it. Ros and Jojo lightly hugged the famous star, and Kim remarked at "how lovely you two are," causing Ros to preen and Jojo to blush.

Nece and Debs shook hands with Kim, said hello, and posed with her for a few camera shots. Chrissie had a handshake like a wrestler, and Kim was hard put to keep from crying out. She was then given a warm hug by Karen. Kim thought it unusual for someone as young looking as Karen to be here, but said nothing. Scott and Dan bowed, telling Kim how pleased they were to meet her, and they loved her movies. Paul, Dan and Bill were very impressed by the famous actress, greeted her warmly and they chatted a few moments. Lilly and Tricia both hugged and welcomed Kim to Shady Grove. Tricia, always impatient, insisted on a photo with Kim, and an autograph. Autographed photos were then passed out, a short visit, then they all went into the dining room for a delicious lunch.

THE END

MEDIEVAL FUN

CHAPTER I

Who is to say when the so-called Dark Ages existed in Europe? Most authorities say it was the period between the fall of the Roman Empire (circa 400AD), and the rebirth of learning, which would be the Italian Renaissance (circa 1400AD). We will let that suffice. No Empire lasted long during this period. Kings came and went, with few heirs to the throne getting that throne. Only the strongest survived.

In the year 510AD the Anglo-Saxons were facing an all-out invasion by the Saxon invaders, who, heretofore had only made sporadic raids on the isles and had been successfuly repulsed by the valiant Knights of the Realm. The heroic deeds of some of these famous knights will be portrayed in this story

Camelot was a beautiful place, The magnificent, high—turreted structure was clean and comfortable, with a huge enclosed courtyard. Green hills, meadows, forests, and streams surrounded the fortress. It was the heart of the Anglo-Saxon Empire.

The colorful pennants flying high on the castle walls displayed large ferocious eagles.

King Mike, of royal descent, was sitting at the head of the massive table, his brow furrowed in thought. The Knights sat quietly around the table waiting for him to speak. Mike had revealed that Sir Bill and Sir Deni, two famous and powerful knights, had returned from a Crusade a few days ago, and had learned of an upcoming massive invasion by the Toras upon their shores. The Toras were mostly ferocious seafaring tribes from the east who had apparently united with the barbaric Saxon-Norlites from the south and were preparing an overpowering assault on the isles. The attacks would probably be from the south and the east, possibly on two fronts. Mike had assembled the Knights to discuss how to defend the isles once again.

Mike sipped his ale and studied his beloved knights, mentally assessing them as he did so. His four swordsmen, Sirs Chrissy, Cathy, Karen, and Deni were extremely powerful warriors who could wield the heavy two-edged swords that in later years were to be called broadswords. These were cutting weapons, not piercing weapons. No European swordsman alive would stand a chance against any of these four. Their medieval body-armor simply couldn't withstand the powerful carbon-steel edges, and their lighter rapiers, and even heavier sabres would be shattered by these powerful weapons. None of his other knights could handle these heavy weapons. He had had some problems with them, though. There was a lot of pride here, and not enough camaraderie. He knew each wanted to prove herself the best, and he had to keep them apart to keep them alive. Born warriors, these four were happy only when in battle.

The bow was a relatively new weapon, loved already by the Anglicans, and it was the only weapon in existence that could strike from a distance. The spear was usually ineffective from much distance, unless thrown by an exceptional warrior. Efforts to build catapults had primarily failed. They were too heavy to transport, and at this time were occasionally used for defense only. The early bowmen were usually very inaccurate, and the shafts were not much more than pointed sticks. the English had started feathering their shafts, though, and were having some success with accuracy. It was to be many years before the more powerful Scottish longbow was to make body armor obsolete in battle. Mike had three Knighted archers, and they were all very accurate. The lethal range of the bow in those days was at most less than 30 meters, but improvements were coming rapidly

His head archer was Sir Dan. Dan had been an outlaw for years, hiding out in the forest between his forays against the rich. He and his men had finally outwitted and overthrown the cruel, corrupt Lord of Surrey, enabling the King to unite almost all of the isle. Dan had knelt at the feet of the King and accepted Knighthood, along with three of his outlaws, one of whom was Sir Cathy, the powerful sword. Sir Monica, another archer, was always the innovative one. She had developed the longer, feathered shaft which had increased accuracy and range immeasurably. His third knighted archer was Sir Georgia, a former swordsman who had been enthralled by the bow. She was probably even more accurate than Dan.

The other Knights were just simply great warriors. They were all skilled with the lance, the sword, the mace, and to some extent, the bow. the Anglican body armor was known as a hauberk, and it protected the torso from most blows. The lighter chainmail came into existence much later. The elongated Anglo-Saxon shields afforded much more protection that the smaller heavier round shields of the Europeans. All in all, Mike probably had the most modern fighting unit in the known world at that time.

Sir Pup was the only Knight of the Table who was not a warrior. He had been knighted because of his relationship to Dawn, the dreaded wizard, who was alleged to be an illegitimate half-sister and student of the powerful sorcerer, Merlin. It was Sir Pup, who, on command from the feared Merlin, had enabled King Mike to obtain the magical and powerful jeweled sword, Excalibur, which was always strapped to the King's side. Merlin, over one-hundred years old now, was on his deathbed, and Dawn was now the advisor to the king, who feared her, but needed her power. Somehow, Sir Pup did not fear the sometimes barbaric and capricious Wizard, and could approach her at will. The King needed Sir Pup.

The attack on the isles came sooner than anticipated, but the Anglicans were ready. The large but cumbersome ships from the continent were met by the faster, smaller English fleet, and shafts rained upon the landing barbarians. The first landing occurred at about where Greater Yarmouth is today, on the eastern seaboard. The English soldiers met the attackers in the water in an attempt to keep them from reaching land, but as more ships came in, they were forced to slowly retreat. The first Knights from the Table to arrive were Sir Ken and Sir Debbie, their swords flashing as they rode into the thick of the battle. The retreat slowed even as more ships arrived. Sir Chrissie had arrived by now, dismounted, and her powerful sword was flashing as she slew Toras, but still they came, with even more ships on the horizon. Sir Georgia swooped in, firing deadly arrows from horseback, and Sir Lisa and Sir Bonnie joined the fray. These were the only Knights assigned here. Sirs Lisa and Bonnie were veteran warriors, having fought two Crusades each. They were both deadly with the dagger as well as the sword.

Suddenly, the remaining ships veered away, tacking to the south, probably to join forces with the attacking Norlites to the south and west, deserting their people on the beach. These were quickly disposed of. Prisoner of war hadn't been invented yet.

Holding a quick conference, the Knights agreed that there would probably be no more attacks here, and, leaving a contingent of soldiers, they headed south with the remaining army. Sir Bob of the Table, the commander of the English boats, had landed, gotten more arrows and provisions, and left in pursuit.

King Mike was preparing to leave Camelot. He had planned to go to the eastern shore, the most likely object of an early attack, but two returing Crusaders had delayed him. Sir Lilly and Sir Doo had refreshed and joined the King. As they were leaving the Castle a courier fron the eastern army had ridden in with the news from Sir Ken. Mike agreed with what they had done, and set out to the southeast. This small but formidable group consisted of the King, Knights Lilly, Doo, and Sir Doug, followed by Sir Pup, a very cranky Wizard, and a small band of elite soldiers. Dawn had been in her formicary brewing a foul concoction of some sort when Pup had told her the King needed her, and she was making things miserable for everyone. Mike figured they would make contact with the other Knights in two days.

CHAPTER II

Military Preparations

Less than four hours had elapsed since the King and his troupe had left Camelot for the south when two Knights of the Table arrived there. Sir Anneke and Sir Tammy had returned from an unsuccessful dragon hunt in what is now Cornwall. Sir Tammy, in addition to being a powerful warrior was, along with Sir Lena, a military tactician. Sir Anneke, on the other hand was a brute—force fighting machine. A former outlaw, she had been known as the "Friar" during her life in the forests. Her favorite weapon was the staff. She literally beat her enemies to death. The Knights refreshed, donned armor, and galloped south and eastward, hoping to soon join the King.

Sir Paul and Sir Don were on an extended vacation on what is now the Isle of Wight, scouting for dragons and doing some fishing. Word of the pending invasion came via an enchanted white falcon, dispatched by the Wizard. They immediately packed up, boated to shore, and rode east. Sir Paul was a veteran Crusader with three to his credit. He was physically big and powerful, and was one of the most vicious hand-to-hand fighters ever known. Sir Don was sort of the ladies' man in court, but he had enormous upper-body strength, and loved to maul his enemies. He had had the Royal Armourer fit him with a metal band around his right hand. It had vicious sharp spikes on it, and he had slashed many an opposing warrior to a horrible death.

King Mike and his entourage had stopped for the night, or for most of one. They had made good time. He had spread his Knights along the shoreline with fleet couriers available to each. It had been agreed at the Table conference that the southern attack would be the one to fear most. The Toras from the east were more raiders than conquerors, and disliked land fighting. The more barbaric Norlites, on the other hand, were vicious, better armed, and would fight to the death. He had sent both Sir Deni and Sir Kathy to the beaches just south and east of what is now known as Brighton. It was a fishing community at this time, and was known as Brighthelmstone, and had good landing beaches. King Mike was sure the main attacking force would land near there. He needed to hold off the attackers until he could assemble more people, and had had to use two of his valuable swords to do it. The other Knights were spaced between there and what is now Dunquerque.

The King hadn't heard from Sir Ros, his remaining Knight. She had been west of Camelot quelling an uprising, and had been overdue at the castle, The wizard had disappeared. She disliked being around people, and had wandered off. Mike sent Sir Pup to round her up. Sir Pup finally found Dawn wading in a small stream and muttering all sorts of evil incantations. Pup shivered, but approached her. When she arrived, King Mike asked her to get a message to Sir Ros, telling her to join them as soon as possible. Grumbling, Dawn summoned an eagle and obeyed. Mike needed all his Knights, and he knew it. Sir Ros was a screaming lethal machine, as deadly and as noisy as a rattlesnake.

Mike had done all he could, He had stationed Sir Lena, along with several couriers, on the coast just about center of where he thought the initial attack would occur. Sir Lena, in addition to being a relentless warrior, was a brilliant military tactician. Basically, she was the General.

Sir Ros had had to hunt, run down, and kill ten or so insurgents, and it had taken some time, but she had finally beheaded the last one. Jail hadn't been invented yet. She was tired, sweaty, irritated, hungry, and dreaded the long trip to Camelot. When the eagle approached, she immediately knew it was a message from the King. She and her mighty charger were magically reinvigorated by the news, and she galloped south and east to join her fellow Knights.

Night fell on the beautiful southern beaches of England. Sir Monica had an assignment; keeping Sir Deni and Sir Cathy apart if they had their swords and had been drinking. Sir Monica was up to the task, She was probably the most respected of all the Knights by the other Knights. She knew if the Barbarians came in, they'd be in bad shape without these two war-machines. They were the only three Knights at this location, along with about two hundred soldiers.

At the eastern end of the "defense" line. Sir Karen was polishing her sword, licking her lips in anticipation of all the killing. Damn, Karen wanted to fight! She looked around for something to kill. Nothing in sight. She'd just have to wait. Sirs Dan and Lisa joined her, and they chatted for awhile. They had had no word from the east as yet. The barbaric Karen realy liked Lisa. Sir Lisa wasn't a prima-donna like those other swordsmen. Lisa was just a good honest killer. They had about one-hundred—fifty soldiers at their command, and had set watch for the night.

The central command post, with Sir Lena in charge was roughly fifteen to twenty miles from each of the others. The only other Knight of the Table assigned with her was Sir Bonnie, but Lena was comfortable with that. Bonnie was a two-legged slaughterhouse, and she also had around two hundred elite soldiers with her.

CHAPTER III
The Invasion

Sir Bill had remained at Camelot, as the King wanted at least one Knight there. A few hours after the King and his troupe left, Queen Vickie summoned Bill. At daybreak Maidens Nina and Carol had taken a picnic lunch and gone, along with two squires, into the forest to play. Vickie, very psychic, felt something had happened, and she requested that Sir Bill check on them. Sir Bill searched the forest and found nothing. He feared the worst, and had decided to go to the Castle to get help, when somethig caught his eye. His fears were well-founded. He instantly knew what had happened. The evil Sorcerer, Mary, had the young people in her clutches. Mary hated the King and had been harassing him for years. A student of sorcery under Merlin, she had been exiled fron England by Dawn and Merlin because of evil witchcraft. Her fortress was somewhere in the Isles to the west and north, which is now primarily Ireland. The more powerful Dawn had always been able to keep Mary out of England, but with Dawn preoccupied and many miles away, the evil Mary had struck. Bill, an expert tracker, found their tracks, and knew they were going south, not west. But why?

Sir Bill returned to Camelot, told the Queen what had happened, and galloped due south as fast as his charger could go. Five hours later, he met and joined up with the blood-spattered Sir Ros, and they exchanged information. They needed to join the King and Dawn as soon as possible.

Sirs Ken, Chrissie, Debbie, and Georgia had just encountered an army sentinel about six miles up the coastline from the easterm encampment. Debbie assigned one of their soldiers to relieve the sentinel, and they accompanied the soldier to the camp, joining the knights there, Still no incoming ships in the channel. Sirs Chrissie and Sir Georgia, refreshed, set out westwardly on the seaboard to reinforce the two Knights at the central command post about fifteen or so miles away. This would provide a powerful sword and an archer at that point.

The invading hordes had assembled and were almost in sight of the English beaches. They knew from experience that they had a formidable foe. The English Knights were the most deadly fighters in the world, but the Saxon—Norlites felt they had the advantage of surprise and numbers, and besides, they would soon be joined by their allies, the Toras.

Little did they know that the Toras probably would never again make landfall on the Isles. They were in full flight at this time with Sir Bob and his small navy in pursuit. They were headed east, not south, and were fleeing for home. The Norlites were on their own. The Toras had lost the element of surprise, and knew the Norlites had, also.

Sirs Dan and Paul were at this time a few miles west of the fishing village of Brighthelmstone, and had joined up with Sirs Ros and Bill. After exchanging information, they were met by an army sentinel—spotter, and received more information. Just then the first attacking ships appeared, about two miles out, and a bit east of their position. Bill quickly sent the soldier eastward to the camp near Brighthelmstone, summoning them.

Concealing themselves, the four Knights slowly worked their way eastward, trying to find a spot of beach where they could take a defensive position. Dan had a goodly supply of feathered shafts and he wanted a good vantage point to launch from. These four Knights were capable of destroying over one hundred barbarian warriors before they tired and began falling, and they were prepared to do so. They finally got in front of the advancing attackers, were fairly well concealed, and were soon joined by some of the nearer soldiers.

King Mike had just about had it with Dawn's surliness and complaining. She was now riding with her head down, and making incantations. Suddenly, the Wizard raised her head, looked around, and then looked westward, all her psychic senses alert. They were about four miles north of the fishing village, and approaching from the northwest. Sirs Anneke and Tammy had joined them a few hours ago, and they were a formidable group now. The wizard suddenly screamed in rage, her clenched hands pointing upward. Her trance, as usual, had given her a vision, and she knew what had happened in the forest near Camelot. Her mystical eyes were almost white with terrible anger, and the King almost feared for his Knights and himself. The two maidens were loved by the irascible wizard, and she was losing control. In addition, the sorcerer Mary was her mortal hated enemy. Even Sir Pup couldn't get near her. As they reached the promontory overlooking the beach, they saw the invaders, maybe thirty minutes from landing. Mike quickly got them back out of sight.

Sir Doo, who was the nosiest Knight of the Table, was perfect for this situation, A natural snoop, she concealed herself where she could see the happenings on the beach, keeping the others informed.

The English soldiers again met the attackers even while they were still in the water. They were outnumbered badly, but they knew the Knights would enter the fray at the appropriate time, The soldiers held for awhile, and then were forced back. Sir Bill hit the right flank of the enemy. His flashing sword never stopping. The trained battle chargers of the English almost seemed to love fighting. Bill was a magnificent mounted figure, both hands on his sword, swinging right and also to the left. Ros had attacked the left flank, and had caused consternation there. The army line had steadied there, so she had turned her attention to a fresh load of attackers farther down the beach to the southwest. Sir Don, his powerful body wielding the flashing sword, had waded into the middle of the first assault, dismounted, and was piling Saxon bodies around him. Sir Dan had coolly dispatched about ten via arrow before he rode into the fray and joined Sir Don.

The blare of the trumpets caused a slight pause in the battle. Looking up, they saw King Mike, waving the magical jewelled Excalibur, followed by two horsemen carrying the large green banner with the ferocious Eagle, charging down from the cliffs to the beach. Flanked by five colorful Knights, and followed by twenty or so soldiers, it was an impressive sight. A tremendous cheer emanated fron the English on the beach.

The Norlites were still pouring onto the beach. Sirs Anneke and Lilly had joined Sir Ros who was fighting an entire boatload The boats were landing to the west, which was bad. The remaining Knights, should they arrive, would come from the east. Sirs Doug and Doo and the King were meeting up with yet another boatload even farther west.

Sir Deni was the first Knight to arrive from the village. Her face was flushed and her blood was flowing. She dismounted at the first opportunity to fight. She waded in with that big sword swinging like a modern ceiling fan, a human lawn mower. The English soldiers and the Knights had moved westward to get out of her way, In no time the remaining Saxons were chopped up, and Sir Deni mounted to go farther west and kill.

Sir Monica and Sir Cathy arrived at the battlefield five minutes or so after Sir Deni. Monica was almost out of arrows, having fired upon approach. She went farther west than Sir Cathy, who had dismounted at the first chance to fight. Monica raced to the side of Sir Anneke, who was almost surrounded by barbarian warriors. Anneke's staff had been cut down so much it looked more like a club, but she was still flailing away. Sir Monica and Sir Anneke soon routed the barbarians, lopping some heads and caving in some others

Sir Cathy, unlike the ferocious and impatient Deni, was a lackadaisical, but methodical swordsman. She slowly dismounted, donned her leather gauntlets, adjusted her shield and helmet, picked up the huge sword, took a couple of practice swings, and waded into a group of about forty invaders. She never even slowed down. Producing body parts at an incredible rate, she waded through the group, reversed course and kept swinging. A few got away, and she calmly moved to another smaller group, which she soon decapitated. Incidentally, Sir Cathy is mentioned in English Folklore as the "Lady Destroyer".

Sir Lena and the Knights from the central command arrived and went to work immediately. Sir Georgia, depleted of arrows, dove in, brandishing her sword.

The original Knights on the scene had tired, and had pulled back for a short rest, and to watch. Sir Lena and Sir Bonnie had joined the King and Sir Doug, who had their hands full with a fresh boatload of barbarians. Sir Doug, usually at the side of the King, was the English equivalent of the modern Secret Service. His job was to protect the King at all costs.

Sir Chrissie, arriving, saw a boatload coming in and stationed herself at the landing spot. Sir Chrissie was, unlike her more savage fellow swordsmen, a real lady (of sorts). She dismounted, wiggled her powerful hips to adjust her leather hauberk, smoothed her hair, glanced around, donned her helmet, motioned for everyone to get clear, hefted that huge sword, and went to work. Fifty barbarians were just a warm-up for Sir Chrissie. In just a few minutes severed arms, legs, and heads were floating in the bloody water, with the surviving attackers fleeing, to be quickly disposed of. From English folklore Sir Chrissie is loosely described as "The Storm Lady".

The battle was almost over. One last boatload was coming in, and so was Sir Karen, galloping toward the landing site, screaming for everyone to get away. These were her barbarians. Sir Karen had no gentility whatsoever. She was one hundred percent vicious swordsman, and she was just about to prove it. She dismounted, spat on her hands, picked up her big sword. adjusted her shield, made sure everyone was in the clear, and went into action. Sir Karen was always hungry, and she was starved. She would end this quickly and get some food. Her big sword was relentless and fast. In just a few moments, half of their comrades butchered, the surviving Norlites fled. Sir Karen is mentioned in medieval folklore also. A villager, witness to the slaughter, writing in Runes, recorded it. Deciphered many centuries later, it was perceived to be somewhere close to "Lady who feeds fish".

CHAPTER IV
Sorcery

The Saxon invasion had lasted for a bit over seven hours. The Knights and soldiers were now downing huge quantities of mead and ale, consuming half-cooked fowl, and relaxing when Sir Pup and the white-faced wizard joined the group. King Mike, always businesslike, requested Dawn to get messages to Sir Bob and to Camelot, and that just about wrapped it up. A soldier rode up to the King, announcing the arrival of yet another ship.

The ship, a small, trim, colorful vessel, approached slowly, cautiously. The helmsman, seeing the carnage on the beach, steered for the area where King Mike and the Knights were gathered. The banners on the vessel could now be seen, and Sir Lilly recognized the colors of her friend, Sir Marc, a Teutonic Knight with whom she had fought shoulder to shoulder in the Holy Land. Telling the king these were friendly Knights, Sir Lilly waded out, welcoming them ashore. The three visiting Knights knelt at the feet of the King, delivering a message. Sirs Marc, Gaet, and Jojo had all fought in the Holy land, and each had previously met some of the Table Knights. Warm greetings were extended, and attention turned to the message the King held.

The message had been delivered to Sir Gaet by an emissary from a dreaded wizard, known only as Vlad, who lived somewhere in what is now the Balkans. The parchment was almost three months old, and was written in Cyrillic, an eastern European tongue. Sirs Pup and Lena, who were literate and knew several languages pored over it. Finally, with a bit of help from Sir Jojo, they had loosely deciphered it.

Vlad, the mysterious sorcerer of Eastern Europe was really more of a prognosticator, He had visions of things yet to come. Seen only at night, he was sometimes called "The Undead One". This mysterious entity had had some loose fragmented psychic ties to the Wizard, Merlin in years past.

Sir Lena related to the King that the missive appeared to say: "The spot of the daemon will show lest the King—"—it trailed off here, as though Vlad had lost his vision. Enigmatc as it was, Dawn knew exactly what it meant. She grabbed Sir Pup by the arm and they went to a secluded spot where Dawn sat on a rock and went into a prolonged trance.

The old Wizard, Merlin, friend and advisor of many English kings, was on his deathbed, usually in a delirious sleep. Visions of leading Mike to the powerful sword, Excalibur, training Dawn and Mary in the intricacies of witchcraft and sorcery, the betrayal of the Evil Mary, and visions of iimpending death permeated his feverish mind. He lay there moaning, half-asleep. Someone was trying to get into his mind, but he was so, so tired. Relentlessly, the signals came, and with effort he opened his still psychic mind. It was Dawn, desperately seeking a bit of information that was sworn never to be revealed Only the frail Merlin could answer her, and he was sworn by his very soul not to do so. Dawn related all of the recent events, including the mysterious message from Europe. Merlin had perked up a bit, and his mind had cleared somewhat. His powers were almost all gone now, and his mind was wandering. He was tiring quickly, but summoned the strength to give Dawn the information she was seeking.

King Mike was in a foul mood. Dawn was the person to handle this strange thing, and she had wandered off again. His Knights were all about half-drunk on ale and mead, and were lounging around swapping war stories with the European Knights. The best part of three hours had elapsed and dusk was setting in when Dawn reappeared, She immediately sought the King and they conferred at length.

The evil Mary, who had been cast out of England, was much feared by the Britons, who occupied a small Northwestern section of the island. Fearing her, they had never been able to unite with the Anglo-Saxons to the east and south. Mary was determined to get the hated King Mike in her clutches, and she was going to use the two Maidens she had kidnapped to do it. If she could destroy the King, she felt she could conquer England. She and about twenty Britons, along with the captive young people from Camelot were settling in for the night about twenty miles west of where the Saxon invasion had just ended and where the King was encamped.

The campfires were dying out, and the tired Knights were retiring for the night. Dawn had taken a potion that would enable her to sleep, but leave her psychic mind open. Some were sleeping in tent-type structures provided by the villagers. The Europeans had retired to their ship, promising to return ashore in the morning.

It was near midnight when Dawn got the mental signal from Mary. Their psychic conversation lasted for some time, negotiating. Dawn did not sleep again that night. Lying still, but deep in thought.

At daybreak the Wizard was seen entering the King's tent. Thirty minutes or so later, a courier summoned Sir Pup, Sir Lisa, and the three archers to the tent.

The King explained what they had to do, and why. Each of them had a critical assignment, and if any one of them failed, it would probably be the end of England as they knew it.

The small group set out westward. The King, followed by Sir Pup, Sir Lisa, Dawn, and the three archers, riding side by side. They rode in silence for about ten miles, stopping at a large rather high boulder. They dismounted and the King unbuckled his beloved sword, laying it in the dust beside the big rock. Unarmed, the King went to the west side of the rock and appeared to be waiting for something. Sir Pup, also devoid of armor, had climbed upon the rock, and was concealed in a small cavity there, along with a large bundle he had brought. The three archers flanked the boulder, facing west. Sir Lisa concealed herself behind the boulder

The evil Witch approached the meeting place where she would exchange the young prisoners for the King. Once this was done, she would rule the isles. She could destroy the damgerous Dawn, somehow, later. The King was unarmed and exactly where Dawn had said he would be,

Not a word was spoken. Mary ordered the Britons to release the young captives, and they ran for Dawn. As soon as they reached her, Dawn could no longer protect the King, by sworn oath. As the young people neared Dawn a scream arose from behind the rock, and Sir Lisa came into view. She looked anything but a Knight of the Realm. She was half-clad in tattered peasant's robes, was dirty, sobbing, and appealing to Mary to help her. Mary was ready to slay her with a bolt of lightning when Lisa looked up and screamed.

Mary, startled, looked upward. There, towering over her on the huge rock was the powerful Merlin, whom she had feared and hated for so many years.

Magnificent in his star-spangled flowing robes, his long white beard, and his conical hat, his stare seemed to penetrate her very soul. She was terrified for a moment, and as Merlin brought his dreaded wand to bear, she instinctively raised her arm in defense. Instantly, three feathered shafts penetrated her wrist, just below her hand. Suddenly powerless, the evil sorceress wailed, cursed, screamed, and died the horrible death of the damned. The Britons, released from her spell, fell at the feet of the mighty King.

THE END

Epilogue—The one mortal spot on the evil Mary's body, alluded to by Vlad, and revealed to Dawn by the dying Merlin, was "the right arm just below the hand." The three unerring Archers of the Table had all hit their mark. Sir Pup had played an impressive Merlin and Sir Lisa had portrayed a convincing damsel in distress. All in all, a great plan had come together. The freed Britons went home with the good news, and King Mike was able to unite the island for the first time in history.

HALLOWEEN FUN

CHAPTER I

The kids were working hard, and they had it right this year. They were going to finally observe the Great Pumpkin on their own terms. Karen and Chrissie, the two biggest and bossiest kids, had come up with a great plan. Instead of fleeing in terror from the Great Pumpkin as in years past, they would be safely entrenched and prepared for the Monster this time.

They were diligently digging a rather large entrenchment in the Pumpkin Patch, and sort of fortifying it, which would protect them completely from the dreaded Great Pumpkin.

Lilly, Pup, Carol, and Bill had dug a rather large hole in the Pumpkin Patch, which was now being covered with old boards and tin, and then it would be covered with dirt and fallen leaves. Mike was a sort of innovative "construction boss", and with Dawn and her little sister Ros swiping material from all over town they had constructed what was really a pretty good camouflaged bunker in which they could lie protected and concealed while observing the Great Pumpkin.

Other kids were now eagerly joining in. Gaet had provided what they thought would be a perfect "door" to cover the entrance, and Chrissie's little brother, Justin, had brought his water gun. Jim had concealed his sling-shot with some small rocks for additional defense, and Lena and Monica, the two smartest kids in town, had gotten interested and had made some great structural suggestions.

All preparations were now in place. The entire group of kids, now joined by Nece, Jojo, and Dan, were gathered enthusiastically in their bunker making their final plans. They would do the usual trick-or-treat to acquire provisions for the long night vigil, because who knew when the Great Pumpkin would appear? As soon as their parents were sure they were tucked in for the night, they would all sneak out and assemble here in their bunker to await the Great Pumpkin. Everyone couldn't fall asleep at the same time or else they might "miss" the Great Pumpkin, so It was agreed that Chrissie and Mike would assign the watches and guide the operation.

It was crunch time. All the kids were quietly in their bunker, speaking only in whispers. Everyone was very excited. This was going to be the experience of their lifetimes. Silence was imperative because Monica, who claimed to know "all" about the Great Pumpkin told them the Monster could hear the slightest sound. No moon tonight. The Pumpkin Patch was in almost total darkness. Almost two hours had passed and no Great Pumpkin. Most of the kids had fallen asleep, and it was eerily quiet in the Patch.

Suddenly a faint orange light appeared in the Pumpkin Patch. The sleeping kids were instantly aroused. This was probably the Great Pumpkin, for whom they were anxiously awaiting! Suddenly, getting closer, they could see another orange light. The lights were nearing the bunker now, and the kids realized the big orange lights were the eyes of the Great Pumpkin. They were getting nervous now. They hadn't figured on orange eyes. An owl began hooting in the pitch-black night and the kids were starting to shake a little, but they held firm in their bunker.

A terribly long, pitiful wail suddenly emanated from the approaching Pumpkin, causing consternation among the kids, but they remained silent. The Great Pumpkin, still groaning as though in pain, approached, stopping right over their bunker. All they could hear was the wailing and a sort of eerie scratching noise right above their heads. Their bunker "roof" held, but was sagging.

Suddenly, the makeshift door to the bunker was thrown open, and scared kids scrambled out and fled for home as fast as their chubby little legs could churn. When the last kid had fled, the tormented wail of the Great Pumpkin turned into a chuckle and the Great Pumpkin quietly disappeared into the darkness.

The End

FOOTBALL FUN GAME IV

CHAPTER I

The day of the big Eagles vs. Lady Eagles game dawned fair, cool, and clear in Eagletown. Last year's game had been a sell-out, and a terrific game. The Ladies had won, knotting the series at one—to—one, with one scoreless tie. Fours hours until game time, and the stands were filling fast. Marc, the town reporter, was interviewing a few early fans, who were really hyped up for the game. One gentleman, who had seen all three previous games told Marc that it "was a lot of fun to watch people play football when they couldn't even play football," whatever that meant. Another said that he liked the way the boys tackled. "Instead of trying to strip the ball, they try to strip the ball carrier." A lady fan said that she liked to watch "how the Ladies managed to keep their clothes on."

The ladie's team arrived at the stadium an hour or so before game time, already in uniform. Dazzling gold and blue. Dawn, the ladie's coach, took the south end of the field for warm-ups. Dawn was a pretty "cool" coach, but Mike, the men's coach, was just devious enough that some of his tactics would cause her to become a bit "unglued". She knew he had a few new players that were pretty good, but so did she. Chrissie, Karen, and Cathy, the center, were the best and most powerful linemen around, and it gave the girls an immense advantage. Dawn's new quarterback, Lisa, could really "throw it", and her two running backs, Ros and Monica, had "moves" most people hadn't even seen yet. Lilly and Nina were back at wide-out and tight end, making her offense an awesome machine. She had also heard that Mike had kicked Pup off the team, and with Pup gone, the men had no speed whatsoever

The men arrived, took the north side of the field, and started warming up. In red and white uniforms, they seemed much bigger than their opponents. Mike had made a bunch of changes, also. Gaet was the new quarterback and Ron, a newcomer, was at running back, along with Ken. Bill and Doug had "beefed up" in the off-season, and hoped to handle the awesome lady linemen a bit better. In addition, Dan, a powerful newcomer. was also anchoring the line at center. Give Gaet enough time, and he could throw and hit his ends, Ed and Chris all day from 40 yards.

The teams had gone to the locker rooms and Mike and Dawn were handing over their rosters and lineups; one to Georgia, the head official, and one to the opposing coach. Mike studied Dawn's roster intently, hoping to find something wrong, but couldn't. Dawn looked over Mike's team roster. Sure enough, she didn't see Pup listed. Why was he here then, and in uniform? Dawn told Georgia about it, and Georgia asked Mike why Pup was in uniform and not on the roster. Mike got out the rule book and pointed out that if there was an injury and the injured player couldn't continue, there was a provision for one roster substitution. Dawn was furious—leave it to Mike to find a loophole. What a sleaze!

The men won the toss, and took over on their 40-yard line. (no one could kick a football, so this was standard procedure). There was pandemonium in the stands. The spectators loved this game.

The first play was a hand-off to Ken, and he got about 4 yards before Anneke, the right tackle, and Nece, a free safety brought him down. Gaet went into the shotgun, and Cathy seemed to come in with the ball, giving the boys a 5-yard sack. Mike was pulling his hair and screaming for blocking. Third and 11. Keith, the right tackle was in motion, and it was third and 16. Gaet lobbed a 3-yard pass to Chris, who was brought down immediately by Lena, the right end. Gaet almost fumbled Dan's snap on fourth down and Chrissie downed him. The girl's were whooping and taking over the ball. Things were looking bad for the guys.

Time out. Bonnie and Pup, the waterboys, were out on the field with Gatorade. The Lady Eagles took over, and moved the ball methodically, Ros and Monica, behind that big line were piling up yardage. They were hard to tackle because their powerful hips were constantly moving. Mike moved 7 players opposite the three big linemen and slowed it down some. It was third and 7 when Lisa threw her first pass. She had plenty of time, and Lilly broke clear. Slightly underthrown, Lilly had to slow a bit for the ball, and Ken tackled her at the 20-yard line. Lilly had to come out for equipment repair, as half her tear-away jersey was missing. She left the field, red-faced and hugging herself, amid tumultous cheering, hooting, and whistling. The ladies were called for motion on the next play and then fumbled the ball away.

The guys took over the ball on their own 17-yard line. Mike was determined they'd move the ball this time. He had sent Harold in for Bill. Chrissie, the defensive and offensive tackle for the ladies, was an animal, and when she blocked you, it was like being hit with a sledge-hammer. Bill was needing a rest and some repairs. Harold was big and strong, and Mike hoped he could help Doug double-team her. Ed, the right end, was tall and had good hands. Gaet just took a quick snap and lobbed it high to where Ed was supposed to be. Ed made a spectacular catch and headed downfield. Carol and Tammy, two swift linebackers, dropped him after an 8-yard gain. The boys were moving the ball now. Ron got 4 over left tackle and on a reverse end-around Ken had another 12. It was looking good until Gaet tried a keeper up the middle. He was hit instantly, and there was a big pile-up. Georgia was carefully watching the "unpiling" and suddenly blew her whistle and threw down a yellow penalty flag. Nece had made the first hit and was lying on poor Gaet, who had his hand inside her jersey. The boys were assessed 15 yards for a bra-strap penalty Gaet was trying to tell Georgia that Nece had put his hand there, but she ignored him.

The guys were tiring fast and Mike only had one more time out. God, he wished it was half-time. You finally get your offense going, and they start putting your hands in their shirts. Dawn was the dirtiest coach in the country. He glared across the field.

The ladies had taken over the ball at their own 35-yard line, and were moving it right on downfield. The guys just couldn't cope with Dawn's powerful offensive line and the swivel-hipped Ros and Monica. four plays later, Nina made a nice catch and ran it over for a touchdown. The two—point conversion failed, and it was 6-0, ladies.

The huge crowd loved this game. One spectator said it was more "grab-ass" than football. All the men could do was try to hold the ball until halftime. Mike would talk to Georgia about this "putting hands in shirts" business then. The guys did pretty well. Ken had a good run over the right side, and he had a good stiff-arm move. Anneke came in for the tackle, and Ken stiff-armed her, removing her jersey, somehow. She made the tackle, though, shoulder pads banging against her bare shoulders. Georgia nullified the play, though, with a disrobing penalty. Unintentional, five yards. Debbie, the middle linebacker, sacked Gaet as the half ended.

The girl's locker room was a happy place. Monica was smirking, and Dawn just couldn't wait to get them back on the field. Lilly was settled down somewhat, asking only that Her picture not "be in the paper" tomorrow. Lisa had followed Dawn's game plan perfectly, and they had just simply worn the guys down. The second half would be a slaughter, and maybe that damn sleazy, over-the-hill Mike would finally quit coaching.

Not so happy in the other dressing room. Mike was foaming at the mouth. He just couldn't understand how a bunch of grown men could let a bunch of women get the best of them. He made a few adjustments and let them get their breath back. He only had two options: one was to hope for a miracle, and the other was to put Pup in. Pup was dumb, didn't follow orders, and couldn't play football, but he had two advantages: he was fast, and the Ladies hated him. Maybe Mike could use that to his advantage. He headed out to the field to find Georgia.

CHAPTER II

Mike had found Georgia at halftime and let her know what he thought about the "paper shirts" the Lady Eagles were wearing. Georgia told Mike sweetly that his people could wear them also. Nothing in the rule-book against it. Mike was fuming when he led his team out for the second half. These stupid officials needed to "get a life" and just let the players play.

The Lady Eagles took over at their 40, and started moving downfield. The Ladies were warmed up now, and the guys just couldn't stop them. After several neat running plays, Lisa called a halfback pass to Ros. Ros was to go ten yards to the 15, cut left sharply, and the ball would be there. Lisa threw a perfect pass, but as Ros cut left she lost stride and was able to only tip the ball. Brandon, the left guard for the guys, was tall and a sort of handsome guy. He grabbed the falling ball and headed the other way. Linemen aren't used to carrying the ball, but Brandon did a great job.

The first Lady to hit Brandon was Lena. She was hanging on to his left foot as Nece grabbed him. Still forging ahead, Brandon was hit by both Carol and Tammy. Slowed to a mere crawl now, Monica and Debbie finally brought him to the turf, his helmet flying off. Several Ladies piled on, and a yellow flag came down. The entire Lady team was piled on Brandon, and Georgia was carefully untangling the mess. Brandon was immobile at the bottom of the pile. Lipstick covered him from his neck clear up to his scalp. He had a peaceful smile on his face, and was breathing regularly, but was unresponsive.

Doctor Jeannie, always at the games, was kneeling beside Brandon, examining him. She finally concluded that he was in a sort of blissful catatonic state, and thought he would be all right. Something had apparently just completely overwhelmed him, similar to an overdose. Mike quickly asked Jeannie point-blank whether Brandon could continue. Jeannie looked at Mike as if he were crazy, and replied, "Of course not." Mike immediately handed Georgia his revised roster, having substituting Pup for Brandon. Dawn was so mad her face was red. She'd known he'd figure out a way to get that stupid Pup in there. If she'd had a pin, she'd have stuck it in that phony possum-playing Brandon

Dawn's problems weren't over. All this had occurred after the play had been blown dead. Georgia carefully paced off the roughness penalty for piling on, thought a minute, and paced off another 15 yards for unneccessary contact. (the lipstick). This brought the nose of the ball to the two-yard line. Dawn was cursing and stomping. Georgia looked at Dawn, blew her whistle, and said "Unsportsman-like conduct. Halfway to the goal," moving the ball another yard.

Dawn called time out, and told the Ladies to just ignore Pup. He would be all over the field, but really was more of a nuisance than a problem, If we just ignore him. he'll probably wind down and just watch, she told them.

The guys scored on the first play, Ken going over untouched. The extra point failed, and the game was tied, 6 to 6.

The Ladies powerful line was tiring a bit, but was taking a terrible toll on the men. Bonnie, now in at right end, Anneke, and Lena were all good blockers and good tacklers. With Brandon on the sidelines, Harold, Chuck, and Keith were getting beaten off the blocks, and Ros and Monica, along with one nice reception by Lilly, had worked the ball down to the 8-yard line. Dan, the big center, had tackled Ros for a loss on one play, but, for some reason, didn't want to get off of her, and Georgia had penalized. the men 5-yards for delay of game.

This close to the goal line, the guys had nothing to lose. They just ALL went to the line of scrimmage to reinforce the blocking. It seemed to work. Three plays later it was fourth—and—goal on the five. A very frustrated Lisa called time out to converse with Dawn.

Mike had seen this time out coming, and his brain was working on all possibilities. The Ladies were tiring some, and if he could stop them here and get a few breaks he could actually win this ball game. He beckoned to Pup, who hadn't been in yet, and had a long chat with him, pointing out on the field and gesticulating wildly.

Pup was kind of a puny guy, but he could run like the wind, and he was a pest. The Lady Eagles knew he couldn't tackle or anything, he just liked to run and jump on people.

Dawn was afraid to try a pass. She decided to have Lisa send Monica over the right side behind Chrissy and Karen, her best blockers. All the guys were doubled up at the line, except Pup, who was about 8 yards deep in the backfield. Just as the ball was snapped, Pup streaked for the line, launched himself over the line, and was coming down on Monica, the ball-carrier. An alert Nece saw him coming and grabbed him in mid-air. Immediately, Georgia flagged the Ladies 10-yards for holding. The Ladies protested the call, but Georgia was firm. "When they're coming at you, hun, you have to block. You can't grab and hold."

On the sidelines, Brandon was regaining his senses. He couldn't speak yet, but was making some sucking sounds and smiling. Jeannie knew he'd be okay. Maybe a bit of mental trauma for awhile from this "unusual" experience, but nothing permanent

The guys had gotten a big break on the holding call, and they took over the ball deep in their own territory. Mike had filled Gaet in on what Pup could do on offense, and it wasn't much. What Gaet needed was someone to give him some time to throw the ball. Pup never huddled before a play. He'd just look around and then line up somewhere just to see what was going to happen. Cathy was so strong at center there was nothing up the middle, and Carol, Debbie, and Tammy were all quick, strong linebackers. They'd just have to grind it out and hope for a break.

Ron was a good ball carrier, but he just couldn't get any running room. He and Ken were pounding the line and getting virually nothing.

Monica and Ros were corners on defense and Lisa was deep safety. All fast, and good tacklers. Gaet had kept the ball on the ground, and he noticed that they were creeping in closer and closer to the scrimmage line.

Pup was in the huddle for the first time and lined up at right end. Gaet took the handoff, noting that Monica and Ros were blitzing the run. Pup took off downfield about 15 yards and Gaet lofted a beautiful pass. Pup caught it just as a charging Lisa flew into him headlong. Pup held onto the ball, raising his other arm in self-defense. His outstretched arm went inside the back of the flying Lisa's pants, and a flag came down. Pup was assessed 15 yards for a "jock-strap violation", nullifying the play with loss of down. Mike got into Georgia's face and said Lisa wasn't wearing no damned jock-strap. Georgia started pacing off the penalty and asked Mike how he knew that. Mike got red in the face and left the field.

Brandon was sitting up on his sideline cot now, looking out on the field wistfully. He wanted to get tackled some more, and they wouldn't let him play.

The guys lost the ball on downs two plays later, and the Ladies started moving it downfield again. When the Ladies were on offense, everyone in the stands would stand and cheer them on. Mike was livid. every time his offense got going, that dern Georgia would come up with a penalty and stop it.

Lilly was fast, and with willowy hips and a good stiff-arm, She was just hard to tackle. Ros and Nina were both good offensive down-field blockers. Lisa faked a handoff to Ros and handed off to Lilly, right behind Ros, straight up the middle. Pup came streaking in, dodged Ros, and got in Lilly's face. Lilly just literally ran over Pup, but had to slow enough for Chuck to bring her down.

Grinding it out like this was too slow, though, and Dawn knew it. Only enough time for about two plays or so, and she sure didn't want to pass with Pup out there. If only Mike weren't such a dirty coach. She gritted her teeth and glared across the field.

Time out, and the stadium was so noisy you'd have thought there was a war going on. Mike told Pup whatever he did, he had to get in Lisa's face somehow as soon as she got the ball. Dawn didn't even want to use the shotgun. Most of the guys were so tired that she felt if they could get into the secondary they could get the last 15 yards and score. Suddenly she had an idea.

Bonnie was tall, with good, long legs (if you know what I mean), and good hands. Lisa, a terrific ball-handler, took the ball from Cathy, and in one smooth motion, sort of scooped it high to Bonnie. Keith got a hand on her but she swivelled away and got into the secondary. Gaet made the tackle, but the Ladies were on the 4 yard line now, and time for another play or two.

Ros took the next hand-off and went left, behind the powerful Chrissie. Chrissie and Karen took Bill and Doug out of the play, and Ros had daylight. Pup came in like a streak, jumped on Ros, and actually wrested the ball from her right at the goal line. Georgia blew the play dead, and then stopped to think. The noise was deafening. Both coaches were running onto the field, and the usually unflappable Georgia apparently didn't know how to rule on this one.

Suddenly, the stadium went silent. Not a sound. Georgia pulled the rule book out, silenced both Dawn and Mike, and studied a moment. Georgia put the rule book away, went to the goal line, and raised both arms. Touchdown, Ladies! The official final score was Ladies 12—Men 6. The stadium erupted, and Mike demanded a rule explanation. Pup had had possession of the ball. How could Ros score without the ball? Dawn was very quiet. She was sure that attitude just might be a factor in all this. Georgia sweetly explained that Pup's feet hadn't touched the ground, and therefore, by Ros having possession of Pup, she also had possession of the ball, therefore it was a touchdown. Mike glared at Pup, glared at Dawn, glared at Ros, glared at Georgia and stalked off the field.

The MVP award went to Chrissie, who had an astounding 26 blocks and 11 tackles. Coach of the Year went to Dawn for putting together such an awesome team, and Lisa was given Athlete of the Year award by Dawn. Post—game activities were concluded, and Eagletown returned to normalcy for another year.

The End.

PORN FUN

CHAPTER I

For the first time in years, Cliff was really excited. The internationally famous pornography director had a script that would blow the charts. His" XXX STEAM" would hit the theaters like a bolt of lightning. This was not a "ho-hummer" with a lot of phony silicon. This was to be the real thing as he was certain many well-endowed famous people would auditioned or apply for the fantastic roles.

Mike, a veteran porn star, would be perfect for the male lead. He could "ooh and ahhh" with the best, and already knew all the "positions". In addition, he was a good actor, having starred in many raunchy R-rated B movies. His rugged good looks and roughness also attracted many of the sadistic type women who paid big bucks to watch these movies.

Cliff had leaned toward Gaet and Scott for the "threesome" scenes. Both were handsome, muscular, and had great stamina. It was rumored in Cannes that Scott was "good" for forty-eight hours, whatever that meant.

He had also selected Chuck, Dan, Bill, and Justin to star in the one big "orgy" scene. Muscular, handsome, and extremely active with their hands, they were good actors, and seemed to love their work. Good "hands on" performers.

Pup had auditioned, for God's sake! No one in their right mind would pay to see him. Cliff liked Pup, tho, and he could safely portray the limo driver in the super-sultry back seat scene. Pup needed the work.

Cliff needed a real pro to play the rapist role, and he had to be very selective here. One of the highlight scenes of the film, the rapist had to sort of personify evil debauchery. Going through the applications, he decided to use Paul, who had a good leer and was experienced in ripping off female apparel.

The last male role went to Doug. He would play the back seat role. Foremost in his field, he was an artist at sliding up a skirt. Nice hands, and a slow, deliberate motion, slowly revealing more and more creamy thigh.

That about wrapped it up for the men. Cliff was getting tired. Tomorrow, he would go through the audition results, watch the clips, and assign the female roles.

CHAPTER II
The Ladie's Roles

Cliff was a feeling a bit tired, despite a good night's rest. Too much midnight oil lately. His voluptuous assistant, Dawn, was already in the office, perky as ever. His coffee was being poured, and the audition results and applications of the ladies were on his desk, along with some film clips. It would be interesting to see who all had applied. He was sure "XXX STEAM" would be an epic, and was hoping some of the top female names in the business had applied.

Dawn was probably the most highly paid assistant director in the porn film business. With many years of experience, she had the uncanny ability to just "sense" when something was (or wasn't) sexily portrayed. Her motto was, "It ain't all skin, hun."

Dawn seated herself, crossed her long silken legs, and they went to work. Cliff was suddenly excited. The famous Lisa had applied for the back-seat role. Known on the continent as "La Langue" (the Tongue), she was a super-sexy box-office hit anywhere. He reminded himself to get a better high definition close-up camera, and to have the rear-view mirror removed from the limo. That stupid Pup would wreck it for sure. Lisa could do more things with her tongue than Tiger Woods could with a golf club.

Dawn was so excited she had buttoned down her blouse a bit and was fanning her face with her hand. She gave Cliff a rather triumphant look and handed him the dossier she had just gone over. Cliff was astounded. The famed British pole-dancer Karen had auditioned. Popularly known as "Thunder Thighs", her performances were always sold out, and she was an indefatigable performer. She never took a day, night, or even an hour off. Highly decorated, she had received knighthood as well as many medals of valor. It was rumored that she performed on a specially designed water-cooled pole to preventing smoking or possible warping. She would be perfect for the action-packed nightclub scene.

Cliff glanced at Dawn, busily reading an application. She had undone another button, and was fingering a fourth. He (almost) wished she wouldn't wear those lace trimmed chemises. Simply too damned distracting. He forced himself to look away and grabbed the next audition report.

My God!! Ros had auditioned! Known as the "Mad Minx" in England, and always in the tabloids, she had her body insured with Lloyd's for millions. Things were coming together now. He would star her with Mike in the all-important motel room scene. A former top lingerie model, she could make a garter belt look more valuable than a sable coat.

Dawn said, "Excuse me." Cliff looked up to see her get to her feet and head for the hallway to the bathroom. Lord! Just watching her walk gave him the flim-flams. When she had retired years ago, the porn industry had almost gone under. He could see why. Every single move she made was sensual.

The next audition result was different, for sure. An amateur trying out for the rape scene. Her name was Lena, and in the enclosed picture she was fully clothed, for Pete's sake! Cliff started to throw it in in the wastebasket, when something caught his trained eye. Peering intently now at the photo. he knew she had the part. Petitely attractive, innocent looking, almost skinny, and utterly defenseless, she just simply looked as though she "needed" raping. Perfect for the rape scene. An experienced, educated, and sophisticated porn audience would go into a frenzy watching her being raped.

Cliff handed Dawn the info on Lena. Dawn looked up, batted her eyes, lowered her spectacles, and examined the papers. Cliff shuddered. How in the hell can a woman adjusting her eyeglasses do so with such a sexual flair? He was losing concentration, and he had one more important role to fill.

The nurse in the hospital scene was a critical role and he had to be careful here. He sneaked a glance at Dawn.

Her skirt had slid up her smooth, white, silky thigh about an inch, and to Cliff it looked like a mile. He shook himself back to reality.

Dawn handed him an audition report. Stella, who had won an Oscar for "Backsides" had auditioned for the nurse role. Stella, nicknamed "Heavenly Haunches" by the tabloids, was perfect for the part, but the part was wrong for Stella. Not enough exposure. He decided to have a marathon race scene, and the camera would follow her very closely around the track, An audience could watch this for an hour, and want more.

He told Dawn about the scene change and why. She leaned back in her chair, her skirt rising a bit more. She fingered her necklace while thinking, her bosom heaving ever so slightly. Finally she agreed. Cliff, completely mesmerized, was calling it a day.

This film was going to be way over budget, with all these big stars, but it would, indeed, set a box office record. He hoped to begin filming a week from today.

CHAPTER III
The Filming

Cliff had a lot to do, with only a week left. He knew Dawn would be out of town for the weekend and he'd have the office to himself. Cliff had sold more porn than any man alive, and he knew how it was done. With this powerful, well known cast available, he had come up with a plan that would make his Eagle Productions millions. Sunday he was busy at the office most of the day.

Monday through Thursday were crucial days. Lots of preparations on the set and a lot of work in the office. Dawn would handle the office work as usual. Long hours, a lot of it on the telephone with various suppliers, and last minute odds and ends to be taken care of.

Shooting started Friday, and the dialogue scenes that set up the "action" were being filmed. The big motel scene was now being set up. Mike and Ros were playing two married people setting up an assignation at a neighboring motel. Cliff and Dawn were in director's chairs as the dialogue was winding

Pup

up. Cliff had the megaphone and Dawn reached to take it from him, then placed it to her lips and gave an order. Watching her sitting erectly, bosom pushed slightly forward, holding that megaphone to her lips, and that dusky, suggestive voice was getting to him. He looked away.

The scene opened with Ros walking down the street. It is now late dusk, and darkening. White, tight, mini-skirt, hair blowing a bit in the beeeze, great legs, heels. Well filmed from all angles. The cameras got it all. On cue, Mike wheeled up in a Mercedes convertible, pulled over to the curb, and they chatted awhile. He finally reached over and opened the door. Ros slowly and expertly climbed in, showing a lot more leg than necessary.

It was almost dark now as they drove into the motel parking lot. Entering the dimly lit motel room, they clutched each other fiercely, kissing and impatiently grabbing at each other's clothes. Just as Ros stepped out of her skirt, the door was kicked open and two men entered. Mike never could follow a script, and he thought this was part of the show. Being the rugged leading man he was, he slugged the nearest one, then turned to confront the other. The second man shoved a badge into Mike's face and advised him that he and this (pausing to sneer at Ros) "lady of the streets" were under arrest for pandering and assault on a police officer. Damn, they had played the pickup scene so perfectly, they had gotten themselves thrown in the slammer!

Dawn got them out the next morning (being filmed, of course), and the judge, captivated by Dawn and conscious of the cameras, admonished the arresting officers for overreacting. Mike, ever the thespian, stalked disdainfully from the courtroom right behind a very disheveled and pissed-off Ros.

Surprisingly, Cliff elected to use the scene. The police intervention had made it a sort of action scene, and the curvaceous Ros, furious and sans her skirt, not wearing a slip, trying to hit a cop with her shoe, was simply too good not to show. A great scene, actually.

Cliff knew exactly what he was doing. He had scrapped the orgy scene and the two threesome scenes, adding the entire cast to the big cocktail bar scene featuring Karen and the pole. The rape scene was being filmed now. This had to be done just right in order to inflame the audience. Paul was the best rapist in the porn business, and he knew how to rape slowly, with great deliberation.

Cliff and Dawn, side by side in the director chairs, watched the scene unfold. Lena, innocent as Little Red Riding Hood, was walking down the deserted dimy-lit street at night. Coming to a rather dark alley, she paused, finally deciding to take the short-cut. As soon as she entered the dark, ominous alleyway, they would add the "Psycho" shower scene sound track. It was perfect. Damn! Dawn had moved her elbow so that it touched his. It felt like a branding iron to Cliff. He moved his arm.

On cue, Paul, wearing dark clothing and a hood, emerged from behind a dumpster and grabbed the now struggling, screaming Lena, covering her mouth quickly with one gloved hand. When he seemed to know she would no longer cry out he released his hold on her face, dropping her to the pavement. He stood above her small, crumpled, defenseless body, leering, hood now in his hand, knowing she was completely terrified and would now submissively accept her fate. Raising the terrified maiden to her feet, he ripped off her blouse in one savage motion. Suddenly Lena went into action. She was just a blur of motion, and almost instantly Paul was hors de combat, lying on the pavement, clutching his midsection.

Cliff roared, "Cut!", and it suddenly came to him where he had seen Lena. She had had a few speaking roles before. She was no amateur. She had co-starred in several martial arts films with Chuck Norris several years ago, and he could remember reading that she had done several other martial arts movies due to her incredible skill. She was sometimes billed as "Lightning Lena". He had unwittingly starred a Ninja in his porn film, sending one of his leading men to the nearest out-patient clinic with a severely damaged groin.

Good film clip, though, and he would run it. He made a mental note to keep Lena in mind for some future roles. Tomorrow, they would film the marathon scene, starring Stella.

They had gotten a city permit to use a rather scenic hike-and-bike trail to film the episode, and two off-duty police officers were hired to keep it as clear as possible for the cameras and filming. In the dialogue for the scene, Stella is portraying a world-class marathon runner training for the Olympics. Chuck and Dan are her trainers, and Gaet and Bill would alternate as her "pacers".

Scene 7 Take 1. Stella is very slowly removing her pale blue warm-up jacket, then even more slowly, her warm-up pants. She is now clad in a rather tight white athletic tank-top, blue hot-pants type running shorts, blue and white running shoes, and her hair is in a pony-tail. Stella opens her workout with a few forward bends with one camera covering her from the side, and five from the rear. Then a few jumping splits, followed by running in place for a few moments.

Chuck was the timer. Snapping his stop-watch, he signalled Stella and Gaet to begin running down the trail. Gaet was a good pacer, but he just didn't have Stella's stamina, and he was soon lagging. The filming apparatus to Stella's rear was a big golf cart type vehicle with big, soft tires holding about eight mounted cameras.

Suddenly spectators began joining the race. Several men and a few women had joined in and were running behind Stella, and more and more bystanders were pouring on the trail. No one seemed to be actually racing. They were there for the scenery. Stella was getting scared now and speeded up. When she speeded up, her "wobble" became more pronounced, and she was now running for her very life.

The two hired cops finally rescued Stella and got her safely away from the frenzied, fired-up mob. She had been pinched and squeezed a bit in the posterior region, but was unhurt. Cliff gave her a snort of Jack Daniels from his flask, and told "Heavenly Haunches" to take the rest of the day off.

Cliff and Dawn agreed that the marathon scene was really pretty good. The cameras had caught everything, right up to and including the rescue. "XXX Steam" was on schedule. Tomorrow they would begin filming the limo rear seat scene, starring Doug and Lisa.

Salaries had to be met, and other bills were pouring in. Making movies is expensive. Paul was still in rehab, with his medical bills soaring. Cliff sure hoped his plan would work. Eagle Productions had staked everything on the outcome.

Lisa was standing on red carpet at the main entrance to what was obviously a rather upscale hotel. She was stunning in a white, silky, rather transparent blouse, mid-thigh light brown skirt, heels, and sunshades. The cameras were getting her from all angles, including from underneath. A voyeur's dream. Cliff knew this scene would be a killer.

Glancing at Dawn, he could see that she, too, was fascinated. She was breathing deeply, fanning her face with that annoying habit she had. He simply couldn't see how any human could breathe like that. It was driving him crazy. He tore his eyes from her just as Pup drove up in the limo, making a nice move to the curb, stopping with Lisa directly facing the rear door.

As Pup was preparing to open the door for her, Lisa sort of sighed slowly and licked her lips, almost as if in anticipation. She was a great actress, and now she was bringing her famous tongue into the scene. A lot of popcorn was going to be spilled.

Lisa made a production of entering the vehicle as only she could. One camera on her face, one behind her, one to the side, and one almost up her skirt. Pup pulled away from the curb, and the cameras now capture the scene in the rear of the limo.

Doug was wearing a tuxedo, as he had been to a formal affair, and he had removed his tie and jacket. Handing Lisa a martini, it was obvious that he had been drinking. Lisa downed her martini in one big gulp, and seated herself on Doug's lap, immediately pulling his face toward hers. Their lips met lightly and Doug's hand went to her thigh, expertly sliding her skirt up ever so slightly.

They both got a bit of fresh air, then kissed a bit harder this time. Doug moved her skirt up slightly and the top of her stocking was beginning to show.

More air, and then harder, more frantic kissing. Doug now had her skirt as high as it would go, and they came up for air again.

Lisa had her lips parted for the next kiss, and Doug opened his mouth. Their faces met, and almost instantly Doug was thrashing violently. Lisa's mouth was working frantically, and Doug collapsed, his hand falling from her exposed thighs. La Langue had struck again!

Cut! Wow! Cliff and Dawn were ecstatic. A classic scene. Doug had now regained consciousness, and wanted to redo the scene. He said he wanted to resume the kissing, but Lisa had triumphantly left the set and gone to her dressing room.

Tomorrow they would film the nightclub scene featuring the entire cast, and they could edit and "can" "XXX STEAM".

CHAPTER IV

Cliff had rented a really nice nightclub for the big scene, Modern, roomy, a big stage with two poles behind the bar, and all in all, just a nice, upscale lounge. They had changed the outside Marquee from "The Copa" to "The Broken Cherry", and were rehearsing now.

Cliff had a friend in Newark who had raved about a pole dancer in one of the big casinos in Atlantic City. Her name was Windy, and they had acquired her for the scene. She had arrived earlier today, and was working out on a pole now. She was the current rage of New England, just as Karen was on the continent. This should prove interesting, indeed.

Cliff and Dawn had agreed that this scene was also perfect for the final casting "victory party". It was leased for the night, so why not take advantage of it and save the expense of another party? Everyone was looking forward to this filming. Free booze and lots of sexy people.

Dawn had noticed Cliff was getting a bit frayed looking. She knew he'd been spending a lot of time late at night in the office, and had no clue as to what he was doing. She usually assisted in the editing and splicing, and that was pretty much caught up. He seemed more rested and alert today. Maybe he'd finished whatever he had been doing.

Scene 1 Take 1. Cameras and mikes were in place, and the scene opened at the lounge entrance. Mike made his grand entrance with a luscious looking Jojo (a very attractive, elegant looking extra) on his arm. Dan, (the club owner), greeted and ushered them in, then turned to greet Paul and the stunning Lisa. Paul was ambulatory now, but with crutches. Lisa was wearing a sparkling red satin cocktail dress, showing a lot of skin, top and bottom. The cameras feasted on this couple.

Scott and Ros arrived next. Ros was in a flesh-colored body-clinging mini, her great legs almost gleaming. She was always a camera-hog, and made a big deal out of greeting Dan. Dan was so overwhelmed he had to go inside and down a shot just to settle down and get the lipstick off. They seated themselves with Mike and Jojo and ordered drinks.

Chuck and Stella approached the canopied entrance with all six portable cameras right behind Stella. Stella, always camera conscious, was finally sort of wiggling through the door very slowly with the cameras reluctantly "peeling" off.

Backstage, Karen had just arrived. Late, as usual, she flounced in with a big bag of "toys" she had just acquired from a nearby adult store. Karen was always in a good mood, and was now in her dressing room donning her costume and applying that olive oil mixture she used to make her mighty, round thighs gleam and glisten.

Cliff was using Pup as a bartender, along with Georgia and Sarah, two great-looking, rather coke-bottle shaped ladies who knew their way around in the porn business. His two cocktail waitresses were Lilly and Debbie, both blond, shapely, and very "pinchable". They were dressed alike in little red and white skimpy outfits, and both had great "underpinning".

The outdoor filming was now completed. Bill had made an entrance almost as grand as Mike's, with the cutest thing you ever saw hanging on to his arm. It was Lena! She was wearing a tight pale blue knee-length gown that was slit up both sides clear to the hip, had makeup on, and was really getting the stares. They started to sit with Paul and Lisa, but Lena said something to Bill, and they sat with Stella and Chuck.

Doug and Gaet came in stag, their eyes roving. These handsome dudes wouldn't be alone long. Doug's problem was he'd wanted to date Lisa, and she had told him she was taken, and to get another date. Gaet was a pickup artist and loved it. They sat at the bar and immediately went into action. Dawn was delicately sipping a drink at the bar and they sat next to her. Cliff was a bit upset at this and he didn't even know why.

Chuck entered escorting a drop-dead unbelievable chunk of pulchritude named Kim. Kim was a classic beauty, with huge, dark eyes that just seemed to say, "Come here, hun." Chuck and Kim joined Lisa and Paul at their table.

Dan was at the mike announcing Karen's first performance, and the lights dimmed even more. the spotlight came on and followed the magnificent Karen across the stage to the pole. She bowed and curtseyed to the audience, and lovingly clasped the pole. Her costume was a white two-piece silky thin material trimmed with a lacy border. She seemed as though she were performing in panties and bra. Her powerful, shapely upper legs were constantly in motion as she put on an unbelievable performance.

Pausing occasionally, she would almost remove a part of her costume, but never did. Fifteen minutes of this, and it was intermission time. The spotlight followed Karen offstage, and a stagehand came onstage with a big basket, gathering all her money from the stage floor.

The applause was deafening, and the cameras flashed to Mike's table, where Lilly had just refreshed their drinks. Some small talk there and then to the camera under the table. The temptress, Ros, had taken off one slipper and was giving Mike's leg a good going over with her toes. Mike was trying to keep his composure, and Jojo was trying to keep Scott's hand off her exposed upper thigh.

Pup was kind of lazy, and he was getting tired of mixing drinks. Gaet had "come on" to Sarah and she had just quit bartending to party with him, and Pup and Georgia were starting to tire. Finally Pup was having Lilly and Debbie take full bottles to the tables, and he'd just fill glasses with anything when they were handed to him. He didn't know how to mix drinks anyway.

Ten minutes before Karen's next appearance, Dan announced the New England sensation, "Wondrous Windy" on the pole and the lights dimmed again. Under the spotlight Windy bowed and waved to the audience. She was wearing a tight, filmy sort of semi-transparent full red Bikini bottom, and a low cut red bra. Windy was a whiz on the pole and her audience, half—swacked by now, was hooting and throwing money on the stage.

With all the liquor Pup was giving everyone, a line was forming at the women's restroom. Ros excused herself and headed for the ladies' room, followed by a staggering Jojo. Ros made it inside, but Jojo collapsed at the door, blocking it partly open. The impatient Lisa was next in line, and just headed for the adjoining mens' room, followed by a camera.

Doug was preparing to leave the mens' room when the door opened and Lisa staggered in. Half drunk, he just grabbed her and started kissing her. Lisa struggled at first, then looked directly into the camera, licked her lips, opened her mouth slightly and in no time Doug was on the floor, happily unconscious. Then she just calmly used the rest room and left him lying there.

Karen usually had about three drinks between acts. She could hold her liquor well. When she made her entrance for her second performance and noticed another pole in "action" she seemed a bit bewildered. Karen went to her pole, spat on her hands, and then calmly walked across the stage, grabbed Windy by the hair and yanked her off the pole. Windy was swinging wildly and cursing Karen, landing a few. Karen was about to unloose a haymaker when Pup and Georgia, probably the soberest people there, broke it up. Cliff screamed, "Cut," and "XXX STEAM" was filmed.

The party never ended there. Before the night was over Paul tried to rape at least three of the ladies to no avail, and Doug, conscious now, was still pursuing Lisa for further ecstatic torment from that mouth of hers. Sarah had tired and left, with Gaet putting the "make" on every lady there. Ros was crumpled at the base of one pole and Stella at the other. The Damage to the Copa lounge was extensive, but Cliff had taken out insurance for the night and, luckily, no one had gone to jail.

CHAPTER V
The Censors and the Climax

Cliff was an expert and he knew "XXX Steam" didn't show enough "skin" to get an X rating. That's the reason he had put the X's in the title; to attract attention. It was a great film, and the censors would be fair and get it right. With all that pulchritude, it would be a blockbuster and it would also be in the mainline theaters where the big money was.

He also knew that Dawn was inadvertently the sexiest thing you'd ever hope to see, and he had capitalized on it, unknown to her. The second weekend before the filming, when he knew she'd be at her condo in Sedona, he'd gone to the office and spent a long day installing spycams all over the place. He knew she'd be there alone all week and he wanted it all on film.

The last several days when STEAM was being filmed, he had gone alone to the office at night, working very late, editing and splicing this film. He wanted to submit it with STEAM,

A difficult film to edit, with no plot, but he was pro. He had inserted about eight water fountain clips. Dawn could lean over a water fountain like no other. Her skirt would rise to exactly the top of her stockings, seams perfectly straight, then she would raise up, take her hands and smooth the back of her skirt down. Then she would turn facing the camera and lick her lips. Then she would brush her bosom with her hands in case a drop of water had gotten on her lacy under blouse.

Dawn was a brown-bagger, and when she ate her lunch, it was a work of art. Editing this film, Cliff knew if he handled this right, he would produce the lowest-budget major film of all time; the only expense being the film.

He heard a ruckus outside, and going to the window, he saw Mike, Ros, Dan, and Karen in the parking lot, arguing about something. Karen and Ros were wearing shorts and heels, and Mike and Dan were dressed like prep kids in shorts and light sweaters. They were probably broke as it was two days until payday. He hurriedly locked the doors as he had film all over the office.

Suddenly they were banging on the door. They were broke and needed some "scratch", and they wanted the keys to the Mercedes. Cliff knew they wouldn't go away, so he handed the Mercedes keys and five hundred through the door, telling them to have fun. Satisfied, the four left, arguing over who was going to drive and what they were going to do.

Cliff had gotten a break the one day Dawn hadn't packed a lunch. She had ordered pizza, and the young fellow who delivered it, seeing Dawn, almost dropped it. His unblinking eyes were fixed on Dawn as he backed out, almost tripping.

The cams had caught her scratching her belly three times, stretching (wow!) five times, adjusting her eyeglasses countless times, and walking to the restroom several times. The unconscious unbuttoning was always worked in, along with the hand fanning her flushed face. He wanted it to run for about an hour and ten minutes, and he was nearly finished.

More banging on the door. God! These people were always broke. Sure enough, Bill and Jojo had spent all they had buying beer at the arena watching the Lakers game and they needed some money to go "clubbing". Sighing, Cliff gave them a few hundred, shooing them away.

It was finished. Cliff "canned" it, entitled it "SEXY SHENANIGANS", filed it away, and would send it, along with "XXX STEAM" to the censors.

Dawn had gone to Sedona the day after the filming was completed, and Cliff hadn't heard from her. He had just gotten to the office, and decided to call her, when Stella and Doug came in. It was obvious they'd been partying all night, They looked like hell, and were barely coherent. Both were trying to talk at the same time, and finally he got their story. Stella had been asked for an autograph by a persistent fellow who had squeezed her "Heavenly" bottom as she was complying. She had slugged the guy, and then Doug had punched him again, resulting in a trip to the Police Station. They weren't booked, but were detained for a while until they became a little less "disorderly", and then released. (Pin-up pics of Stella were all over the police station barely minutes after they left).

Broke, hungry, and hung over, they had walked to the office. Cliff made a pot of coffee, settled them down, and gave them a few hundred for "taxi money" after they promised to go home and sleep it off.

The two films had been at the rating and censorship board for several days now, and Cliff should hear from "BARF" (Board of Approval and Rating of Films) any day now

A phone call to Sedona revealed that Dawn had gone to Las Vegas accompanied by a gentleman, and it was unknown just where she (they?) were staying. Cliff gritted his teeth. Well he would just fill her in later.

Cliff carefully opened the envelope from BARF. This was going to be bad news, as usually the messages came along with the returned films, and the films hadn't been returned.

Eagle Enterprises
Santa Monica, CA

Dear Sirs:

We regret to inform you that at this time
we are unable to rate either film as titled.
However, we are reviewing criteria that may
enable the films to be rated and released
for viewing. There could be a considerable
delay. Thanking you for your patience.
                    BARF

Cliff gritted his teeth, picked up the telephone and
called Justin, who worked at BARF. Justin was not
available, and the sweet voice asked, "Could anyone
else assist you, sir?" Cliff hung up, just as Lisa and
Scott walked in, looking pretty chummy.

They wanted to go to Las Vegas for the day and a
night, returning late tomorrow to get paid, and they
needed an advance on their salaries. Then they
added that they needed to use the Mercedes to get
them there. Cliff had just about had it with these
profligates always wanting money, and he was just
about to tell them to get lost, when Lisa, always a
hugger, grabbed him, giving him a big, long, wet
smack on the cheek. He melted, gave them a grand,
and told them to take the limo, adding that that wild
idiot, Mike, had the Mercedes.

Dawn called later that afternoon. Her sultry voice just
radiated happiness. She said she would be away

Pup

another week, as she would be honeymooning in Vegas with her latest (10th) husband. Before Cliff could say anything, she said, "Hugs and kisses, hon. See You later." Good Lord! All this crap going on, and now Dawn goes off and gets herself married. Suddenly Cliff hated show business.

Five days later, the long-awaited package arrived from BARF. The films were rated, censored, and could now be released. Cliff anxiously opened the envelope.

Eagle Productions
Santa Monica, CA

Dear Sirs:

Congratulations! Your films have been approved for distribution. We are extremely sorry for the delay, but certain criteria must be met before a film can be released.

The film you submitted as "XXXSTEAM" did not receive an X rating, therefore we changed the title to "ATTEMPTED SHENANIGANS", which aptly describes it. We also had to come up with a new content category, as you will see.

Our recommended caption for this film is as follows: ATTEMPTED SHENANIGANS (new title) (2011)—mild violence, adult situations, language, sheer stupidity (new category)—Comedy. PG

As to your second film, entitled SEXY SHENANIGANS, we had to play in a totally different ball park, so to speak. First, there is no plot, which would normally make it a documentary, which it it not. Secondly, we had never seen anything quite like it, and consequently we viewed it many times. Our findings are as follows:

XXXXSTEAM (title change) 2011—overpowering sexuality (new rating)—XXXX(new rating) very adult adults only (new rating)

We found the films to be (ahem) entertaining, and very little was censored. If you disagree with any findings, feel free to contact us. Good luck at the box office, and, if you would, send us a complimentary copy of XXXXSTEAM, please.

BARF

Cliff was kicking his heels. He knew he would make millions on these two. He immediately called his press agent, Donna, making an appointment for her tomorrow morning.

Donna had loved the films, and they were discussing the various marketing possibilities. Cliff was watching her as she, tapping her pencil eraser against her even, white teeth, was musing just how to get this thing started with the media. He tore his eyes away. Never again would he go through this torture. No one had the right to read and think like that.

He heard voices as the door opened. Dawn and Paul entered, looking radiant and happy. Dawn hugged Cliff, then stepped back to show him her big wedding rings. It was obvious that these two were very happy. Congratulations and hugs from Cliff and Donna, who already knew both well.

Dawn handed Cliff her resignation, saying she was retiring from the business to become a homemaker. Shocked by this, Cliff stammered," But, Dawn, you have a lavish life-style. How will you manage without your salary?" Dawn answered that She and Paul had discussed all this, and they felt they could make it just fine on their savings and that Paul also made a lot of "rape" money.

They left, arm in arm, and Cliff turned to Donna, asking her if she would mind being his assistant "just until he could find someone."

The End

PREPPING FUN

CHAPTER I

Orientation

The Eagletown Academy for Young ladies was an expensive school. The reason it was always fully booked was simply that it was the best. A two-year Academy, it accepted only those young ladies who showed promise of being in the upper echelons of society later in life. When young ladies graduated from this Academy, they were actually fought over by the Registrars at Vassar and other prestigious universities. Other perks consisted of modern, roomy three-lady dormitories, good, wholesome food, and various recreational facilities, including a 35-foot swimming pool. In actuality, an ideal institution with an impeccable reputation.

It was the first day of school at the Academy, and Georgia, the head registrar and Dean of English, was going over the transcripts of the new students. There were twelve High School juniors, the maximum enrollment allowable. This exclusive two-year Academy taught twenty-four, no more and no less, each year. Each applicant was required to have a GPA of 3.5 or more, and all did except one.

Tricia had a GPA of only 2.8, but, according to her transcript, she showed "much promise" in other fields and she had been accepted, primarily because her wealthy father had agreed to "endow" the academy to the tune of eight and one-half million dollars.

The twelve seniors were an exceptional class of ladies. They were all from wealthy families, and were on the verge of becoming gracious, beautiful women. Dawn, the headmistress and drama professor, was a "Ladie's Lady", and she was sort of a "mother" to the seniors. She had no sense of humor, and she was all business—always prim and proper. A stately, graceful woman, she could stride with a full cup and saucer on her head and never spill a drop of liquid. Chrissie, the school's best athlete, was president of the senior class, and also a mathematics major.

The Academy had Three Europeans. Karen, from England, was a senior, and had been set back one year, so it was her third year here. She had had a problem learning the words to "How now, brown cow", and was also prone to bad slangy language when upset. She was responding well, though, and was expected to graduate this year if she slowed down on her night life. Monica, from The Netherlands, was a newcomer. The only daughter of a wealthy "old money" Dutch family, she was sent to a private school far away from home, as her parents loved to travel, and they didn't trust her at home alone. Ros, also from England was a newcomer this term. Her grades were excellent, second among the newcomers, and she showed extraordinary traces of future beauty and grace, braces and thick glasses notwithstanding.

Grace and poise sometimes is inherent in a young lady. If not, it can usually be taught. Mike, a teacher extraordinaire, was the master of that. For many years he had unfailingly taught the young ladies to walk just like Dawn, stately and with purpose. He was well-liked by the young ladies and had a large capacity for patience. His biggest problem now was Doo, a senior and excellent scholar, whom he had conditionally "passed", and was taking remedial classes with Mike. She was just simply uncoordinated and couldn't walk a straight line.

Lilly, a newcomer, was a pretty young lady, She had very good grades and came from a prominent banking family in New England. Her parents wanted her to go to "Haaahvud" when she left Eagletown. She was assigned a dorm room with Monica and Nece. Nece was a very talented Junior. as she had already been published. A very popular book of children's stories and poems. She was an avid learner, as well as being one of the prettiest young ladies in the school.

Lena had the highest GPA of the Juniors, at 3,9, almost perfect. Petite qnd pretty, she was annoyingly meticulous in everything she did. It took her almost an hour to eat lunch. Her assigned roommates were Josee and Debbie.

Chuck was the speech mentor for the young ladies. His perfect English was perfectly enunciated, and he wanted it that way from his students. He almost always had a conductor's baton in his hand, and if a young lady made a grave error, she was usually smacked lightly on the hand or wrist. A teaching aid, he called it, and it seemed to work. He was chatting with and getting to know the twelve new ladies and suddenly his head snapped up and the baton in his hand twitched. Debbie was from North Carolina, and Chuck had never heard such a "horrible" accent. He had his work cut out here, he knew. This pretty young blond lady needed a lot of work. He sighed: seemed there was always one in every class.

Jojo was the only daughter of a prominent surgeon, and she wasn't a bit interested in medicine. Attractive and intelligent, she had a very analytical mind, and excelled at mathematics. Pup, the advanced mathematics professor at the Eagletown Academy, only taught two advanced courses, advanced calculus and analytical geometry. He had had already scanned the transcripts of the newcomers and had accepted Jojo eagerly. Jojo was assigned to room with Tricia and Lisa, a first-year student from New York. Jojo was the only new student he accepted. Lena, with little interest in advanced math, had not applied.

Lisa's father was a Senator from New York state, and partner in a large law firm there. She had spent two high school years in a private exclusive up-state school, leaving with honors, excelling in the theater arts. She was eager to meet Dawn, her new and famous mentor.

Bill, the advanced history professor at the Academy had accepted three of the incoming Juniors. Josee, Nina, and Kim. All three seemed to love academics and probably would attain advanced degrees, possibly remaining in academic work. Josee was from a very wealthy family in the supermarket business. Newly rich, they were very politely shunned by their financial peers, and they were making sure their pretty little daughter wouldn't have that problem.

Kim, a very pretty young lady, had also been accepted to the advanced foreign language class taught by Professor Scott, who had the ability to teach a half-dozen or so young ladies five or six different languages at the same time in the same room. He was a sort of handsome gentleman and the girls would flirt with him on occasion just to make him blush. Kim was assigned to share a dorm room with Ros and Nina. Nina was an artist, and had already sold many paintings. The history of art intrigued her, and she spent many hours of research in the Academy library.

Bonnie was a Senior, and she assisted Mike a lot. She was as graceful as a swan, rivalling even Dawn in the social graces. Mike's class was in session and she was free so she joined in for some volunteer work. All twelve Juniors were in attendance as this was a requisite, along with Doo, still trying to learn how to walk gracefully. Mike was having some problems so he assigned Bonnie the more advanced students. Lisa was no problem. Her aristocratic family had trained her well. Bonnie spent almost an hour trying to show Debbie, Tricia, and Kim the proper way to be introduced to another person; the exact and proper way and exact time to extend the hand, murmuring the proper words just the proper way, the proper smile, and they were starting to get the hang of it. Doo, bless her heart, was walking and walking, trying to get it right. Mike was very satisfied with the first day. It had gone well, and he automatically knew where his problems would be. He thanked Bonnie graciously, as usual, and she responded graciously.

The advanced Calculus class was going well, Not being a required course, Pup only had four students. Chrissie, an exceptional math student, was working on a tertiary problem she would easily solve in about 20 or so minutes. Jojo was looking over her new text, and Doo, an exceptional mathematician, was working with some equations on the rear blackboard. Elaine, another senior, was puzzling over a bunch of long equations she had conjured up from somewhere. Pup was placing a difficult problem for them on the board, and as he was prone to do sometimes, his mind wandered, and he began placing formulae related to spatial physics on the board. Suddenly Jojo was at the board pointing out a possible error in Pup's jottings. Pup studied it momentarily, made a few gestures with his chalk, erased it, and continued placing their problem on the board.

The first few days of a new term were always the hardest for Chuck. Getting to know the new Juniors and discovering what he would have to do for each and every one took a few days at best. He had finally gotten Karen familiar with remembering the words and properly enunciating "How now, brown cow", but it had taken its toll on his mind. All twelve were very attentive and (thank God) none had a lisp. Monica, with a Dutch accent, spoke perfect English, however, and Chuck felt he could tone down the accent, possibly eliminate it. Ros wore braces, but spoke well through them. Lilly, from New England, had an accent, but a desirable one in this case.

Debbie was his problem this year. He gritted his teeth, asking her to repeat the "How now" bit again. That Appalachian accent was just wrong for those words. Grrrr. Well, he'd figure something out. Tricia could be a problem, also. She had a wandering mind, and sometimes just didn't focus. In Chuck's class you HAD to focus.

CHAPTER II

Finishing the "Finest"

Dr. Gaet, the Superintendent of the Eagletown Academy, looked across his desk at Dawn and Georgia and gritted his teeth. The Academy had no principal, per se, and Dawn or Georgia usually assumed the role when one was needed. The students had voted to do a version of "Gone With The Wind" for the annual drama presentation and some problems were arising. Nece had written an excellent abridged version of the famous story in three acts that would play out in just a little over an hour. The current problem was that Debz and Lisa had both screened for the leading role, Scarlett O'Hara, and it had been a toss-up. Both young ladies were consummate actresses at the age of sixteen. Discussing it at length, no solution was reached. They had a few days left to assign the role, and shelved it for now. Dawn, director of the play, leaned toward Debs as she was a senior, and Georgia, co-director, was just simply waiting for a break. She knew either would play the part perfectly.

It was mid-term now, and Ros had taken the school day off. She would be at the dentists' office for half a day or so having her braces removed, and the other half at the ophthalmologist getting her contact lenses. It was a muggy, chilly winter Friday with intermittent rain.

Lilly was an exemplary student due in part to the fact that she had been gifted with a photographic memory. It was dark and rainy outside, and Georgia, being in a competitive mood, had contrived a spelling bee. A real old time bee. Lena and Lilly were the sole survivors, Nina being last eliminated. Dr. Gaet, on his rounds, had dropped in and stayed to watch. He and Georgia were at a computer happily selecting rare long words for the two to spell. The bell rang ending the match with no clear winner. Dr. Gaet was always amazed and very proud of the intelligence of "his" young ladies. He gave Georgia a "well-done" high-five and left.

Michael, an honor graduate from Stanford, and a former collegiate track and field champion, was the Academy physical fitness director. Normally, a gym period consisted of a few ladylike calisthenics, a short lecture on fitness, diet, and hygiene, followed by a free swim, or maybe a bit of diving competition from the few who chose to participate. Today Michael had set up the volleyball net, and they were eager to play. Choosing up sides, they then happily played for the better part of the period. Chrissie excelled here as she usually did in anything involving athletics, but today it seemed that Lilly was making saves all over the court, the taller Bonnie and Josee making kills, and Chrissie's team lost. Lots of fun, though, and good sportsmansip, followed by congratulations to the winners.

Calculus class was in session, with Dr. Pup reading some formulae from an esoteric math book written by a little-known British mathematician many years ago. He came to an interesting theorem that he was placing on the board for them when, nearing the end of it, he suddenly put the book down and kept writing equations on the board. Coming to the part where Jojo had found a possible error, he stopped and was deep in thought, all four students at his elbow. Suddenly Pup started again, rapidly jotting on the blackboard. Suddenly he jammed his chalk into the board, turned to the ladies and said: "At last. I've finally done it"!! Chrissy knew these advanced equations had to do with the space-time continuum, but to what end? She was still studying it. Jojo was nearly to the end, and she was taking notes. She had an idea, but that was impossible! Doo was already studying it on another section of blackboard, and Elaine knew it had something to do with the speed of light, and was making mental calculations. The mathematical prodigy, Jojo, suddenly turned white in the face. If her calculations were correct, Dr. Pup had just laid the mathematical groundwork for a time-travel machine!

Dawn was assisting Mike in Mike's classroom with six of the Juniors. These six would practice a formal dinner for the first time. Monica was first.

She answered the door, properly greeting Mike and Dawn, the visiting couple. A bit of small talk, and then being properly escorted into the room and introduced. Monica did it perfectly, and it was Nece's turn. Also perfect. Tricia had to go through it three times, but finally got it. Lisa, as usual, was perfect, and Lena was next. Lena knew the moves, but was so deliberate in her greetings they made her do it again, a bit more fluently. Kim was a born hostess. She quickly had them in and introduced in a very congenial and formal manner.

The table was set for six, and Mike and Dawn seated each of the young ladies, making sure they sat properly. the young ladies sat primly, engaging in small talk as their food was served, always from the left side. Even napkins were to be handled properly, Proper utensil selection at the proper time with the proper portion size was very important. The ladies did an excellent job, with a bit of coaching from Mike and Dawn. Mike was pleased with the outcome and gave the ladies the rest of the period to do as they liked.

Chuck was at his wit's end with Debbie. Her Southern accent was so ingrained he just couldn't eliminate it. He was having her practice on the word "floor". She was showing some progress and had progressed from "flowaah" to "flaw", and he was getting excited. Recitals were the norm in his classroom, and the young ladies at the lectern were also getting accustomed to public speaking, a must for these young ladies. Ros, the shy one, was away today, but she had been taking to the podium easier each time. Tricia was reading the eulogy by Mark Anthony at Caesar's burial, and Chuck closed his eyes. Every word was perfectly enunciated, with no haste nor eliding. A masterful reading. The class applauded.

The Advanced History class was in session, Debz, Doo, Bonnie, and three Juniors-Nina, Josee, and Kim in attendance. Dr. Bill, an excellent professor. had given each a five page condensed history of Portugal to study for fifteen minutes. At the bell, they then then had twenty minutes to write their own summation of it, Their grade for the period would be on their summation. Bill couldn't believe their response. Not a question was asked. They just went to work and did it. He already knew how it would come out. An easy assignment for these six. Nina's would be lengthy, leaning heavily on Portugese art. Debz' would be short, concise, mentioning only the flow of history due to internal and international events. Doo was so fast she could almost do the entire thing in twenty minutes. leaving no detail out. Bonnie would lean a bit on the romantic side of it. The royalty, and their accomplishments. Nece would be a bit more geographical, and add a bit of her own knowledge, also. Kim, the analyst, wold pick it over, find the faults and the triumphs, and make an interesting and complete short summary.

Dr. Scott really liked Kim. She had the ability to learn a new language and speak it with very little accent. She seemed to just "know" how it was supposed to sound. French, Spanish, and Latin were the most-taught, and most of his students knew these by mid-term. Monica, the young Dutch lady, had an advantage here, as she was well-travelled, having vacationed abroad many summers with her parents. It was a nasty Friday outside and they were just playing Scott's game. Just an intelligent chat in foreign languages. Rules were: When it was your turn, you must continue the conversation in an intelligent fashion, in a different foreign language. Actually, a very good drill.

It had been a wet nasty and dark Friday. Tomorrow was Saturday, and most of the young ladies had plans for tomorrow—shopping being high on the list. Eagletown had a very well-stocked Emporium, and it was beckoning.

Tennis season was whenever the weather would permit, The Academy played mostly intramural—among themselves, but scheduled three or four practice matches against local high schools.

Auditions were over for the annual Drama presentation, and roles would be assigned when classes ended Monday.

CHAPTER III
Retail and Relaxation

The citizens of Eagletown were an honest, hard-working bunch, and they all knew that at any given time when the Academy was in session, the twenty-four wealthiest people in town were probably the twenty-four students there. That was one reason Saturday was such a good retail day. These young ladies never asked how much anything was. They just got it if they wanted it. When they descended on Main Street it was a merchant's paradise. This was to be such a Saturday.

The huge Emporium in Eagletown wasn't cheap, but it prided itself in handling only quality items, and it had a customer satisfaction ratio second to none. Doug had been a salesman there for several years now. Strictly on commission, he was by far the store's highest paid employee, and his sales returns were surprisingly low. He was an extraordinary salesman and had the gift of making people happy with a purchase. Surprisingly scrupulous, he had turned down many offers to sell new cars, stocks and bonds, insurance, and other high—commission items.

Saturday was a beautiful day, and Doug would be in Ladies' Shoes, as sales had been lagging there. Around mid-morning, a quite lovely young lady entered. Poised and seemingly in no hurry, she was looking around at various shoes. Doug immediately assumed her to be one of the young, wealthy ladies from the Academy, and he offered to assist her. Sitting, Doo removed her shoes and Doug measured her foot. She already had her proper size in a box she'd chosen, and Doug professionally placed them on her feet. Very nice slipper-type shoes and very expensive. The young lady has taste, he thought. Doo arose, walked to the full-length mirror, and Doug noticed a slight, almost undetectable "lurch" as she walked. Doo, satisfied, seated herself, and Doug removed the shoes. Doug asked Doo to place her ankles and knees together while sitting. It was just as he thought. Her right leg was about one-fourth of an inch longer than the left, causing the slight imbalance while walking. Pointing this out to her, he asked if she'd ever noticed this before, and asked if she had ever heard of prosthetic shoes.

Doug only had one pair of prosthetic shoes in stock that fit her prescription, and he had her try them on. Just then Elaine, Lisa, and Lilly sauntered into Ladies' Shoes. Doo was at the mirror looking at herself and turned to greet them. Mike's training was deeply ingrained into her now, and she walked over to hug her schoolmates. Elaine noticed it instantly.

Doo was walking every bit as stately and forcefully as she had been taught! Doo was ecstatic, and before she left, she had ordered one dozen pairs of variously styled prosthetic shoes, swiped her wealthy father's credit card for $3857.89, and had forced a $50 tip on Doug.

The four young ladies next went to the Jewelry Department, and "oohed" and "aaahed' around for a half-hour or so. Lilly finally nonchalantly purchased a beautiful gold necklace she "just loved" for just a tad over $2200 and they left. Five minutes later they met Dawn and Georgia in the lingerie department. Dawn and Georgia were amazed and excited about Doo's experience. Watching her walk, they both agreed that Doo could now walk as elegantly as anyone in the Academy. By now they had been joined by Bonnie and Debz, both lugging shopping bags from the Emporium. They, too, were so happy over Doo's good fortune they just kept hugging her. After purchasing a little over $800 in lingerie they all went to the Taco Bell for a fabulous lunch.

Karen was as adventurous as a young lady could get, and Tricia wasn't far behind. Almost every Saturday they could be found in the Billiard parlor on Pogo Street. There was a space-age type pinball machine in there with a built-in computer that recorded the high scores. If you were good enough or fortunate enough to get a high score, you entered your name after it, and it was automatically recorded it for all to see. All of the top ten or fifteen scores had Tricia or Karen as the player. They would try to beat their own scores, taking turns. The machine had no free play feature, so they just piled up enough quarters to play awhile and when they ran out they would get some more. This particular machine was very popular, and some of the young men and ladies watching would usually join in, and invariably get beaten. Laughing and happy, they always had a good time.

Nece and Jojo loved to bowl, and it wasn't unusual for them to get in ten or fifteen lines on a Saturday afternoon. Both averaged over 180, and on many occasions bowled well over 200, a benchmark score, even for men. The Eagletown Lanes had twelve "alleys", and Ed, the cigar-chewing owner, would schedule a few Saturday afternoon events for the two. A small tournament or two, and some prize bowling. Nece and Jojo usually took top honors. Other young ladies from the Acadamey would make it a point to drop in for awhile and cheer them on.

Bill, Scott, Michael, and Chuck had just gotten back to town. They'd gotten up early and bagged a few birds with their shotguns. Hungry by now, they'd stopped at Taco Bell, and met up with Dawn, Georgia, and company. Doo's good fortune had made their day. They all happily hugged her. She had tried so hard for so long.

Monica, Debz, and Josee, decked out in western jeans, shirts, boots, and hats were getting out of their taxi at the stables at the edge of town. The stables were owned by Dan, a handsome ex-rodeo circuit star. He loved horses and he really liked these girls from the Academy—they treated horses with great respect, as he did. All three were excellent riders and always insisted on doing their own saddling up. He always checked for safety reasons, but they were good at it. Everything was properly done and cinched just right. He had packed some saddlebags as he had promised to guide them into the foothills today. The young ladies were excited at the prospect of a real "trail" ride. Dan had told them to expect a lot of single-file travel. They should arrive back at the stables around dusk after a campfire meal in the hills. Biscuits, bacon, and canned beans.

Ros had spent over three hours in Dr. Justin's office Friday. He carefully removed her braces and immediately knew he'd done an excellent job. Not allowing her to see her teeth yet, he had his hygienist give them a complete cleaning, whitening and polishing. Checking Ros' teeth for the final time, he was amazed at her dazzling smile. She needed to do something with that straight hair, though, and get some contacts lenses. He said nothing. Ros studied her image in the mirror and with her hands she raised her hair up just a bit, moving it around and thinking.

The contact lenses were ready, so Ros went directly to Dr. Tammy's office. Dr. Tammy spent almost two hours with Ros, explaining how all this worked. Getting them in and out of the eye required a bit of practice. Proper use of the solution and storage in the case provided also took some time. Dr. Tammy couldn't remember when she'd seen such a potential beauty and casually asked her what she intended doing about her hair. Dr. Tammy recommended a salon on Main Street, and a particular beautician there named Neil. Ros jumped at the chance and a phone call resulted in a ten o'clock apointment with Neil Saturday morning. She had gotten permission from Georgia for a sleep-over with a girl friend in Eagletown, and didn't return to the Academy Friday night.

Neil was a bit nonplused at first, He had to bring out the extraordinary beauty in this young lady and keep her looking her age at the same time. He decided on a bob, a subtle upsweep, no tint, keeping well within the Academy guidelines. Ros had agreed, so Neil professionally and carefully did the makeover. After studying herself intently in the mirrors at length, Ros paid her bill and tipped Neil twenty-five dollars. Then the "new" Ros very self-consciously walked out the door into the sunlight and the sights of Main Street.

CHAPTER IV
A Busy Monday

Dr. Chuck had worked and worked with Debbie. Her accent was barely noticeable now, but still had a trace of Appalachia in it. Actually, it was perfectly subtle. She was at the podium reading now, and, coincidentally, it was a passage from "Gone With the Wind". Dawn and Georgia were spending most of the day in Chuck's classroom. Secretly, they both wanted Debbie to play Scarlett O'hara in the annual play because of her accent. It was perfect, but could Debbie act? Normally, she was one of the most unemotional girls in the Academy. They were here to find out. Interrupting, Dawn gave Debbie a copy of a scene from the play, asking her to read only Scarlett's lines, and she, Dawn, would read Rhett Butler's lines. Two hours and a lot of work later, Dawn, Georgia, and Dr. Chuck had Debbie relaxed and emoting quite well. Debbie was at the "haoww naoww, browwn caoww" stage, and it was perfect. Just enough drawl to be authentic. Debbie happily agreed to play the part.

Dr. Gaet had summoned Doo to his office during the first period, congratulating her on the wise decision to wear special shoes. The only pair she had now were a low pump. Not a school oxford, but he gave her permission to wear them if she liked until she got her others.

Next, he called in the shy Ros, wanting to get a look at her, as news had spread quickly, and the school was buzzing. He was more than amazed by her appearance. Ros would be a while overcoming her shyness and Gaet gave her a fatherly talk, knowing she'd emerge, and hoping she didn't "overdo" that part of it.

Nece's publisher had contacted the school, informing them that her children's book was now in its third printing, and there was strong demand for more of her work. Gaet had passed this on to Nece, and had congratulated her on her success.

Duke University had been in contact with the school offering Chrissie a full scholarship in tennis and volleyballl, and many other offers were pouring in for these fabulous seniors. A busy time of the year, and the Administration office was swamped with mail and phone calls. Georgia had handled all this for many years, and she always unhurriedly did what she thought was best for her talented young seniors.

It appeared Bonnie (committed to Vassar) would be Valedictorian this year, and Georgia estimated either Debz or Nina would be Salutatorian. MIT was sending mail almost daily now regarding Doo and Chrissie, being interested in both. Karen would probably go to Oxford. Debz would probably commit to her mother's alma mater, Vassar. Elaine was headed for either MIT or Stanford. Nina was still undecided. Her parents wanted her to go to Colgate, as it was near home. Georgia placed their records aside for now, as more mail was coming in. The phone began ringing and she almost cursed. Another greedy University registrar, probably.

Debz and Lisa had graciously accepted the fact that Debbie would portray Scarlett in the drama presentation, both agreeing the part was perfect for her. Lisa was to play the role of Rhett Butler, and Debz would play Ashley, whom Scarlett was in love with, but he was married (to Melanie), who would be played by Monica. Lilly was assigned the role of Scarlett's loyal maid, an important role. All other players had more minor but important roles. The first rehearsal was mostly discussion as Dawn and Georgia were always open to suggestions. It would be a grind now for over four weeks—costumes had to be acquired as well as backdrops being made. Nece always attended, modifying her script slightly on occasion to accommodate anything that came up. They were destined to get along well, and have a lot of fun preparing this play.

Grammar was of the utmost importance to these future socialites, and two years of intense English were a requisite at the academy. Georgia taught mostly Juniors, and Dawn usually fine-tuned the Seniors. The class size at the academy (usually six or even less) gave the students an enormous advantage. Karen and Tricia were probably the two most emotional young ladies in the Academy, and they had a tendency to "slip" on occasion. Karen's British slang would emerge sometimes if she were highly excited, and some of the words had no meaning to the others at all. Dawn thought it was a bit humorous, really.

Monday afternoon an informal tennis match was played against Eagletown High School. Chrissie, Karen, and Bonnie were just too much, and the Academy won every match except one, an overwhelming win. Jojo and Elaine both had won Internet chess matches against ranked competition earlier this afternoon, and the overall morale at the Academy was very high.

Dr. Gaet held a faculty meeting in the office every Monday. Short meetings, and usually all faculty attended. This Monday, the meeting was called to order, and the first discussion concerned the upcoming drama presentation. There would be five public showings, the last one being in the large Eagletown Theater. In a normal year, entertainment media from the national press would pour into town for the last two or three showings.

Classroom problems were then discussed, if there were any. They all knew how self-conscious Ros was with her new "look". They discussed it, knowing it would wear off. Her grades were excellent, and she would soon be able to concentrate on academics again. Doo's good fortune was mentioned, and Mike admitted he hadn't even considered a problem of that nature, although he would in the future.

Michael mentioned the possibility of a softball team, but they decided against it, because of the number of players required. The Academy just wasn't into major sports. Pup reported that Tricia was catching on to the geometry well now. Tricia was now a 3.4 student. He had been a bit worried about her. Debz, the popular senior, really liked Tricia, and had helped her a lot.

Security was discussed, as usual. These young ladies were all from very wealthy families, and there was always the possibility of something happening to one of them. The school was drug free and there was no loitering on the premises. No kidnapping attempts had ever been made, and the Academy spent a lot of money on quality insurance to protect themselves and the young ladies.

All the young ladies at the Academy had taken, or were taking French. Around mid-term, Scott would have "French" days or maybe "Latin" days. Today was a "French" day and all written and oral communication was in that language. He loved to make them play games, as it made the course work easier, and also fed their competitive spirit. Each young lady was given ten minutes to study a short story in French, which contained ten subtle mistakes in grammar, spelling, or usage. They were to find and correct the mistakes, then recite the entire piece in perfect French. Not an easy test. Monica aced it, smirked at the others, and the rest did an extraordinary job. Dr. Gaet was sitting in and before leaving the classroom, he told them he was honored to have them as students.

Mike never left a stone unturned. He had eight of the young ladies outside in the parking lot, and a crowd had assembled. His purpose was to teach them exactly the proper way to enter and exit a vehicle. It seemed as though half of Eagletown had gathered to watch all this. Hooting and whooping, they showed appreciation for a bit of extra leg showing or a skirt inadvertently scooted a bit high. Mike had been through this before. Ros got hooted at and turned red in the face. Thirty minutes later when she got hooted, she beamed, The deliberate Lena got hooted at and just smiled, waving to the bystanders. Lilly had the shortest skirt, and she was the "star" of the show. It was good for the young ladies to go through this, and Mike kept them at it. Opening the door just right and escorting a lady from an automobile seat was an art, and Mike taught it that way. When Mike "finished" you, you were well prepared for society.

CHAPTER V
The Play, the Painting, and Pup

"Gone With the Wind" was a love story set in the Civil War South. Scarlett O'Hara owned a large plantation named Tara and she was deeply in love with Ashley, but he was married (to Melanie). Scarlett married, but her frail young husband died from an illness. Later, she married a Confederate soldier, who was killed in the war. Through all this tragedy she still loved Ashley, who now lived in Atlanta. After the war was settled, Scarlett had taxes on her plantation that she just couldn't pay, so she went to Atlanta to ask Ashley's help, She met Rhett Butler there, who was not of Southern society, but very wealthy. He paid her taxes and fell in love with her. They married and had one child, a daughter, who, when she was six or seven years old, was killed when thrown from a horse. After the accident, Scarlett realizes she really does love Rhett, but now he now no longer loves her. Their rather enigmatic parting at the end is the big scene.

Costumes had arrived, and the preparation of the drama was almost complete. The first dress rehearsal was shown only to the faculty and staff of the Academy. The audience was intent on the performance, and it went well. Dawn and Georgia had really overdone it here. With this power-packed cast and the fantastic script by Nece, this could be the best presentation ever by the Academy. Dawn was seated front row center next to Dr. Pup. Old Pup just attended things like this because it was expected of him. He had no interest in the performing arts, and would be glad to see it end so he could leave. Nece had written it in three acts, and Act III was ending. Dawn glanced at Pup. Surprisingly, he was unusually intent on the performance. Debbie (Scarlett) was sensational in the final scene where she, in her soft southern voice, emotionally professed her love for Rhett. Lisa (Rhett), no longer loving her, turned her down, and when Debbie pleaded, Lisa uttered the famous "Frankly, Scarlett, I don't give a damn." with so much emotion there was a pause after the curtain came down. Then applause, and lots of it. Dawn glanced at Pup, who was wiping the tears from his eyes. That was when she knew they had a blockbuster,

The piano had sort of gone the way of the dinosaur, but the Academy had two in the usually vacant music room.

There were no music nor art classes, per se, taught at the Academy, but they were there for the young ladies to pursue at their leisure. Josee and Lena had both had formal piano training from pre-school age, They both were willing to work with any others who wanted to learn the instrument. This was usually between four and five-thirty PM, after regular classes. Three or four would go to the music room and they would have a great time for an hour or so.

Tammy, a renowned artist, primarily an illustrator, and a well-paid one, lived in Eagletown and worked pro bono with a few of the young ladies. She loved young people and she loved art. She and Nina, the art lover, had become fast friends. Chrissie was a surprisingly talented painter, and she was fast. She and Nina had made many of the backdrops used in the play, and they were very realistic. Chrissie had just completed a portrait of a seated, smiling Ros. Ros had been a good, but very anxious model. The finished portrait of Ros was an amazing piece of art and Tammy immediately had Chrissie paint in a rather somber outdoor background. Tammy and Chrissie immediately named the portrait "La Gioconda Giovanile", and it was to appear on many teen magazine covers. It immediately drew the art world like a magnet. Tammy knew many magazine publishers as she did so many illustrations for them. Before the school term was ended offers for this painting would be in the tens of millions of dollars.

Georgia was at her wit's end. She had to handle a dozen of the hottest high school graduates in the country, make sure their transcripts were perfect, work with the presentation, and now this! She had to fend off over twenty phone calls every day from some art lover or collector who wanted a showing of Chrissie's' portrait of Ros. The staff had discussed it and decided to place the painting in a bank vault in Eagletown. A lot of possible legal problems here. Was the painting Chrissie's, the Academy's, or did it belong to Ros?

Chrissie and Ros were so well-known now that people in Eagletown stopping them for autographs, and Chrissie had to incessantly answer "Yes" when asked, "Did you really paint that?" Any shyness Ros had had was long gone. Vanity was the next stage, but the faculty at the Academy would have none of that, and Ros's ego was contained, at least for the time being.

Pup, in a telephone conversation with an old colleague at MIT, had inadvertently mentioned that he thought he had completed a mathematical theory on time travel, and all hell broke loose. His colleague had leaked it and the Defense Department, the CIA, the FBI, and the White House were clamoring for Pup's formulae. Dr. Gaet was on the telephones with Georgia constantly fending off these agencies. Pup had refused to release it. Fame meant nothing to him. He was concerned with possible international consequences, and even the social, religious, and ecological problems worldwide that could result should the machine be built. Dr. Gaet had agreed and they were determined to keep it a secret as long as they could.

The first official showing of "Gone With the Wind" was shown in the small Academy auditorium, and was so well-received that it was reviewed in more than a few of the large city newspapers. The New York Times review stated proudly that the talented Lisa was "One of their own". The next showing was to be at Eagletown High School in three days, and the five hundred tickets had been snapped up, an extraordinary amount from out of town.

The day of the play at the high school dawned with every hotel in Eagletown full. Automobile traffic into the town was the heaviest on record, and all the Academy students were locked-down on campus until this thing got sorted out. Don, the police chief, had several officers trying to keep order at the gates to the Academy as well as trying to keep traffic flowing through the small town. There were approximately one-hundred-fifty show biz people and art lovers, mixed with big-city reporters clamoring at the gates of the Academy, and the crowd was growing.

About ten AM it really hit the fan. France had almost declared war. The French were so incensed over Chrissie's painting that they had lodged a lawsuit in International courts over the name and nature of the painting. The American Ambassador to France said the French were storming the American Embassy at this time. Back at home, the governor had declared Eagletown a disaster area and had called in the National Guard to try to keep order. If Chrissie or Ros had set foot in France, they'd have been guillotined. An International Incident of the first magnitude.

Monica's parents had called from Pago Pago to remind the school they'd paid a lot of money to educate their precious and talented daughter, not to put her on the front pages, and hung up. Lena's father, a long-time powerful Congressman, had called saying he hoped they could handle all this "scandal" or there would be a Congressional investigation. Anyone but the unflappable Georgia would have panicked, but she just took the calls, handling them as diplomatically and efficiently as possible The Prime Minister of UK called and said that the painting belonged in Britain as Ros was a British citizen, and if that painting fell into French hands, diplomatic ties with the United States could be severed.

The troupe was escorted to the high school and performed admirably on schedule. Not a dry eye in the entire audience. "Encore, encore" was the chant after the performance. The happy players were escorted back to the still locked-down campus, and every phone line in Eagletown was swamped for most of the night.

The Eagletown police had been able to keep Pup and Jojo hidden from all the Feds with search warrants up to now, but it was inevitable they would be found. Don had gotten legal advice and had the local magistrate draw up papers that would (they hoped) keep the two in Eagletown. Meanwhile French lawyers and art experts were to arrive in Eagletown overnight.

CHAPTER VI
The Hearing

The four French gentlemen arrived via limousine about 8 AM. Unable to find lodging, they went to the Dairy Queen, refreshed, and spent a lot of time on the telephone. Two were art experts from the Louvre, one was an attorney representing the Louvre, and the fourth was a French diplomat. He was in charge. About 9:45 Chief Don and one officer pulled into the Dairy Queen, introduced themselves, and agreed to escort them to the judge's office in the court house.

About 10 AM a white limousine containing two art experts from the Tate Musuem, a British attorney, a British diplomat, and Ros's very upset father pulled up to the court house steps. Ten minutes later, an Air Force helicopter requested transportation for four to the court house and landed on the Eagletown football field. Don sent escorts for the Secretary of State, a federal attorney, and two Secret Service agents.

The three Tammy's in Eagletown were sometimes referred to as the "triamvirate". The three were professional women, very successful, and close friends. Judge Tammy was a pretty judge, and she was a good one. She had never before had this much pandemonium in her office. France clamoring for court orders, Britain clamoring for court orders, and now the Secretary of State was there possibly wanting court orders.

She banged her gavel, got silence, and told everyone to be seated. Everything was going to be done orderly, and if it took some time, well, just get yourself as comfortable as possible. Explaining that this was not a trial, she said it was a hearing to get things sorted out a bit here. She would issue no writs until a hearing was held. She requested the French attorney to address the bench.

The French attorney said basically that his government, and the Louvre, in particular, were concerned that a young lady at the Academy had painted, for commercial purposes, a portrait that possibly compromised the Mona Lisa, a French treasure. This was an insult to the French nation and to the French people. They wanted to see the painting, meet the artist, and have it withdrawn from the public. The French government was offering seven and one-half million Euros for it should it prove to be the authentic painting. They insisted on seeing the painting as soon as possible.

The British attorney, representing Ros's father and the British government explained that Ros's father loved his beautiful young daughter and that the portrait must hang in the Manor with other historical family portraits, and the British government was indignant that the French would even consider confiscating a portrait of one of their subjects. They, too, wanted to see the painting, and meet Chrissie and Ros. In addition, he said Ros's father was offering ten million Euros for the painting should it prove authentic.

The federal attorney said he was here to make certain that the portrait never left American soil until the situation was resolved to the satisfaction of Washington.

Tammy recessed for twenty minutes and then told everyone she was going to try to resolve this right here in the courtroom. They would reconvene at 2 PM. Court dismissed.

As soon as the courtroom cleared, Tammy called Dr. Gaet at the Academy and they spoke at length. Then she called the Police Station and requested Chief Don to come to the courtroom. Then she wrote a legal document, stamped it with her seal, and placed it in an envelope, handing it to Don. She then called her close friend, Tammy the illustrator, insisting on lunch together.

The mob had returned to the locked-down Academy. Some had never left, snapping pictures of everything that moved on the campus. Most had gone to the courthouse and done the same thing there. No news to speak of, and they were getting impatient.

At exactly two PM, the doors opened to the courtroom and everyone filed in. There was a large easel just to the right of the Judge, but no painting on it, A buzz went up, and the room had an air of expectation.

Tammy explained again that this was a hearing only. Should litigation arise over this situation, this would serve to clarify the proper legal procedures. Just then the door to the courtroom opened and three people were ushered in. Two strikingly pretty ladies and a impressive appearing gentleman. The judge introduced the three as Vickie, the mayor of Eagletown and wife of Professor Mike at the Academy, Dan, the city attorney, and Tammy, the painter-illustrator who was present when the painting was being completed.

A moment or so later, the doors opened again, and two dozen of the loveliest young ladies you could ever hope to see decorously entered, and sat. Brown oxfords, knee-high white stockings, knee-length pleated tartan skirts, white starched blouses with the Academy emblem on the left breast, and small tam type tartan headwear. A very impressive and well-behaved group.

They were followed by the entire faculty of the Academy, and Dr. Gaet approached the bench, saying something in a low voice to the judge. Tammy looked at her watch, cleared her throat, and said the hearing would commence in approximately ten minutes, and would Ros and her father like to retire to the chamber behind the bench to exchange greetings.

It was exactly ten minutes later when the door opened and a very handsome, statuesque lady entered, carrying what appeared to be a covered portrait, followed by Don, the police chief and two oficers. Anneke, the banker, placed the painting on the easel and sat. Don and the two officers left the courtroom.

A happy Ros and her father, both a bit teary-eyed, were summoned, and Tammy looked around, Satisfied that everyone was here, she banged her gavel to commence the hearing, and the door opened again. Two men wearing dark suits approached the bench, and spoke with the judge a few minutes, showing her some papers and some identification. She studied the papers, grimaced, glanced at Professor Pup, and told them it would have to wait. They could sit and wait, or be back at four-thirty PM, dismissing them. They left the courtroom.

The French delegation, relaxed now, in no hurry, and gallant as always, asked to be introduced to the lovely ladies. Tammy acquiesced as she was curious herself, so Georgia introduced each young lady to the assemblage. There was quite a bit of interest as Chrissie stood and was introduced as the painter of the portrait. Ros, now a very striking young lady, also drew a lot of interest. Jojo and Elaine, both chessmasters, drew ahhhs of approval. After the introductions, Georgia added proudly that each and every one of these young ladies was fluent in French, drawing yet another nod of approval frim the French assemblage.

Tammy told the courtrom that it was time to examine the painting as to its authenticity. The bailiff removed the cover and it appeared to be the painting in question. The four experts eagerly converged on the painting, studying it at length, passing around a magnifying glass. Even the back and the frame were closely examined. Not a word was spoken, but the four moved around the painting studying it from every angle, excitedly pointing out and studying small nuances. Seeming loath to take their eyes off the painting, they finally all walked away and conversed. Four or five minutes later, they seemed to be in agreement, and one of the French experts asked to address the bench.

These had been very tense, crucial moments for both Chrissie and Ros. Both felt their stomachs in knots, almost to the point of nausea. Dawn was seated directly behind them, with a hand on each young ladies' shoulder.

The expert stated that they had agreed that the painting was authentic. Done in oils, properly framed, and obviously a new painting. It was indeed the painting in question, and it would probably someday be a classic. The Louvre was now offering twelve and one-half million Euros for the painting.

Tammy, the judge, wanted to establish outright ownership of the painting. Should it be sold, she wanted no ensuing lawsuits over the ownership. Tammy the painter took the stand.

Tammy said briefly that the two young ladies were fast friends, and that Chrissie had agreed to paint a portrait of Ros, presumably for Ros. She described Chrissie as a very talented painter and a very fast painter. This portrait had been completed in two sittings, This statement seemed to bewilder the art experts. Tammy said she was present when the painting was completed and Chrissie had finally allowed her and the eager Ros to view it. Tammy said that she herself had been amazed by the intensity of the likeness and had suggested the somber background which she felt would not detract from the remarkable portrait. Then, the name of the painting just fell in place. They had agreed on it instantly. Tammy, herself, laid no claim to the portrait, and assumed it belonged to either Chrissie or Ros, or both.

Regarding the commercial use of the portrait, Tammy had felt the portrait was simply too good not to go public, and she had allowed it to be seen via several teen magazines, where knowledge of it had been picked up by the mainstream media. The proceeds from all this were to date around ninety thousand dollars which she had deposited in a separate account in the Eagletown bank. The Academy was unaware of the money, and it was undetermined exactly to whom the money belonged.

At this time, Anneke approached the bench, delivering to the judge the bank's complete history of the account. It was as Tammy had stated, and there was an extended silence in the courtroom. Tammy declared a twenty minute recess and disappeared.

Everyone in the courtroom was milling around the portrait, and an excited buzz was going on. Professor Pup went directly to the Secretary of State, who had been remarkedly quiet after being introduced, and they were having a long conversation, speaking quietly, but seriously. Ros and her father were admiring the portrait, and she was animatedly telling him all about sitting for it. The art experts from France seemed a bit bewildered, and kept going back to the painting and Ros, studying both. Chrissie, never shy, was still a bit uneasy over all this. The British attorney asked her if possibly she could do his wife in oils, and he wasn't kidding. The last thing the adventurous Chrissie wanted to do right now was become a painter. One of the British art experts was with Jojo and Elaine. They were playfully exchanging oral chess moves and laughing.

Everyone was having such a good time that a groan went up when the Judge came into the courtroom and ended it. The gavel banged down, and Chrissie was the next to testify.

The press clamoring outside the Eagletown courthouse was starting to get a bit antsy. Not one word from the courtroom, and it was almost 3:20 PM. They'd gotten some good shots of the young ladies as they filed in, and that was about it. Anneke had left the courthouse, being escorted back to the bank, but she wasn't talking.

Inside, court was in session. Chrissie had stated that as far as she was concerned, the painting belonged to Ros, and the money generated belonged to Tammy, the painter, and, or, Ros. The French attorney had tried to pin her down by asking her how familiar she was with the famous Mona Lisa painting by Da Vinci, but Chrissie said she painted Ros as she saw her, and didn't copy anything or even have anything else in mind. She stepped down, and Judge Tammy thought a few minutes and cleared her throat. Ros was not called.

Tammy told the assemblage that she had reached a decision, and if anyone disagreed with it, they had the court's permission to present their differences. She told the court that she felt Chrissie had painted the portrait in good will and given it to her friend, Ros, and therefore the painting belonged to Ros. She was open to suggestions as to the ownership of the money in the bank account, but was leaning towards just dividing it equally between Tammy, Ros, and Chrissie. Looking directly at the French delegation, she said she understood their concern about their famous painting, and suggested Ros and Chrissy could possibly change the name of Chrissy's painting to their satisfaction. The damage done by the publicity prior to locking up the painting was minimal, and would soon die down. Then she declared a fifteen minute recess.

The Secretary of State followed the judge to her chambers, wanting to have a few words with her, and the others in the courtroom were animatedly discussing the verdict. The French delegation was grouped around the painting again. The French love beauty, and they love art.

Word had gotten into the courtroom that almost all the young ladies' parents were in Eagletown, and were at the Academy at this time. Monica's world-touring parents had been on a small remote island in the Pacific that had no airport, and were forced to wait for a helicopter from Australia to get them. The young ladies were happily milling around now, and admiring the painting. Professor Scott introduced himself to the French group in French, and some of the young ladies joined in to the pleasure of their Gallic visitors.

The French spokesman said the ruling seemed fair, but the French still desired the painting, and were now offering fifteen million Euros for it. The British agreed the decision was fair, and the secretary of State said the ruling was fair, but he felt the painting should hang in an American museum, possibly in New York City, for six months, at the least. The painting had never had a public showing, and he felt the American public deserved that right. Tammy said that arrangement would be between the American government and Ros and her family, not here in court. Chrissie and Ros seemed to be relieved at the outcome. The city attorney, Dan, stood briefly, and on behalf of the mayor, Vickie, welcomed everyone to Eagletown, and thanked the court for making a wise decision.

CHAPTER VII

The Final showing

The National Guard was doing a good job of keeping order in Eagletown, and kept the exodus from the courtroom orderly. The press were promised a conference at 4:45 PM on the courthouse steps and the phone lines were being set up now. The camera crews were scampering for a vantage point.

At exactly 4:30 PM, the two FBI agents entered the courtroom, to meet with Judge Tammy. Pup and Jojo had remained, as well as the American delegation. The Secretary of State conversed with the two agents at length, and finally the two approached the bench. Tammy gave them back their warrant, and they left. Dr. Pup thanked the Secretary and the judge for defusing the situation, and he and Jojo set out on foot for the Academy, five blocks away.

The big final showing of "Gone With the Wind" was two days away, to be staged at the Ritz Theater, Eagletowns' largest and finest, Curtain time was at 2:30 PM. Sold out, it was to be televised live by PBS.

Nece and Tricia had become very close friends. Almost always together, they shared most of their girlish secrets. Nece, ever curious, had been amazed at Tricia's transformation from a C-, underperforming public school student into the superb academic she now was. The wealthy Nece had never been in public school, and had no idea what they were like. She had picked Tricia's brain, so to speak, and methodically taken notes. The more she discovered about the public school system, the more curious she became, and she did an enormous amount of research on the subject, past to present.

All this had ended up in book form that she submitted to her publisher. Nece was appalled and outraged at her findings after all this research and fact-finding, and she let it show. The cover was blazing red, and the center was a black-edged white circle, containing the words: PUBLIC /SCHOOLS, with a diagonal black line across the circle. She ripped into the powerful teacher's unions, the underperforming teachers' incessant demands for pay raises. lack of punishment resulting in disorderly classrooms, undeserved tenure, methods of financing, waste, even fraud in some cases. Her book had been quickly published, and had become a public sensation almost immediately.

No classes were held on Friday. The young ladies and their parents were having a very happy open house at the Academy. Dr. Gaet had catered the three meals of the day, including more than a few adult beverages, and everyone was just having a great time. Monica's parents had finally arrived, and the tired, handsome couple were received with open arms. The parents all had front row center seats compliments of the Academy, and all were looking forward to tomorrow afternoon. Tired and excited, they all retired early.

The Ritz was located one block south of Pogo and Main, and was filling rapidly. The television cameras were in place and it was almost curtain time.

Dawn, Georgia, and Dr. Gaet were the only adults backstage. The troupe was eager to perform, especially with their parents in the audience. Debz performed perfectly as Ashley, ever loyal to his wife, and Monica portrayed Melanie equally well. Lilly, in black-face, played the difficult role of Scarlett's loyal maid and confidante magnificently. When the final curtain came down, a lot of handkerchiefs were wiping a lot of eyes. The rather enigmatic, unexpected parting of Scarlett and Rhett had been performed so dramatically by Debbie and Lisa that the audience was sort of stunned. Then, amid thunderous applause and flash bulbs, the cast appeared back on stage for a final bow to their audience.

A week or so later Nece almost had to be sequestered. Her book had caused, if possible, more uproar than Chrissie's painting. Every public school in America was screaming foul, and the big, powerful teachers' unions were trying to sue Nece, her publisher, the Academy, and anything else that moved. The unions hadn't filed anything yet because they couldn't get a court to take the case. Almost every judge in the country had, or had had, their children in private schools because of exactly the things Nece had exposed.

With the play, the painting, and now the book, there were always at least a dozen or so paparazzi at the gates of the Academy at any one time, hanging around to find out what was going to go down next.

The End

RIVERBOAT FUN

CHAPTER I
The EAGLE

Mike was very proud of his EAGLE. She was the Queen of the Mississippi; a very fast and very proud stern-wheeler. She had beaten the ROBERT E LEE in the big race in '85, and hadn't been challenged since. Mike charged the highest prices of any boat on the river for fares and freight up and down the waterway, and could get it. People were proud to ride the EAGLE—a floating luxury hotel, complete with casino.

The stern—wheelers were the elite of the river—faster, bigger and with more and better accommodations than the slower freight-hauling side-wheelers. Fares were much lower on the freighters, but poor accommodations, frequent stops, poor food, and low-class cabins were the norm.

Mike also had a very well-trained professional crew. All the big boats carried two pilots. Pilots were necessary, because they knew the hazardous river like the backs of their hands. Stern wheelers had the paddle wheel to the rear where it was somewhat protected from floating debris, or from a possible reef that could damage it. The pilot's job was to keep this from happening. Mike's two pilots were Deni, who was born on the river, and Pup, who had studied and charted the river. Both were veteran and very highly paid pilots.

The EAGLE was on a downstream cruise, and had stopped in Natchez for loading, unloading, and fuel, when Mike first heard of a possible challenge to his supremacy on the river. A bit unnerved over it, he sent his purser, Bob, to find out what he could. The EAGLE left Natchez as soon as possible. Mike was in a hurry to get to New Orleans, get his hands on a newspaper, and get to the telegraph office. Bill, Mike's Mate, was in charge of the engine room. He told the stokers, Chrissie and Tony, to pour the wood on all the way to port.

Mike's fears weren't unfounded. It seems a British expatriate named Dawn, who was some kind of wealthy English nobility, wanted to rule the river as her country ruled the seas. She had hired the famous Dutch shipbuilder, Monica, to design and build a stern-wheeler that was supposedly even bigger and faster than the EAGLE. The river limited the size, but Monica and her engineer, Anneke, knew just what to do, and a magnificent ship was soon to emerge from an out-of-the-way shipyard in St. Louis.

When the EAGLE arrived and docked in New Orleans, the forward gangplank was lowered, and

Mike tore ashore. Stern-wheelers, ever protective of the precious paddle-wheel, always docked prow first, a special gangway was thrown over, and the on-and-off traffic moved over the gangplank.

The crew had finished their chores, and headed ashore. Pup, Bob, and a few others stayed aboard. Mike came back a few hours later, and he seemed very pre-occupied. Mike told them he knew now, for sure, that a boat possibly equal to the EAGLE would be on the river soon, and the owner of the other ship was already advertising for freight and passengers.

Thirteen or fourteen miles per hour was about maximum speed for the big boats. They ran on steam, and burned wood. The best and hottest wood was oak, and the cheapest was cottonwood. The big furnaces could use an enormous amount of wood. There were docks all along the river where wood could be purchased by the cord. Wood is heavy, and weight is a factor on the river. Mike would usually stock more fuel when they were going downstream.

The EAGLE was leaving soon. Three crew members were missing. Tony and Chrissie, the two stokers, and Doo, a bartender and dancer, who, along with Lisa, a very voluptous singer, were the EAGLE'S attractive, vivacious female entertainers. Bill soon found them. Chrissie loved to fight and she had started one, as usual. She and Tony were both a bit beaten up, but still ambulatory. He found Doo getting a damned tattoo at a kiosk near the dock. Bill practically shanghaied the three and hauled them aboard. The Eagle then weighed anchor and headed upstream.

CHAPTER II
The ICE CREAM

The ICE CREAM was due to be christened in two days. Monica and Anneke were inspecting the boat, making notes on some possible changes. A shake-down cruise to New Orleans was scheduled in a week or so, and would tell them a lot.

Meanwhile, Dawn, along with her captain, Karen, was interviewing for crew members. They had one pilot, Lilly, under contract. Lilly was an old Cape Cod fisherman, and had been on the river several years now. Karen came from a British seafaring family, and had spent most of her life on the water. She had left Britain at Dawn's request to captain the ICE CREAM. The adventure intrigued her. The Dutch maritime engineer, Anneke, had agreed to a one-year contract as purser. The pursers on the boats handled an enormous amount of money. The receipts from the dining room, the bar, the casino, and other incidental expenditures from passengers, as well as fares. The gift shop alone was a large enterprise. They were also responsible for paying the crew, which was usually in cash. Anneke was very good with money, and up to the job.

They had just interviewed and hired a very pretty and capable woman named Jeannie to be in charge of the bar and casino area. Jeannie was interviewing for her staff now. She had hired the renowned French chef, Katie, who was to hire her own staff. Dawn and Karen were still looking for an honest, experienced mate and a second pilot, and they would basically have a full crew.

The ICE CREAM made her debut to the River Authority amid a flourish of publicity. The press in late 1800's was as avid as it is now. Champagne flowed, and many interviews were held. The big question was: Would Dawn challenge the EAGLE to race? Dawn dodged the question for now.

The ICE CREAM was by far the most impressive boat on the river. Brilliant white with pale-blue trim, 3 stories high, two stacks, and a huge foredeck for cargo and promenade. At 155 feet long and 33 feet wide, with a 35 foot paddle wheel, she was one of the largest ever built. Being new, she was a beauty of a boat, and the newspapers headlined her up and down the river. The faster boats also hauled the mail, and Dawn was getting mail contracts already.

The ICE CREAM was to leave down river on Saturday Sept. 14th at 11AM for New Orleans. The River Authority logged all arrival and departure times. The schedule was a matter of pride to the captains and owners, as promptness usually warranted higher fares. The 43 staterooms had been booked already, and downstream freight and provisions were being loaded now. Monica had agreed to act as mate for the shake-down cruise. The boats had to have at least two pilots, as one was in the wheelhouse at almost all times. These riverboats had a draft of only four feet or so, as the river could be very shallow in spots. With no below deck holds, freight was placed on the foredeck, secured, and covered.

Meanwhile, Jeannie, at an enormous cost, had contracted the famous St. Louis singer, Lena, and an exotic very well-endowed dancer named Tammy, who had had prior experience aboard the EAGLE. A bit of luck came their way when a young fellow named Doug approached Dawn, showed her his pilot's credentials, amd proof of previous experience on the EAGLE. He was put under contract in a heartbeat. Monica had found two experienced stokers in a bar near the dock, and Cathy and Don were hired, which pretty much filled the crucial positions.

Downstream mail was brought on board at the last minute, and the ICE CREAM set out on her maiden voyage. Anneke had insisted on overly-large boilers in case extra speed was needed. An overload could explode a boiler, and on a boat teeming with people, loss of life could be enormous. About three hours out, Karen, who was at the helm, asked for more speed. Passengers and crew were lining the rails as the stacks bellowed black smoke. The ICE CREAM picked up speed, and soon Karen asked for more speed. The fire-boxes could take no more wood, so Monica had one container of lard added. The big boat surged forward, and a resounding cheer went up. Lilly and Doug were both in the wheelhouse, showing Karen where possible hazards on the river might be, and trying to keep in the center of the river. The lard quickly burned out, but now they knew what the ICE CREAM was capable of. Doug told Karen he had no doubt that the ICE CREAM was faster than the Eagle, and the EAGLE's old boilers would never hold up in an all-out race.

The ICE CREAM had a few minor incidents on the trip, but overall had had a great and very profitable maiden voyage.

Dawn, ever eager to rule, made her challenge public from New Orleans. The telegraph was buzzing, and thousands were being bet on the outcome already. Mike had to accept the challenge or step down.

When word got to Mike, the EAGLE was preparing to leave Memphis for St.Louis. Mike called Bill, Bob, and the two pilots to the wheelhouse, showing them the telegram. Mike also had heard that Doug, one of his former pilots, had signed on the ICE CREAM and he was furious. Mike also knew he needed new boilers for an extended high-speed race. He opted to turn the Eagle into a shipyard right here in Memphis, accept the challenge, and would agree on a date as soon as the EAGLE was refitted with new and bigger boilers.

CHAPTER III

The Race

Mike wasn't the type to lose money. The EAGLE, for a few months, was the biggest attraction in Memphis. The EAGLE cuisine was as fine as anything in Memphis, and the luxurious staterooms became hotel rooms for a time. The yard where they were docked for repairs was near an upscale area, giving them an affluent clientele. Mike had lost a fabulous dancer when he left St.Louis, when Tammy missed the cruise. Paul, his director of entertainment, had received word from her that she had signed on the ICE CREAM at an enormous salary. He decided not to hire another dancer at this time, as Lisa was a tireless performer. Doo was such a great entertainer-singer that she was temporarily the rage of Memphis. When the refurbished Eagle finally embarked for St. Louis Mike had more than met all expenses.

Mike took Deni and Bill with him to negotiate the contract for the big race. The meeting was held at the River Authority office in St.Louis. Dawn was accompanied by Lilly and her captain, Karen. The

River Authority had mandated a date be set on or before June first. All terms would be haggled over by the owners and the Authority. Many intangibles here. From where to where? Upstream or downstream? When to race was a big factor. Spring thaws affected the current and the river levels. Weight; fully booked, or crews only? The owners always wanted to make money.

It took several days, but an agreement was struck. They would race downstream from Memphis to New Orleans. This was a very tortuous route. The Mississippi south from Memphis had more bends than a pit of snakes, and would test both boats and crews at the higher speeds. Staterooms were to be half-booked, due to some peril at the higher speeds. No mail and no freight. Fully fueled, with five barrels of lard each. They would race before the spring thaws by leaving Memphis simultaneously at dawn on March 1. Their prior schedules would be such that both boats would be in Memphis slightly before that date. Mike and Dawn, distrusting each other to the fullest, signed the papers, shook hands, and the deal was done.

Mike and Dawn had to establish new schedules. The EAGLE would work upstream from St. Louis until it was time to head for Memphis. The ICE CREAM would operate only between Memphis and St. Louis until late February.

The odds on the race fluctuated. Mike, of course, was the most experienced skipper. Deni was arguably the best pilot on the river for that area. She had been born near Natchez, and knew the river as well as anyone alive. The press heralded the ICE CREAM as possibly the fastest Mississippi boat of all-time. Experience was a factor, but Dawn had really assembled a great crew.

Dawn was approaching, and the two boats were awaiting the foghorn blast from the Authority. It came, and the anchors were weighed. The race was underway!

Dawn never took the wheel. Karen or one of the pilots was always on the helm. Mike was his own Captain, and he was spelled only by his pilots, or Bob, on occasion.

Soon, the ICE CREAM edged slightly ahead. Getting far enough ahead to pull in front was a huge advantage, and Mike was determined this wasn't going to happen. If he could stay even until they started into the tortuous part of the river, he felt he could prevail, but if he were several lengths behind, he would be hard-pressed to overtake the fleet ICE CREAM. Here is where Lilly and Deni were so invaluable. Both knew that part of the river: where it was deep enough to "cut a corner" and where possibly they could trap the other boat into a shallow, slowing it considerably. A big factor here was other boats. Upstream boats had the right-of-way, because their slower speed made it more difficult to maneuver. The foghorn was blaring almost constantly, because no one knew what was around the bend, and there wasn't a straight stretch of river the rest of the way.

Karen had a slight lead, but the EAGLE stayed close enough to keep her from getting directly in front. The current wasn't a big factor as the river was over a mile wide in spots. Karen had used some of the precious lard, but Mike had apparently done the same. Lilly was really concentrating on getting the shortest route possible by negotiating the bends in the river. The extra length of The ICE CREAM was a bit of a hindrance here. Dawn, a bit new to all this, was a bit perturbed that they weren't just simply running away from the EAGLE. Another problem was that early spring rains had put a lot of debris in the river. Both boats were constantly having to dodge large logs.

Dusk had set in, and the boats had slowed considerably. Neither even considered the safety of anchoring until dawn. Mike cursed himself for using Deni first. She was tired, and Pup would have the conn shortly. Pup was a formally-schooled pilot, and he had made charts of the river. He navigated by his charts, taking into consideration river levels and other factors. Mike liked the old-school pilots the best, but Pup had never let him down.

On the ICE CREAM, Dawn was finishing a shrimp cocktail. She loved shrimp, and sort of nibbled at it all day. Still upset at the lack of dominance, she remained outwardly calm, leaving things to Karen, Doug, and Lilly. Doug was relieving Lilly for the night watch, and the boat had slowed for what looked like a long night. The Eagle was about one-half boat length to their stern on the port side, and would probably be there at dawn. Everyone was praying for no fog, which could require stopping altogether.

Approximately 400 miles from Memphis to New Orleans meant that the race should end about mid-afternoon tomorrow. Doug estimated that they were a bit ahead of schedule, The night hours just might determine the outcome.

Kerosene lanterns were all these boats had, and they were placed so the boats could be seen, providing very little aid to visibility. Pup had to see his charts, so the wheelhouse of the EAGLE was lit. Pup had charted the river and kept his charts upgraded. He knew where the river was the widest, the deepest, and where it would give them a chance to possibly gain a bit on the ICE CREAM.

Karen was still at the helm of the ICE CREAM. 35 or 40 hours was nothing for her. Three times during the night she had had to order more speed to fend off the EAGLE. Finally Doug figured out what the Eagle was doing, and they then knew when to use more wood, even beating the EAGLE to the punch once. All night long this jockeying went on at speeds of usually less than 5 miles per hour.

Daylight saw light fog on the river, and the stately ICE CREAM maybe less than ten feet ahead of the EAGLE. Now, into the final ten hours or so of the race, Mike and Deni took over on the wheelhouse, and Mike knew the time to race was now. If the ICE CREAM were the better boat, so be it.

The Mississippi River into New Orleans runs almost due east. The last 12 miles or so were fairly straight, and the river was wide. They entered this stretch of the river with the ICE CREAM ahead by about five feet.

On both boats it was all-out to the finish now. Anneke, the Dutch engineer, had her slide rule out, with Doug at her side, keeping her posted on the distance remaining. At the appropriate time, Anneke would signal the use of their last container of lard.

The EAGLE had a bit of an advantage being on the port side of the ICE CREAM—the last bend turning eastbound gave them the shorter turn, and Mike had taken it full speed, picking up about 10 feet. He had one container of lard left, and had to use it at exactly the right time.

Seven miles to go. The dock in New Orleans was jammed with people, who, until now had had to follow the race via newspaper. The railings of both boats were lined with passengers and crew also.

Four miles to go, and the ICE CREAM was still slightly ahead. Monica was the designated spotter for the final run, and she never took her eyes off the EAGLE. The smoke from the EAGLE's twin stacks suddenly went from black to white, and she signaled the EAGLE was using lard. Cathy and Don on the ICE CREAM had their last container of lard ready.

The EAGLE surged forward, gaining ever so slowly on the ICE CREAM, finally taking the lead. Doug told Anneke, "Three miles." Both stokers waiting for Anneke's signal. No signal fron Anneke. Karen, at the helm, wondered why they had let the Eagle pass. Finally, with just under 3 miles to go, Anneke gave the signal. The stacks on the ICE CREAM began issuing white smoke, and she was gaining speed. The EAGLE was losing speed now, and with about 300 yards remaining, the ICE CREAM took the lead for the last time, and won the race.

New Orleans was going crazy. Never had a river race been as exciting, nor as close. The crews intermingled and congratulations exchanged. Doug and Tammy were happy to see their old friends on the EAGLE. All in all, not a harsh word was exchanged. Both teams had done a great job.

Dawn and Karen had gone ashore and were swarmed by the press. Gracious and happy, flushed with victory, Dawn praised the EAGLE and both crews. Suddenly, a courier burst through the throng, and handed Dawn a telegram. She opened it, and her face turned white. Karen, at her side, took it from her, and read: STERN-WHEELER WING NUT LEAVES MEMPHIS SHIPYARD STOP ESTABLISHES SPEED RECORD TO ST.LOUIS.

THE END

MONASTIC FUN

CHAPTER I

A monastery is a religious institution dedicated to prayer, research, meditation, and is also the habitation of the Monks or Friars who do their work there. This story is of a monastery in the Basque mountains of Spain in the year 1928.

The ancient buildings of Monte Sangre were of bleached, unpainted, stark white stone and one building rose to three stories above the rocky land. Two miles or so above the small village below, it nestled into the surrounding mountains. The Monks who lived and worked here were sworn to lives of poverty, celibacy, and toil. The more literate and educated were involved in constant religious research and study. The illiterate Monks worked at supporting the monastery, usually through an agricultural effort of some sort. We will delve into the heretofore unknown lives of a few of these dedicated, devout Monks.

The Monks were orderly seated around the big table noisily downing their midday meal. The noon meal was usually the largest of the day. The Abbess, Dawn, sat at the head of the table, which was raised a bit so she would be above the others. Prayers were always intoned during the meal, so there was no conversation. The Monks had designed a sign language to overcome all this, however, and quite a bit was silently going on.

Friar Scott had gotten his hands on several liters of wine that he had promptly hidden, and he was quietly getting the word out, and Friar Karen was getting up a swimming party for this afternoon at their secret spot in the river. Friar Nece, always concerned for the much older Friar Jojo, had saved the frail Jojo a bit of her pudding. There was a sudden commotion at the door, and Friar Chrissie entered. She was late and she was hungry. Chrissie had been a Hermit Friar, lost is solitary meditation for many years, when they had found her in her cave two years ago, half-starved and very near death. She had been cleaned up, brought back to health and placed here in the dormitory with the field Monks. Friar Chrissie, who seldom spoke to anyone, downed a bowl of pudding as the bell rang for prayers

The agricultural complex of the monastery, except for a pittance from the Church and a few small contributions, enabled the monastery to financially exist. Under Abbess Dawn's supervision, they now had a wine press and a cheese factory. The delicious goat cheese and silky Monte Sangre wine were to be found on some of the finest dining tables in Europe.

Friar Karen was first to hit the cold water, followed by Friars Tina and Tricia. The small pond in the river had cold, clear water and was ideal for swimming and bathing. Friar Monica threw off her cumbersome robe and joined. Nudity meant nothing to the celibate monks, and they happily played and swam in the frigid mountain water. In an hour or so they would join Friar Scott and Friar Chuck and drink wine until they had to attend Vespers, the lengthy evening prayer service.

Friars Pup and Bonnie were goat-herders. Tending a flock of mountain goats is not an easy task, but they were good at what they did. Friar Pup could run almost as fast as the elusive goats, and the two Monks always managed to bring them home for milking late in the day. One young frisky goat had gotten down near the river, and they both went to corral it and get it back in the herd. Nearing the river bank, they heard laughing and screaming. The two goat-herds had stumbled onto the Friars' swimming hole. They waved to their Brothers in the water, and sat on a rock to watch the frolicking. Suddenly Friar Bonnie's robe was off and she, too, was naked in the water. Friar Pup watched for awhile, bid them farewell, and returned to his flock.

The Monte Sangre wine cellar was a huge room. Centuries old, it had originally been a dungeon of sorts, and had been remodeled after a fashion. Over eighty casks of the delicious wine were aging in the cellar at any given time. Friars Lisa and Dan, who were literate, had toiled here for years. Each monk knew the exact age of each cask of wine and they kept remarkably accurate records. The monastery had one phone line to the village, which was in the Abbot's office in the main building. When a cask was ready to be sold, they would get word to the Abbot, Mike.

Abbot Mike, who did very little work, would have Friar Tammy, who basically ran his office, call the wholesaler in the village below, and the wholesaler would send a truck and crew up the tortuous road to the monastery to get the cask and pay for it. Immediately after calling, Mike would then take his favorite goblet to the wine cellar and he and the two Monks would "test" the product until it was picked up.

Friar Lilly was literate and her pallet was in a dormitory in the main administration building. Friar Lilly was basically the purser of the monastery and her job was to keep provisions replenished. Every ten days or so, Friar Lilly and Friar Brandon would ride the donkeys to the village, taking any checks for wine, cheese, or any donated checks to the bank for deposit. then they would "shop" for the monastery and get the mail from the Post Office. The precipitous trip back to the monastery could not be done at night. Their business finished, they usually wined and dined on monastery money, and then slept it off all night on a pew at the village church. Friar Brandon would sometimes get more than a bit romantically inclined while drinking and Lilly usually had to protect any village ladies who got near him.

Friar Elaine, a comely and very devout young lady, was a musical enthusiast. Well educated, she spent most of her waking hours poring over and amending religious pieces of music. Some of the oldest and less frequently used hymns she had edited and they had regained some popularity. Gifted with a beautiful voice and an ear for the organ, she and Abbess Dawn usually led the monastery choir in praise of their Lord. The monastery choir, at best, was terrible, and any changes they made seemed to make it even more horrible. The impetuous Friar Elaine loved wine and she loved to talk. Her young blood ran hot, and she had a secret crush on Friar Doug, a handsome young Monk who worked in Archives, constantly studying the history of the church, making mountains of notes.

Friar Doug worked with and was training a young Monk, Friar Jam. Friar Jam, only recently ordained, was a quick learner, and their work went smoothly, despite frequent lengthy visits from Friar Elaine.

It was about 2 PM when the big alarm bell in the monastery square began ringing. Friar Pup had raced from the fields to report that the frail, older Friar Jojo, who worked in the office near the vineyards, had wandered off and fallen into a rather steep rocky ravine. She was alive, but in pain, and Friar Pup sped back to the scene. Friar Tammy phoned the village operator, requesting the village doctor immediately.

The Monks were peering down into the deep rocky chasm. They could see Brother Jojo, and it appeared she may have broken an arm. Abbot Mike arrived, assessed the situation. and ordered Friar Pup to go to the monastery and get a long rope. Friar Chrissie, who worked in the nearby stables, seemed to appear out of nowhere. She had been given the assignment because of her love of solitude. She removed her sandals and lowered herself into the chasm. In a matter of moments, the Friar had reached the injured Jojo and had carefully gotten Jojo onto her back. A few minutes later Friar Chrissie emerged from the hole, deposited the injured Jojo on the ground and left for the stables, never saying a word.

Friar Scott's wine "party" started about 5 in the afternoon. The delicious Sangre wine was heady and it was going fast. He and Friar Chuck had been joined in the clearing in the cornfield by Brothers Karen, Monica, Tricia, Tina, and the uninvited, but welcome, Pup and Bonnie. It is a bit unclear what all happened at the "party", but it ended with a group of rather "relaxed", pleasantly tired Brethren clinging to one another and staggering back to the monastery for Vespers.

The Bishop, Gaet, and Abbot Mike were old friends, having attended the same seminary. Mike always looked forward to the Bishop's extended visits, and Abbess Dawn dreaded them. Mike and Gaet wouldn't draw a sober breath for a week, and she, Dawn would have to "run" the entire monastery. Thank The Lord (she crossed herself) Tammy was so efficient. The Bishop would arrive Monday, bringing his snooty Vicar, Debbie, with him.

CHAPTER II

The Visit and the Vision

The Bishop, Gaet, and his vicar, Debbie, had made a timely arrival at the monastery, along with tons of luggage and supplies. The Bishop was one who loved luxury, and as there was very little at the monastery, he brought his own. After two days of inspecting the lush vineyards, gardens, and fields of the monastery, the Abbot and Bishop, discarding their cassocks and in civilian dress, went to the village for a few days. Dawn gritted her teeth and crossed herself. She had to run the monastery now, while those two chased whores in the village, and with that nosy Vicar, Debbie, here, she had to watch her tongue.

A vicar is not really a figure in the hierarchy of the church. A Vicar is a representative of one, as Debbie was a very loyal representative of the Bishop, Gaet. If Bishop Gaet chose not to attend a distasteful function, Debbie attended in lieu of the Bishop. As he preferred to party in the village with his friend, the Abbot Mike, his business at the monastery would be conducted by the Vicar, Debbie.

Dawn and Debbie entered the cubicle where Friar Carol kept the monastery log. Carol submitted a comprehensive report to the Vatican monthly through a courier who picked up the report directly from her and delivered it to Cardinal Lena in Avila. Friar Carol obtained the financial report from Lilly or Brandon and the agricultural report from Nece, the only literate Monk in the fields at this time. The wine report usually came from Lisa, and all this was meticulously logged. In addition, any papal punishment administered and any unusual circumstances were recorded and entered. The church kept good records. The Vatican was actually receiving a monthly diary of the monastery. Debbie was impressed. She told the Abbess, Dawn, that Monte Sangre had really impressed her so far, making the Abbess feel a bit guilty.

Their next stop was the garden area. Lush rows of melons and vegetables were being tirelessly tended by the Friars Monica and Karen. Debbie had never seen such large, vibrant plants before and she asked the Friar, Monica, if they had always had a crop this bountiful. Monica, who had a peculiar smirk when she spoke, told the Vicar that the last two years had been the finest years they'd ever had. Debbie was loath to leave the beautiful garden area, but followed the Abbess to the apiary where Friars Tina and Chuck collected and produced the fine, rich honey.

Friar Scott made some of the finest goat cheese in Europe. He and Friar Tricia had mastered the art of adding spices, such as pimiento, chives, and even onion, and these flavored cheeses were in demand all over Europe. The two Monks produced a loaf of French—style bread and the four had a delicious lunch. Debbie thought it was the most delicious lunch she'd ever eaten and graciously thanked the two Monks, Then they went to the small office where Friar Nece kept her agricultural records.

Friar Jojo, too old to toil in the fields, assisted Nece, and, having miraculously recovered from her fractured arm overnight in the infirmary, had not missed any time in the office. Dawn was surprised to see Jojo there and examined her arm. It seemed to be completely healed, with no remaining pain, not even a bruise mark. Hugging the older Monk, Dawn crossed herself. A miracle, indeed! God is with us!

The Vicar was really inpressed by the massive vineyards. Not much activity here today. Dawn and Debbie leisurely walked a long row, stopping to pluck and munch on a few riper grapes. They could see Friars Pup and Bonnie in their long ankle-length robes and long, crooked staffs. carefully watching the grazing animals in the field to the east. It was getting hot now, and the two just waved to the Monks, deciding to go on to the stables.

Friar Chrissie was almost a mute. She had spoken so little for so many years that the effort to do so just wasn't in her. Dawn introduced the Vicar to the Monk. and Chrissie acknowledged with a nod, made the sign of the cross, and resumed shoveling into her wheelbarrow. For some reason, Debbie was watching the Monk intently. Chrissie had hit an object with her shovel and knelt to remove it. Debbie paled. Shaking herself mentally, she bid the Monk good day, and she and Dawn returned to the cool monastery.

After being asked, Dawn told the Vicar all she knew about Friar Chrissie. She knew that Chrissie was literate as she had had a hermitage for years, When they found her two years ago she was so near death that about all they could do was get a bit of broth into her and pray. Dawn said that the puzzling thing about it was that in less than twenty-four hours Chrissie was up and about. Debbie already knew of the incident in the ravine and the rescue of Jojo, and something was bothering her. She shrugged it off, bid Dawn good afternoon and went in to nap.

Mike and Gaet returned to the monastery about noon on Friday, refreshed, donned cassocks, lit cigars, and Bishop Gaet, all business now, wanted a report from Debbie. For some reason, Debbie was hesitant to report in front of the Abbot, so the two retired to the Bishop's quarters. After giving a glowing report on the state of the monastery, she told the Bishop of her vision.

One night, prior to leaving Seville for the monastery, she had had a very powerful, disturbing dream. It was a dark night and an injured or dead animal was on the ground. Suddenly a hooded robed figure appeared over it. The cloaked figure knelt for some time over the animal. The animal suddenly arose and bounded away. The hooded figure remained kneeling for some time as though in meditation or possibly prayer, then arose. The hooded figure was now winged! She told the Bishop of going to the stable with Dawn, and she just KNEW that the mysterious Friar at the stable was the hooded figure in her dreams. (She had now had the recurrent, vivid dream several times). She also related the mysterious healing of the Hermit Chrissie herself. Arising in a matter of hours from almost certain death, and now we have the miraculous recovery of Friar Jojo after her accident.

Gaet's brow furrowed in thought. Finally, he spoke: "God's ways are mysterious. If the heavens have sent us a Saint we must know for sure. The Vatican will send investigators. First, I think we should speak with Friar Jojo. Also, I, myself, need to meet this Friar, Chrissie. We must learn all we can before we present our case to the Cardinal."

Work at the monastery sort of just dwindled off around noon on Saturdays, and the Monks just prepared themselves for the Sabbath, when work was minimal and prayer was maximal. The fun-loving Scott and Karen already had scheduled a swim party followed by a wine-orgy in the cornfield for later in the afternoon.

The Bishop, Gaet, wanted to visit the stables, but Mike wanted to go to the fields and hit a few golf balls. From their position in the green, goat-cropped pasture, they had a clear view of the stables, several hundred yards to their left. They could see the tireless Friar, Chrissie, constantly shoveling and depositing the straw and goat dung onto a huge pile, where she would mix it some, and resume digging. Surprisingly, after almost two years, Mike could tell the Bishop very little about the strange Monk. Most Monks are assigned by the diocese, arrive with credentials, and are assigned work and quarters. Friar Chrissie was sort of "adopted", and Hermitage records are usually almost non-existant. The dedicated Monk had even moved her pallet to a small room in the stables.

The frolicking and romping in the pool had been great fun and very invigorating. The Monks had all retired to the clearing an hour or so ago. Lisa and Dan had smuggled out several gallons of the powerful, delicious El Vino Sangre and Friar Jojo had already happily passed out after two glasses, her gray hair pillowed on Friar Nece's ample lap. When the Monks were drinking, they sort of paired off, and it is unclear what actually occurred at these functions, but eventually the clearing would be devoid of certain Monks, with a lot of "rustling" sounds going on in the adjacent cornfield. Friars Brandon, Chuck and Scott would usually leave the clearing several times, as would Brothers Lisa, Monica, and Karen. The Monks always managed to consume the wine and totter back to the monastery in time for Vespers.

Monday morning Nece and Jojo were summoned to the Abbot's Quarters. Mike, Dawn, Bishop Gaet, and the Vicar, Debbie, were in the small conference room and bid them good morning and seated them. Mike said they wanted to ask Jojo a few questions, and began by asking Jojo if she remembered Friar Chrissie rescuing her from the chasm after falling. Friar Jojo said she had never lost consciousness, and she remembered it well. Brother Chrissie had picked her up and gotten her in a "piggyback" position and climbed out with her. The Bishop interjected here, asking Jojo how she had been able to cling to the Monk's back with a broken arm. Jojo thought for a minute and replied that her arm "hadn't hurt" at the time. The pain returned at the infirmary, where she was sedated. The next morning her arm was fine.

Bishop Gaet was getting excited now. He exchanged glances with Debbie and continued, asking Jojo if anyone was with her in the infirmary for the night, and she replied that Brother Nece had spent the night with her in her room. The Vicar took over here, asking Friar Nece if anyone had entered the room during the night, and if anything at all had occurred there. Nece thought, looked around, almost said something, checked herself, and said no. Then she said she wasn't sure. Bishop Gaet was as excited now as a man can get, but he wisely said nothing. Dawn and Mike were on the edge of their seats. Debbie, who had put on a hood, told Nece to watch closely, and she knelt in just the exact way she had seen in her dreams so many times, meditated for a few minutes, and arose. Nece's face was pale."

Yes, but it was only a dream." She had had it in the infirmary, and she had feared for her friend and Brother Jojo as the cloaked figure was kneeling over her. The dream had been so vivid she had awakened in a cold sweat. The Bishop asked Jojo one more thing. Was there anything different about the figure when it stood up? Jojo answered: "Yes, Sire, it had big wings."

Abbess Dawn was suddenly remembering some things. Jojo and Nece had gone back to their office and the four clergy were ecstatic. There was a possibility that they had a Saint among their very own! A few months ago, Pup had reported an injured young goat. He had carried it to the stable, and was administering to it when Friar Chrissie had waved him away, motioning that she would take over. Friar Pup had acquiesced and left the stable. As Pup left, he saw the Monk kneeling over the injured animal. The next morning the animal was completely healed.

The four felt they had enough evidence to notify the Cardinal. If Cardinal Lena felt it sufficient to warrant an investigation, her office would handle that. Bishop Gaet called her later that afternoon, and was requested to get their evidence to her in Avila in writing as soon as possible. Meanwhile, she would send an envoy to the monastery.

CHAPTER III

The Devil's Advocate

Cardinal Lena didn't joust with windmills. She knew Bishop Gaet well, and if he thought there were possibly some divine occurrences going on at Monte Sangre, something unusual WAS happening, and the Church needed to know what it was. She had finally received a rather bulky summation of all this from the Abbot's office in Monte Sangre, and had read it with interest. It appeared to her that there may have actually been some divine healing, but who or what had healed the dying Hermit, Chrissie? And the wings? No Saint, to her knowledge, had been winged. Lots of unanswered questions here. She was so intrigued, she had to resist an impulse to visit the monastery, herself. The potential discovery of a Saint in their midst was one of the most important happenings in the Church and was taken very seriously.

The Cardinal had immediately dispatched Monsignor Kim to the monastery to find out what she could. Should they begin the Canonization process, Monsignor Kim would be the Devil's Advocate. This means that Kim would argue against Canonization, even if she felt it was justified. It was Church Law that both sides be represented. God's Advocate would be another ranking clergy to be appointed later.

Monsignor Kim loved the scenic mountainous monastery already. It seemed peaceful beyond belief, and the massive centuries—old structures were cool and roomy. After a lengthy visit with the other Clerics, she told them she would need access to the archives. Friar Doug welcomed her, introduced her to Friar Jam, his assistant, and to Friar Elaine, who came bubbling in. Kim had never seen a Monk as pretty and vivacious as Elaine before, and told her so, making a friend for life.

The Monsignor found it pleasant working with the handsome, efficient Monk, Doug. His record-keeping was comprehensive and orderly. Friar Jam, quick and efficient, could already place her hands quickly on almost any document they needed.

Kim explained to Doug that she would be taking a lot of notes, probably, and needed to actually see the documents in question. Jam had quickly been able to produce the necessary archives and they were able to determine that Friar Chrissie had established her Hermitage at the cave, less than two miles from the monastery, almost seven years ago. She had lived in solitude for almost five years. A long time, really. Most Hermit Monks gave up much sooner than that, moving into a nearby monastery, or leaving the Church and just melting into society. Kim made several lengthy notations from the documents and they were returned to the archives.

Kim asked Doug if the monastery had provided sustenance for the Hermit during this time, and the Monk, surprisingly, wasn't sure. He assumed they had, or she would have perished. Kim made a note. The dying Hermit had been discovered by Friar Bonnie, a goat-herd. Friar Bonnie had probably been the most frequent visitor of the Hermit throughout the years. Asked, Doug told Kim that Friar Bonnie just exuded love. She loved everyone, and her outgoing personality and beatific appearance just made her loved by everyone. She was probably the closest person on earth to the aloof Monk, Chrissie. Kim made a note.

Monsignor Kim wanted to immediately interview Friar Bonnie, but, first things first. The next morning she appeared in Friar Lilly's office, where Lilly and Friar Brandon were going over inventories and receipts. Introducing herself, she explained she was interested in the period when Friar Chrissie had had her Hermitage at the cave. The Hermitage being an adjunct of the monastery, had she any records of sustenance being supplied to the Hermitage? Friar Lilly could remember the period well. She told Kim that there were no records of it, but, yes, the monastery had indirectly supported the Hermit, through Friars Nece and Bonnie.

Sheltered somewhat by the higher mountains to the north, the monastery near the foothills still had severely cold winters, and she, Lilly, had periodically issued blankets and warm new robes to Nece or Bonnie to take to the cave, and Brother Bonnie (and Brother Nece, or Pup, on occasion) had been seen many times through the years on the steep trail to the cave carrying a basket, presumably bearing food to the cave. Kim made some notes, and asked Lilly and Brandon if either had ever been to the cave. Neither had ever been to the cave. She thanked them and left.

At the Bishop's insistence, Mike agreed to accompany him on a trip to the cave. Stopping in the field, they had a pleasant chat with Friars Pup and Bonnie. On a hunch, the Bishop asked Pup if he had ever been to the cave. Pup nodded. Many times. The Bishop asked the Monk if he would accompany them, guiding them to the cave, and Pup agreed. Something about the Friar Bonnie bothered the Bishop. He had never seen a countenance so serene and complacent,. He resisted an urge to kneel at her feet. She almost radiated holiness. He was going to have the Vicar find out a bit more about this Monk.

Less than a mile from the herd in the field, they entered the cave. The Holy Bishop suddenly had a profound eerie feeling, and glancing at Mike and the Monk, He knew they were feeling something also. Mike avoided the Bishop's eyes and was fingering his beads. Pup's eyes were almost closed and his lips were moving as though in prayer. Bishop Gaet felt as though he were in a sacred shrine, but a shrine to what or to whom? The two small rooms inside the cave showed very little sign of having ever been occupied, and they soon left, silently, almost reverently,

Monsignor Kim entered Friar Carol's pleasant, small office, introduced herself, and they chatted for awhile. Kim asked Carol if she kept copies of the reports she sent to the Cardinal. Carol replied that every single one was on file chronogically. The Monsignor asked for and was presented with the log for the date the Hermit, Chrissie was found dying in the Hermitage and the subsequent logs for the next two weeks or so. Scanning the documents and making notations on her pad, Kim suddenly asked for the logs for the two weeks BEFORE the incident.

Reading these with interest, Kim suddenly became almost animated, and started copying from some of the reports. Thanking Carol profusely, the Monsignor left her office. With just the information she had collected so far, Monsignor Kim had a lot of work to do. She would now telephone the Cardinal.

The Bishop had indefinitely cancelled his departure from Monte Sangre, and the inquisitive Vicar, Debbie, (unknown to the Monsignor) was still nosing around. Debbie was good at talking with people, and she was doing a lot of it. She had formed some sort of relationship with the goat-herds, Friars Pup and Bonnie, and spent more than a little time in the fields and at the stables.

Friar Bonnie had finally reluctantly agreed to escort the Vicar to the cave, and they were nearing the entrance single-file on the narrow, rocky ledge, the Friar leading. Bonnie entered the cool, dark cave and instantly knelt, fingering her beads. Debbie walked around Bonnie and into the cave, An aura of something not of this world permeated the cave, and she involuntarily knelt and joined in prayer. They silently left the cave and not a word was spoken during their return to the field.

Friars Karen and Monica had just helped the villagers load their truck with the huge melons. Nece was charging by the melon and a bit of haggling was going on. It was mid-afternoon and they decided to go to the river, clean their robes, and cool off with a nice long swim. Pup, Bonnie, and Chrissie were already in the pool, their robes drying on a rock in the bright sunlight. Surprised to see Friar Chrissie there, they cleaned their garments and happily hit the water. Chrissie soon left for the stables, as other Monks appeared.

The Cardinal, Lena, placed the telephone receiver on it's hook, relaxed in her chair, and went into deep thought. The situation at Monte Sangre was, so far, going better than expected. She shivered in anticipation of Kim's next call. Soon, she would have to inform Rome.

When the Vicar told Bishop Gaet of her visit to the cave with Bonnie, and the awestricken reverent feeling she'd had there, he related to her the events of his visit with Friar Pup and the Abbot. The Bishop said it was akin to being in a Holy Sepulchre, but no one, to his knowledge, had died or been entombed there.

The Abbot, Mike, and the Bishop had requested to speak with Kim as early as possible the following morning, when they asked if it would be possible to sit-in when she met with either Friar Nece or Friar Bonnie. The Monsignor said she would be pleased to have them attend, and would let them know. Mike asked Kim if she had been to the cave, and she said no. The Abbot gave her an odd look, but said nothing.

Sainthood is awarded posthumously. The preliminary investigation at Monte Sangre would, however, probably determine whether the Canonization process would begin. All the information gathered at Monte Sangre would be on hold for many years, but it was imperative that it be done.

CHAPTER IV
The Revelation

Cardinal Lena had called Rome and given them all the information she had on the events at Monte Sangre. The Bishop of Rome had immediately dispatched Archbishop Georgia to the monastery. Georgia had been there three days now, most of that time being spent with the other potential Advocate, Monsignor Kim. Georgia was a rather serious, unflappable person, and was, secretly, a bit dubious of the entire thing. Some puzzling things were going on, though. One was that the Vicar, Debbie, was spending a lot of time at the stables, and why? Another was that everyone, including Bishop Gaet, seemed to be in awe every time the Hermitage was even mentioned.

Georgia insisted on going to the cave, and Kim agreed. Friar Nece had been to the cave many times, so they asked her to escort them early tomorrow. Friar Nece seemed reluctant, but agreed to do so. Once they had visited the cave, they planned to get with Abbot Mike and Bishop Gaet to schedule an interrogation of Friars Bonnie and Nece.

The last eighty or so yards to the cave were very treacherous. A narrow rocky ledge had to be traversed single—file, Friar Nece leading the way. Nearing the entrance, they could see that a rock slide had partially blocked the entrance. Nece, nervously fingering her beads, partially climbed the rubble and peered inside. She felt they could crawl inside, but was not sure. Georgia impatiently pushed the ashen-faced Monk aside, climbed the rubble and stuck her head inside the cave. Suddenly the Archbishop froze, raising her hands as though in supplication. Bowing her head, she began praying. Kim, four feet or so from the partially blocked entrance, could still feel the overpowering presence. She resisted the urge to kneel and moved farther away. She knew she was not going into the cave. A few minutes passed and a trembling Georgia beckoned for Nece to assist her down from her perch on the rocks.

Very few words were spoken on the trip back to the monastery. As they passed the stables, fifty yards or so to their right, they could see the Vicar and Friars Pup and Bonnie in the corral seemingly in an animated conversation with the normally mute Friar, Chrissie.

There was little that went on at Monte Sangre that Abbess Dawn was not aware of. She knew of the swimming hole and she was aware of the clearing in the cornfield, and she was aware of some other things. The Clerics were assembled, scheduling the meeting with Friars Bonnie and Nece, Dawn dryly remarked that it might be a good idea to include Friar Pup and the Vicar, Debbie. Monsignor Kim made a notation on her pad and looked questioningly at the Abbess. Dawn said no more. They were pretty much in agreement that Monsignor Kim would primarily conduct the meeting. They scheduled it for one PM the following Saturday.

Friday night the heavens rumbled, and nearby lightning, thunder, wind, and torrential rain struck the monastery. Saturday dawned soggy and cloudy. Friar Bonnie arrived at the stables early and Friar Chrissie was nowhere to be found. She shrugged, Pup arrived, and they took the herd to the field. Being Saturday, they returned early, around midday. Still no Friar Chrissie. Friar Monica met them there, advising them they were to be in the Abbot's quarters in an hour or so.

When Friars Bonnie and Pup arrived at Mike's quarters, the efficient Tammy ushered them into the larger conference room, seating then at one end of the long table alongside Friar Nece. Then she closed the door, sat, and took out her stenographer's pad. Every spoken word would be recorded.

The Clerics were at one end of the table, and the three Monks at the other. The Vicar sat in between, near the center of the table. After a brief prayer, Bishop Gaet stood and introduced Archbishop Georgia, stating she was from Rome, and that the Church needed more information from the monastery concerning the discovery of the dying Hermit, Chrissie, in the cave. He did not say why. The Bishop then turned the meeting over to Monsignor Kim.

Kim opened by introducing herself. She explained she had been sent here by Cardinal Lena in Avila, and she had been asked to discover all the facts she could concerning the incident in the cave. She began by unnecesarily asking Friar Nece if she had ever been to the hermitage. Nece said she had been there many times. Kim said she had ascertained from monastery records that, just prior to the incident, there had been severe weather at the monastery. Nece remembered it well. It had been severely cold, with an ice storm. It was difficult to even keep one's footing outdoors, and the ice would not melt in the cold for over a week. Kim asked Nece if she had thought of the Monk in the cold cave during this period. Nece said they had prayed for her constantly, as they could not get to her to help her.

Kim gave Nece a look of approval and asked Friar Bonnie if she had gone to the cave as soon as the ice melted. Bonnie replied that they had not waited, They had feared for Chrissie's life, and, roping themselves together for safety, they had made it to the cave over the icy rocks. Kim then asked her who had gone with her on this mission. Bonnie said that Brother Lillie had bundled up warm clothing and blankets and Friar Nece carried them to the cave. She, herself, carried a large basket of food and wine. Pup had lashed a large bundle of firewood to his back. Roped together, Friar Pup had led the way.

They had made it to the cave slowly, but without incident.

Kim paused here, as though to regroup. Then slowly, she asked Bonnie to remember and tell her exactly what happened when they entered the cave. Friar Bonnie was starting to break down, losing composure. Bonnie finally related that Brothers Pup and Nece had stayed in the larger room to unpack Chrissie's things and to try to build a fire. She had gone on into the smaller room where Chrissie slept, fearing the worst.

Monsignor Kim paused again, feeling the pain that Bonnie was going through. Finally, taking a deep breath, Kim asked in a soft, almost humble voice, "What did you find there?" Bonnie finally answered. She had found Chrissie covered with her blankets, and she appeared lifeless. Sobbing now, she was being comforted by her Brother Monks.

Friar Bonnie said that she had never before felt such intense grief. She had loved the lonely Hermit. Chrissie's forehead was cold, and her hand was lifeless. Bonnie had taken Chrissie's cold hand in hers, and, clasping it, her outpourings of intense grief, love, loss, and prayer were so powerful the other two Monks had joined in. Suddenly, the lifeless hand she held clasped her hand! Startled, she opened her eyes and looked at Chrissie. Chrissie's eyes were open and alert. She was alive!

Everyone in the room was stunned, Kim almost fell. There were tears in Georgia's eyes, and the Bishop and Abbot Mike were were sitting with bowed heads. Dawn was tearfully fingering her beads.

Chrissie had partial use of her limbs, and, covering her for warmth, the three Monks had been able to get her down to the infirmary. Strangely, the rocky trail to the cave was no longer icy and the return trip was relatively easy. There was an intense silence in the room, as though no one knew what to say or do next. Then there was a knock on the door.

Friar Chuck entered and went to the Abbot, speaking in a low tone. Mike then asked him something and the Monk nodded, Mike thought a few moments, asked Chuck something else. Then the Abbot thanked the Friar and Friar Chuck left the room. Mike seemed to be searching mentally for something to say. He finally stood and said Friar Chrissie had left the monastery. She was nowhere to be found. They had even searched the cave. The entrance was now partially blocked but they had been able to crawl in. There was no trace of the Friar anywhere.

Archbishop Georgia was the first to speak. She asked the Abbot if Friar Chuck had said who had climbed into the cave, and the Abbot said no. Georgia said they must find out. Ten minutes later Friar Karen, who had crawled into the cave was present. Kim asked the Monk if she had felt a spiritual presence of any sort upon entering the cave. Karen said it was dark and a bit eerie, but, no, nothing like that.

The Bishop and Mike exchanged glances, as did Kim and Georgia.

Everyone seemed to be waiting for the Bishop to speak. Finally Gaet stood. He said that it was improbable that Friar Chrissie could have left the monastery during the storm, but apparently she somehow had. But why, and to where? No one said anything. The Bishop sat, conferring with Mike and the Archbishop, Georgia. Beckoning the Monsignor, they conversed at length. Bishop Gaet finally stood and said that apparently all their investigations had been in vain, and he was officially closing the investigation. Since no one knew where Chrissie had gone, he would call the Cardinal, informing her of the events and his decision. This could always be resumed if she were to be found.

There was a brief silence, and the Abbess stood, saying that she knew where Chrissie was! She paused, letting it sink in. Raising her hand for silence, she said that the Vicar, Debbie had come to her quarters just before dawn, cold, wet, and distraught. She had comforted Debbie, they had prayed, and Debbie had related her experience of the night before. Dawn had known that the Vicar and the lonely Friar, Chrissie, had become close friends, and that she, Friar Pup, and Friar Bonnie knew things about Chrissie that no one else was privy to.

All eyes in the room were on Debbie. Debbie, obviously very shaken. looked at Dawn, bowed her head in prayer, composed herself, and began speaking. This is her narrative: Chrissie had expired in the cave many hours before she was found by the three Monks. She was in the arms of God in Heaven. The devout Friar Bonnie had experienced such loss and grief while clasping the lifeless body of her friend that the heavens had relented and sent Chrissie back! The Vicar, now in tears, said that for almost two years now Chrissie had been on earth, but as an Angel. Her place in Heaven had been secured, and her time on earth was limited. Chrissie had known that yesterday was to be her last day on earth and she had told her friend, the Vicar.

Somehow, Debbie knew that Chrissie would visit the cave before leaving, and at dusk she had gone alone up the narrow, treacherous trail to be with her friend. The entrance was partially blocked now, she noted, and Chrissie was just crawling over it into the cave. She waved and shouted, but just as Chrissie disappeared into the cave, the Heavens erupted. The storm seemed to hit the cave area with all it's fury. Debbie finally made it to the entrance, and, shielding herself from the rain and wind as best she could, she had prayed until she fainted.

She awoke, cold and wet, but otherwise unhurt. Determined, she managed to crawl into the cave. She had a tin of matches and she was able to illuminate it enough to determine that her friend had, indeed, returned to the heavens. Debbie stopped here, bowing her head. She could say no more.

Mike, the Abbot, visibly shaken, arose and led them in a long prayer of dedication and love for the departed Friar, and the meeting was over.

Tammy had called the village and determined there had been no storm at the village below them. No one there had even been aware of a storm at the nearby monastery. When Mike heard this, he said it was as he suspected. The storm had been a divine welcoming of Chrissie's return to the heavens.

Cardinal Lena sent all this to Rome, and in less than a year, the cave was declared a Holy Shrine to the Angel, Chrissie.

THE END

A FAIRY TALE
(Stolen by Pup)

Once upon a time there was a magical kingdom, ruled by a very beautiful, but vain Queen. The kingdoms around her had fallen on hard times, but the Queen prospered. She was beautiful and knew she was the fairest in the land, because she was in possession of a magic mirror that told her so. The Queen was very vain about her beauty. Every morning after she brushed her long, gleaming hair, she would ask the magic mirror who was fairest in the land, and the mirror would reassure her that she was. Then, Dawn, the Queen, would go about ruling her great and prosperous kingdom.

Years went by and the kingdom prospered, even as the kingdoms around her grew poorer and poorer. Dawn was very selfish and refused to help her destitute neighbors.

One morning after she finished brushing her magnificent long hair she went to the mirror and, as usual, asked who was fairest in the land. The mirror answered that it was no longer her, the Queen, but a maiden named Ros. Dawn was furious and demanded to know who this Ros was. She was an orphan who lived with her wicked stepmother, Chrissie.

Summoning her servant, Bill, she set out for Chrissie's cottage. Arriving, She discovered that the maiden had fled a week or so ago, and the wicked Chrissie had no idea where she'd gone. Furious, the Queen immediately ordered all her minions to find Ros at all costs, promising a reward of five gold pieces. Chrissie, knowing what the problem was, told her Queen to bring Ros home and she wouldn't be fairest in the land much longer.

The mean Chrissie had used Ros for nothing but drudgery. Dressed in ragged and dirty clothing, Ros had to empty the slop buckets, clean the chimneys, scrub floors constantly, and Chrissie fed her very little.

Under cover of night, Ros had fled from the village into the forest, where she became bewildered and lost her bearings. Tired and cold, deep in the dark forest, she finally collapsed. Many hours later, she was found lying in the forest by a pretty little dwarf named Monica, who would constantly smirk and then sneeze. Monica hurriedly summoned her fellow dwarfs and they carried Ros to their cottage, where they revived and fed her.

Ros awoke in the small cottage with seven small dwarfs surrounding her bedside. Startled at first, they soon allayed her fears and soon had her warm, fed, relaxed, and comfortable. The dwarf named Lisa was always happy. She hugged Ros and made her welcome, introducing herself and the others. The dwarf, Dan, who wore tiny spectacles, was sort of like a doctor to the others, always fussing over and helping them with any ailment. Mike, the largest of the tiny dwarfs, was always pessimistic and a bit grumpy. but actually smiled and welcomed Ros to their home. Karen, a pretty little dwarf, was always a bit lethargic, appearing sleepy all the time. Pup, the smallest dwarf was terribly bashful, hiding his mouth when he spoke. The seventh dwarf, Scott, always had a blank look, appearing a bit dopey at times.

The dwarfs were miners, and a trail from the cottage went directly into the mountain where they went every morning to mine. Chanting "Hi-ho, it's off to work we go", Ros now chiming in, they would leave for the mine. Ros was beginning to love the kind, merry dwarfs, and she loved the routine.

Ros was picking berries in the forest one day when a handsome stranger on a magnificent white charger came upon her. Stopping to chat with the winsome Ros, they fell in love instantly. His name was Neil, and he was a Prince from a much poorer neighboring kingdom. When he discovered her name was Ros, his face grew white.

He told her she was in grave danger and must leave the kingdom quickly. He would take her now from the clutches of the evil Queen. Ros was loath to leave her friends in the cottage, so she and Neil went to the cottage and he related the events leading to her being here, and the Queen's jealousy.

Now, these seven dwarfs had mined the mountain for many years, and they led Ros and Neil to their cache in a room inside the mountain where gold was piled everywhere. Neil had instantly liked the dwarfs and offered to get them, also, safely from the evil Queen's clutches. Loading their gold onto pack animals, they all set off at nightfall.

Dawn, the Queen, had had her alchemist, Lena, concoct a powerful, lethal poison and had poisoned an apple with it. The apple was intended for Ros, and the Queen had just learned of the dwarfs and their mine in the mountain. She arrived too late, though, and went back to her castle furious and frustrated.

Neil was King now, and many years had passed. The dwarfs, who loved to mine, had found a mountain of gold and were happily mining and caching their gold. Neil and his Queen, Ros, with all their gold, soon had their kingdom flourishing. The generous Neil had also helped his needy neighbors, and all the kingdoms were now prospering.

Dawn was growing older now, and the passing years had tempered her vanity. She had invited a neighboring King, Neil, and his Queen to her castle for a visit. When they arrived, she discovered the Queen was the mysterious, beautiful Ros whom she had hunted for so many years. Dawn now had no animosity. She welcomed them to her castle, and later invited Ros to her rooms. The two beautiful Queens were standing in front of the magic mirror, and Dawn, knowing it would say Ros, asked who was fairest in the land. The mirror said "Jojo".

Queen Ros was furious and demanded to know who Jojo was.

They lived happily ever after.

With apologies to the Grimm Brothers.

The End.

NAVAL FUN

CHAPTER I

It was May, 1942, and it was hot. The USS EAGLE, a destroyer assigned to protect the USS HORNET, was patrolling off the port stern of the big carrier, sonar and radar alert for enemy both in the air and underwater. The American fleet had met the Japanese in the Coral Sea, and, temporarily at least, had slowed the Japanese expansion in the Southern Pacific. They were just now leaving after securing the area.

They were to rendezvous with several more carriers and a major task force fromPearl Harbor and were expecting to engage most of the remaining Japanese fleet somewhere near Midway, 1200 miles or so north of Pearl Harbor, and an American Naval Base at the time. This story will reveal some of the extraordinary feats of some of the crew members of the EAGLE before and during the battle of Midway, which definitely turned the tide of the naval war in the Pacific.

The American fleet had taken the Japanese head-on in the Coral Sea north of Australia, but had suffered huge losses. At this time, the HORNET was the only American carrier afloat west of Pearl Harbor, and nearly half of her aircraft had been destroyed. Supplies were low, as were munitions.

Commander Dawn, the captain of the EAGLE was almost always in the chartroom, leaving Lieutenant Nina the wheelhouse, or bridge, command. She and Radarman Chief Petty Officer Tricia had killed many a pot of coffee together. Lt.Lena, the Radar and Communications officer almost lived in there, also.

The EAGLE had uffered extensive damage, and Chief Boatswain Georgia had her people working 12 hours on and 12 hours off repairing and refitting. The engineering officer, Lt (jg) Gaet, had suffered little damage below decks, and he and his people were assisting. The repairs were nearly completed.

The EAGLE was fortunate to have a radioman as good as First Class Radioman Elaine, one distinct advantage being that she was fluent in Japanese. Almost always in the radio room, she was occasionally able to intercept a message from the enemy. Then she and Lt. Ed, the Intelligence officer, would attempt to break the Japanese code.

The crew of the EAGLE fought hard, played hard, and ate well. Chief Petty Officer Monica was arguably the best cook in the US Navy, and she kept her mess-hands, Seamen Bonnie and Pup, busy making delicious meals for the crew. Her battle station was as gunner, and she had uncanny accuracy with her 20mm twin- mount. She had to her credit three Japanese planes shot down, and one torpedo exploded enroute to target. Pup and Bonnie helped load one of the forward 5"-38 big guns in the forward array during battle. Her shipmates called Monica "smirk shot", as she had a peculiar smirk at times.

Chrissie was a Gunners Mate Second Class, and a sharpshooter. She had five stripes (notches) on her 20mm.gun turret, the most on the ship, and had probably saved the EAGLE a serious hit when she faced a suicide pilot coming straight in about 30 feet off the water and blew it up. Two other 20mm gunners were Dan and Paul, both Petty officers. Dan was a Hospital Corpsman Second Class, and worked under Nece, the First Class Corpsman on the EAGLE, and acting ship's doctor at this time. Paul was a Gunner's Mate Third Class.

Bob, Chief Yeoman, manned a 40mm during battle. The Bofors 40mm twin-mount cannon was a much larger gun than the 20mm, and was primarily an anti-aircraft weapon. Bob had two kills to his credit. Debbie, a Seaman Gunner's Mate, also manned a twin-40, with one enemy craft shot down.

The HORNET kept three aircraft aloft at all times for surveillance, and one of the pilots had just radioed coordinates of a Japanese oil tanker he'd spotted. These tankers were a MUST kill, as the Japanese had to import all of their oil, and a complete embargo could shorten the war immeasurably.

Lisa, Radioman Second Class, also trained as a 5"-38 gunner-crew member, handed the coded message to Elaine, and Elaine retired to the code room with Ed. The EAGLE was the least damaged of the ships who survived the battle, and had been selected to intercept and destroy the Japanese tanker. Dawn verified through code, and ordered flank speed. Lena had already calculated contact in a bit under seven hours. The EAGLE, with her powerful turbines and two screws could reach speeds of about almost 40 knots in good weather.

Commander Ros was a survivor from another destroyer that had gone down in the Coral Sea. At this time, she was acting as part-time Radar officer and part-time Navigator. Five hours and thirty minutes later Radarman Tricia had the tanker blip on the screen, about 35 miles away. If they hurried they could sink it before dusk or they could wait for dawn. Dawn radioed the HORNET, and was advised to try to finish it off and return as soon as possible. BATTLE STATIONS and a short briefing went out on the intercom 20 minutes later.

Lt, Commander Mike, Executive officer and Gunnery Officer on the EAGLE, was in charge of the 5-inch guns. Mike knew the Mark IV fire-control system as well as any man alive, and he would coordinate, aim, and order the firing. Lilly, Chief

Gunner's Mate, was an expert 5-inch fire director, and her crews were always well-trained. At the appropriate time, they would turn broadside and sink the tanker from several miles away.

It was approximately 7:30 PM when Dawn gave the order to slow and broadside the tanker. The 5"-38 was probably the best naval gun of all time for what it was designed to do. It was rapid—fire, and had a range of around ten miles with a projectile of over 50 pounds. The tanker couldn't see the EAGLE, but probably knew it was there. The big guns roared, and the big projectiles sped westward. The target was a little over 6 miles away, visually obstructed by the horizon. Mike waited exactly two minutes, fired another salvo, and the EAGLE sped toward the tanker. Radar showed very little there now. Anything substantial still above the water would be torpedoed. Fifteen minutes later they could see the remains of the tanker, and there wasn't much. A dozen or so survivors, lots of smoke, and some debris. Reporting to the HORNET, and changing course, Dawn reported tanker sank and they should rendezvous within 18 hours. Mission accomplished. Ros asked Dawn later if the HORNET had inquired about survivors, and Dawn said she 'hadn't noticed."

Elaine had hooked up a small motor, geared down, to rotate the tuning condenser of her best radio receiver, hooked it up to an oscilloscope, and also to a wire recorder. This gave her the primitive equivalent of a Radio Intercept System.

Shortly after sinking the Japanese tanker, an unknown new frequency popped up on the scope. It was in Japanese code, and she began recording. Four hours later, she and Ed were close to cracking the Japanese coding. Knowing they needed assistance from Naval Intel in Pearl Harbor, they excitedly called Lisa in and sent word that Mike was wanted in the code room.

Commander Mike was astounded at what they'd discovered, and authorized coded radio transmission to Pearl Harbor on the seldon used highest—priority frequency. They hastily got their lengthy message together, and Lisa, extremely fast and accurate, began sending the message. Unknowingly, they had just saved the American fleet from a clever Japanese trap near Midway.

Naval Intel in Pearl Harbor kept one frequency open to the Eagle, working with Ed and Elaine. The HORNET was told to change to a more easterly course, and the USS ENTERPRISE left Pearl Harbor with a full contingent of warplanes, accompanied by a small task force.

Dawn, Ros, Lena and Mike were having a meeting in the chartroom. If all calculations were correct, they could possibly be within range of Japanese aircraft by about mid-morning tomorrow. The HORNET had no planes aloft now, and the ENTERPRISE was still several hundred miles away. By mid-afternoon tomorrow, or so, they might be able to assist each other somewhat. They decided to run a few drills, make all possible preparedness, and fill in the crew in the morning.

Ping!!! Ping!!! Sonarman First Class Anneke straightened in her chair and analyzed the "sighting". Several hundred yards aft and starboard, and obviously a submarine. The EAGLE was east and north of the Japanese shipping lanes, where most of the American subs were assigned. She called Lt. Lena immediately, and plugged the sonar screen into a PPI in the chartroom, and another on the bridge. Captain Dawn was reluctant to call General Quarters, and decided to just keep an eye on it for a while. Anneke was good at what she did. She kept it focused on the screens. The sub commander seemed to just want to "tag along", probably because of an extremely dark night with good cloud cover.

Visibility was still poor as daylight approached. The Japanese sub had moved a bit during the night, and it was becoming obvious that it was after the Hornet. Dawn and Nina were on the bridge with Chief Quartermaster Karen, who also was a trained 20mm gunner. LT. Nina was intently trying to penetrate the murk with a mariner's telescope. Ros was in the chartroom, and Mike was concerning himself with gunnery right now. If that sub rose to attain periscope depth he was sure one of his sharpshooters could eliminate the periscope. They received a signal from Anneke, and they knew the Japanese sub was now making it's move.

CHAPTER II

Bo'sun Mate Second Class Doug, appointed Master-at-Arms by Commander Mike, unlocked the heavy door, and Seaman Doo (formerly Gunner's Mate Third Class) emerged frim the brig after 5 days of bread and water. Doo had swiped some apples, sugar, and yeast from Monica and created herself a fine bunch of "applejack". She had inebriated herself to the point that she had passed out, gotten caught, and gotten herself a Captain's Mast. A Captain's Mast at sea is a formal maritime trial for minor offenses. The Captain weighs the evidence and delivers a verdict. In Doo's case, Dawn had given her 5 days confinement, and demotion of one stripe. (In a battle zone, a mild verdict, probably). She had been reassigned to work with Chrissie, and now reported to Chrissie for duty. Doo was fun-loving, well-liked, a good sailor, and was warmly welcomed back to duty. (The officers didn't know this, but Doo had shared a lot of the delicious, powerful applejack with a lot of crew members before she got busted).

Lt. Norm, Captain of the USS MYSTRA, DE735, had hidden behind the long hull of the HORNET and changed course to obtain a position directly aft of the now rising Japanese submarine. A Destroyer Escort is smaller than a Destroyer, with much less firepower and speed. The Mystra sported two 5" guns, four 40mm Bofors cannon, and 8 20-mm anti-aircraft guns. More importantly, she was equipped with depth-charges and had an excellent, well-trained crew.

Petty Officer Anneke had been tracking the sub now for many hours. It was now about 100 meters deep, and slowly rising, speed about 4 knots, facing the Hornet, but, at 1600 meters, much too far for good torpedo range, When a submarine gets to periscope depth, approximately 25 to 30 feet under water, it becomes difficult to handle, because it becomes a bit too buoyant. Most authorities say they handle best down about 400 meters or so. When a periscope breaks water, it leaves a wake, and is visible to radar and to the naked eye. The sub was well below periscope depth at this time, but rising, Calculations were being made on the EAGLE and on the HORNET.

Lt. Lena calculated they had fifteen minutes or so before they'd make their move. When the sub was at 15 meters depth and 600 meters from the HORNET, the HORNET went full—speed, hard port, the EAGLE went full-speed, hard starboard, and Norm ordered full—ahead on the MYSTRA. The MYSTRA deployed depth charges at the designated spot, then the EAGLE sped through, dropping another group. Dawn made a hard turn, and, assuming they'd missed, dropped a third group of charges where they thought the sub would now be. There were no survivors.

It was just about this time that The USS YORKTOWN and a large naval task force was heading north from Pearl Harbor, approximately 48-hours behind the ENTERPRISE

The Admiral on the HORNET had gotten orders from Pearl Harbor to slow speed and wait to rendezvous with the Enterprise under radio silence. Rendezvous was expected early morning day-after-tomorrow. Dawn welcomed the respite, Some needed repairs could be made, and the crew was tired. Unknown to them, this change of orders had possibly saved their lives, as there was a major change in plans, due to interception of Japanese naval messages. Japanese radio traffic was very heavy at this time. Naval Intel knew the Japanese had something working, and, unknown to the Japanese, the Americans had now completely broken their radio code.

Corpsman Nece had her hands full. The EAGLE had picked up over twenty survivors from other ships, and some were critically wounded. Most had been transferred to the infirmary on the Hornet, but three remained, and one had taken a turn for the worse. There were four doctors on the HORNET, and she could contact them for advice, but, under radio silence, she had lost this advantage. The only means of communication now was semaphore; the use of two specially designed flags in the hands of skilled Signalmen. After nightfall, a series of powerful shuttered beacons were used, blinking out a code similar to Morse. The small fleet was almost at a standstill now, and the HORNET had lowered two small boats with medical supplies and two doctors. Help was on the way for Nece. Dan was a capable corpsman, also, and they kept their patients as comfortable as possible. The three would probably be moved to the large infirmary aboard the HORNET.

Chief Petty Officer Lilly and Gunner's Mate Chrissie had just cleaned up in a crap game and a poker game, respectivelly, and it was light's out on the EAGLE. In eighteen hours they would be in contact with the enemy.

Intel at Pearl Harbor had made their decision. Radio silence was lifted and the task force was ordered to Point Luck, about 350 miles friom Midway. Officers Ros and Lena, in the chartroom, knew enemy contact could be at any time. At 1600 hours an aircraft appeared on the radar. The General Quarters gong sounded just as Georgia had finished lashing a lifeboat that had worked loose. American aircraft were now airborne over the HORNET, and the Japanese reconnaissance plane fled. The enemy now knew where they were, and it would be many hours before anyone would leave their Battle Stations. They were now near enough to the ENTERPRISE to be sure of some additional air cover, enabling them to continue.

The complete American task force assembled, got into formation, and, knowing the enemy strength and location, was steaming toward Midway by evening, June 2nd. The Eagle had taken on stores, fuel, and ammunition, all meticulously recorded by Chief Bob, who directed most of the distribution.

At dawn, June 4, the Japanese were in position, and struck Midway Island. With eight carriers, Admiral Yamamota had air superiority, but he made a mistake by making an all-out aerial assault. Too many planes had to return for fuel at the same time, decreasing the air cover for his carriers, and he lost two carriers to American torpedo bombers from the naval base on Midway.

The EAGLE had been reassigned to the ENTERPRISE, Admiral Yamamoto was determined to sink the American carriers, and Captain Dawn was commanding from the bridge. Monica was happy, she was smirking, and she was piling up cannon casings all over the place. Three planes down, and that last one had been exciting. Dawn had cleverly maneuvered the Eagle to within 100 yards or so of the ENTERPRISE and turned so that Chrissie and Monica's guns would be facing the incoming enemy planes, Pup, reassigned to Monica's 20 mm mount as helper, kept begging her to let him "shoot some Japs". Monica handed Pup her.45, smirked, and said "go ahead". Chrissie also had three more planes to her credit, and had the same problem in that Doo kept wanting to "shoot".

Commander Mike, always judicious with his big guns, was well aware of their anti-aircraft capabalities, and his gun crews took out many enemy aircraft before they even got close.

The Japanese had sent two cruisers along with the aircraft assault, and ship-to—ship gunfire was now erupting. The American cruisers were still a bit too far away to be effective, and the Japanese cruisers were almost within firing-range of the American carriers. The Americans had few choices. Retreating was not an option, and the EAGLE and three other destroyers were ordered to engage the cruisers in a delaying tactic.

Mike was glued to his Fire Control radar. Dawn had headed at the cruisers full—speed using an inconsistent zigzag—type course, making the EAGLE as small as she could, target-wise. Mike estimated 4 minutes until he'd be in range to fire. Japanese aircraft were busy protecting the cruisers from American bombers, and the Eagle was temporarily free from aerial attack. Big shells were falling near the EAGLE, though, and Dawn continued her erratic course. When Mike had begun firing, Dawn thought it was the sweetest sound she'd ever heard.

Mike began firing the forward batteries at almost 10 miles away, and never let up. Radarman Tricia reported the grim news that two of the American destroyers had disappeared from radar. The American aircraft had done some damage to the two heavy cruisers in that a few gun mounts had been disabled, and a few fires reported. The cruisers were almost in sight now, and the EAGLE was miraculously unhit. Mike was well within range now—almost too close. The 5-inch projectiles from the EAGLE had taken a terrible toll on the Japanese cruiser. The superstructure was ablaze, and the bridge appeared to have taken a direct hit. Dawn never slowed. At three miles, she ordered torpedo tubes readied. Mike had his big guns lowered about as low as they would go, and the EAGLE was too close now for the big Japanese guns to be effective, Japanese planes were now peeling off and attacking the EAGLE. Every gun on the EAGLE was firing, and it seemed as though Dawn was going to ram the enemy cruiser. Suddenly, the EAGLE went full astern. Coming to a near stand-still, and a sitting duck for the Japanese, the Eagle fired all twelve torpedoes at the heavy cruiser at point-blank range. The entire port side of the Japanese cruiser seemed to erupt, and she was beginning to settle in the water. The EAGLE was wallowing in the force of the explosion, and American shells were now whining overhead.

The Japanese ended up losing four aircraft carriers and two heavy cruisers at Midway. More importantly, they were now on the defensive. Their hopes of taking Pearl Harbor, their only chance of winning the war, were all but gone. The Yorktown was the only American carrier lost at Midway, and she was readily replaced.

The heroes on the USS EAGLE were to be involved in much more Pacific warfare, but not as prey this time. The EAGLE was the hunter now, the raptor for which she was named, and by sinking the Japanese heavy cruiser the entire crew of the Eagle were to be awarded the Navy Cross, authority of Admiral Chester Nimitz.

THE END

PIED PIPER FUN

CHAPTER I

Eagletown had developed a rat problem. It had started out mildly with some chewed up plumbing, and gotten worse. Almost everyone in town had then gotten cats, creating a cat problem. Yowling cats all night, then half-eaten rats and spilled garbage all over town to clean up the next morning. The citizens were sick of it, and went to the mayor, Mike, demanding something be done. Mike, the owner of the Eagletown saloon, had been mayor for many years.

Mike was well aware of the problem, and he had been on the computer in his office trying to find a solution. He had Googled "Pest Eradication", had had to enter the Eagletown ZIP Code, check "Within 50 Miles", then the amount, where he tentatively entered $750. Entering all this, he got only one result.

"Pest Removal. All types. From fleas to elephants. No job too large. Quick, efficient, clean service. No poisons used. Will negotiate. Results guaranteed. Call Gilles at 1-(BYE)—BYEPEST."

Eagletown had a pretty nice City Hall, and the council was assembled for the emergency meeting concerning the cat and rat plague. Georgia, an accountant, represented the West Ward, where the most affluent citizens of Eagletown lived, and she had a bit more clout than any of the others. She was smart and she was innovative, but sometimes she could be just downright bull-headed.

Chrissie, an insurance agent, represented East Eagletown, the poorest section of town, and she represented them well. Her Ward had well-paved streets, and if even a street light burned out, it was replaced tomorrow. Councilwoman Chrissie was no one to fool with.

South Eagletown was represented by Pup, who worked at the cemetery. Pup was probably the worst Councilman in the country. He'd bring a crossword puzzle book to council meetings, not pay attention, and vote yes on anything they presented. Pup just didn't give a damn.

The Northern part of town (Second ward) was represented by Councilwoman Lanita, who published and edited the weekly city newspaper, the TALON. Lanita was a difficult person to go up against because her mighty pen could swing the populace to her way of thinking.

There was a big attendance today because of the current animal problem, and Mike brought the meeting to order. Mike was a popular mayor because he did a lot of favors for the citizens of Eagletown. He knew everyone in town, and if he wasn't "fixing" a ticket for someone, he was probably buying them a drink at his establishment.

Mike explained to the attendees that he felt the city was in need of professional help with this thing, and he had contacted a person named Gilles, who operated a pest removal service. Gilles had said he could easily and quickly solve the problem, and would contact them soon. As to the expense, Mike said he was trying to keep it under $750, but no contract as yet. As to the method, Mike said Gilles would probably set traps all over town, as he didn't use poison.

People were starting to get upset. Lilly, who worked at the hospital, said no damned traps were going to be placed at her house. Others were starting to grumble now and the meeting started going downhill fast.

The intercom buzzed, and the sultry, suggestive voice of Dawn, the voluptuous City Hall receptionist, came on, announcing the arrival of a gentleman named Gilles. Mike said to send him in.

Gilles was a rather strange looking fellow as he was wearing such colorful clothing. His trousers had one blue leg and one yellow leg. His shirt front was red on the left side and brown on the right side, and he wore a sort of weird tasseled cap that was multi-colored. The citizens of Eagletown were taken aback a bit, and it was suddenly very quiet in the chamber.

Mike introduced himself, made Gillis comfortable, and started his interrogation by asking Gilles if he thought the removal of several hundred cats and thousands of rats and mice might be too big a job. Gilles stated that this was a small job, really. Mike then asked him how he planned to do this, and Gilles calmly said he would lure them away. Mike asked politely, "What type of bait would lure both cats and mice?" Gilles replied he didn't use bait.

Gilles told the assemblage that he had in his possession a magic fife from which he could produce the tones necessary to lure the pests from the city. Georgia, always impatient, immediately spoke up, telling Mike they had a charlatan here and they were just wasting time with all this.

Gilles looked at Georgia rather strangely, and produced a small brown fife from inside his shirt. He placed it to his lips. Soft melody was coming from the fife as Gilles suddenly struck a rather discordant note, then soft lilting notes again. Georgia had risen and was approaching Gilles, when he suddenly stopped playing. Georgia seemed to awaken as though from a hypnotic state, slightly disoriented.

Mike, having witnessed this, wanted to give Gilles the go-ahead, and suggested, if they can come to terms, to put it up for vote. Chrissie seconded the motion. Gilles said his normal fee was $500, and

Mike jumped at it. Gilles raised his hand for silence, adding that $500 was for one pest, but they had two. He could remove the rats and leave the cats, or whatever. It was up to them to decide.

Lanita asked Gilles if he would remove both the rats and the cats for $750. Gilles thought a few minutes and said he could, but he would only take them five miles, and some could possibly return. They needed to be taken ten miles, and it would be $850.

Mike agreed, asking Gilles if the city could pay $500 when the pests left the city limits and the remainder when the job was finished. Gilles thought for some time, finally agreeing to a contract with those terms.

The townspeople in attendance were quiet, actually a bit awed by this strange fellow. Somehow, they felt Gilles could do the job, despite his appearance and his unusual modus operandi.

Putting it to a vote, Georgia and Lanita voted no and Chrissie gave it the go-ahead. Pup was day-dreaming about something and when it was his turn he just voted "yea", as usual. Mike cast the tie-breaker, and Gilles had his contract with the city. His contract read he was to relocate them to the open spaces ten miles south of Eagletown.

The city clerk, Jojo, issued a check for $500 to Gilles, and, to protect the city, she was to position herself one mile south of Eagletown, When Gilles actually had the pests that far out, she would give him the check when he passed by. Gilles agreed, but insisted on cash, so Jojo was to go by the bank first and cash the check.

Jojo was young and adventurous, and had saved enough to buy a a brand-spanking new yellow convertible from Stella's agency. After cashing the check Jojo went by the agency to see if her car was ready. Stella told her the car was ready, but there was a matter of $300 for closing costs that was due upon delivery. Jojo, being young, was eager to get her car, and told Stella why she needed it.

Stella was intrigued by the story of the council meeting and the agreement with this unusual gentleman, Gilles. She agreed to release the car for $150, knowing Jojo would get the remainder to her soon, on the condition she could accompany her. Jojo agreed, and, having no choice, gave Stella the money from the city money. This Gilles seemed a reasonable enough person, and she would explain to him what had happened.

Jojo and Stella hadn't even gotten out of the driveway before they were waved down by Karen. Karen was one of Jojo's closest friends, and also a close friend to almost every single, young man in Eagletown. After admiring Jojo's new car and finding out where they were going, she just hopped in, saying, "About time something exciting happened in this bloody town."

Two blocks later, Ros was in the car. Ros worked the night shift at the hospital, and spent her daytime hours fending off most of Eagletown's eligible young males as well as some older, not-so-eligible ones. The four stopped off at the Dairy Queen for take-out lunch, and headed south for the rendezvous point.

As they left Eagletown, they could see that almost everyone in town would be at the south city limits soon, to see this magical thing unfold.

CHAPTER II

A pretty good-sized crowd was already gathering near the southern city limits of Eagletown, and Gilles had, so far at least, done absolutely nothing. He was just sitting on a bench near the intersection of Pogo and Main as though waiting for something.

Mike and the hour-glass shaped Dawn had left city hall and walked south on Main street, which was also the highway through town. Nearing the city limits, they could see that Jojo had finally gotten delivery on her new convertible from that thief, Stella, and that it was parked just off the highway about a half-mile south of town in Jim's driveway. She also had some other people with her. Mike was suddenly starting to get an uneasy feeling about this whole matter.

Jim was a farmer. A chicken farmer. He sold chickens, he sold eggs, and he sold fertilizer. He had a really nice layout. Nice home, good, large, well-built outbuildings, and his bank account was one of the largest in town. His farm was located on sixteen acres of the best farm land near Eagletown. Jim was also probably the most eligible unmarried male in Eagletown, and very well known by all four of the young ladies parked in his driveway.

Most of the townspeople were now by the side of the highway leading south out of Eagletown, and all eyes were on the enigmatic, colorful Gilles. Suddenly he stood, walked to the center of Main Street, took out his fife and placed it to his lips. The notes from the tiny fife carried well, and Gilles was the master of it. Suddenly he hit a sour note, paused, then resumed. Nothing was happening! Mike was getting a sinking feeling in his stomach. Thank God they hadn't paid him yet.

Gilles hit another bad note, and suddenly rats and mice were appearing from all directions moving slowly toward him. He back-pedaled slowly, suddenly hitting another loud, discordant note. Cats were now converging on Gilles as hs slowly worked his way southward. Seemingly satisfied, he turned his back to his "following", and, placing both hands on the fife, he increased his pace, tootling merrily southward. Gilles had a way of walking that was more of a march, really. His knees came up high, and he had a long stride.

As he neared the townspeople, they began cheering, and the ladies were blowing him kisses. Seemingly oblivious, Gilles continued tootling southward out of town, with the closely packed vermin, followed by the cats, at a leisurely pace right behind him.

Jojo was getting nervous. In her eagerness to get possession of her pretty car she had possibly gotten herself in a big mess here. She knew Stella had locked the missing $150 in a drawer before they left. She also knew that Karen and Ros never had much money, as they were two of the most expensive, demanding dates in Eagletown.

Jim was her only chance. If Gilles wanted the entire $500, Jim would loan her the rest, she was sure. Gilles was about a quarter-mile away now, and she was mentally getting her story together. Her heart was fluttering.

Jim and Lisa had joined the group at the convertible. Lisa was another of Eagletown's "heart throbs". She wasn't as voluptuous as Stella and Karen, nor as "leggy" as Ros, but she was, as was Jojo, a head turner with a lot of class. She candled eggs and supervised their packaging for Jim. When Jojo hit him up for 150 bucks in cash, Jim told her he'd gone into town and made a deposit earlier, but he'd be glad to give her a check. Jojo was really worried now. She just knew Gilles wouldn't want a check.

Gilles and his "caravan" had reached the group in Jim's driveway when Lanita and Chrissie joined Mike and Dawn. Mike was a bit more relaxed now, as things seemed normal. It was obvious that there was a very good discussion going on at the convertible. Gilles suddenly waved his arms, turning to look back at Eagletown. What was going on here? Lanita, always the reporter, was making shorthand figures like mad, and everyone looking at Mike and the council members, expecting them to do something.

When Gilles approached the group at the convertible, Jojo climbed out and handed him the envelope, explaining what had happened, and not to worry, he'd get his money in full. By now the group from Eagletown were all out of the car, surrounding Gilles. Gilles studied the group momentarily, thinking. Finally, he spoke, "Many, many years ago, I was not paid for a removal much like this, and I had two options. I must do as I did then."

Stella sort of wiggled (in a delightful way) when she walked, and she sidled up to Gilles, their hips touching. She asked in her most seductive voice, "What are your options? You know you'll be paid in full."

Gilles, obviously still thinking, responded. "I must be sure of my money. I can either return the vermin and the cats to Eagletown and keep this money I now have, or, as I did many years ago, I will finish the job." Then he added, "But I must have collateral to do so."

All five of the young ladies were around Gilles now, begging him to complete the job and thanking him. Gilles faced north, waved to the townspeople aggregated there, and placed the fife to his mouth. Beautiful notes emanated from the tiny fife. Gilles was good! The caravan proceeded southward and when it had gone 25 feet or so Gilles produced a terrible note from his fife. Then sweet melody again and the five young ladies were marching southward. Gilles was taking his collateral!

A lot of townspeople had followed the caravan out of town, and the first to approach the bewildered Jim was Lilly. Jim had tried to prevent the southbound exodus of the young ladies, but they had seemed oblivious to him. A last faint discordant tootle from the fife wafted over them, and Lilly, suddenly transfixed, was marching southward. Jim was almost incoherent as Mike and Dawn and the townspeople approached him.

When Jim related the conversation at the convertible, Mike became furious. First of all, he could have shot Jojo for acting like a little kid over that damned yellow car. Then he was mad at Stella, She always insisted on that last "closing payment" when she sold a car. Then he was mad at Ros and Karen. Those two were always trouble, especially Karen. And now that damned Gilles was taking a half-dozen of the prettiest young ladies in Eagletown with him to parts unknown.

CHAPTER III

Lilly had caught up with the other young ladies and they were all silently marching southward with that peculiar high-knee stride. They were entering the first bend in the road south out of Eagletown and were disappearing from view.

Jojo had left the keys in the ignition of her new car, and just as the caravan disappeared from view, Jim, Mike, Pup, and Chrissie jumped in and sped southward in an attempt to rescue the ladies and get them safely back to town. As they took the slight turn eastward, Jim just slammed on the brakes. The roadway was clear! Not a sign of anything. Not even a stray rat.

With a great sense of loss, especially felt among the young men of Eagletown, the townspeople returned to a now quiet, very somber Eagletown.

The next day was Wednesday and the weekly TALON hit the stands. Lanita had published a powerful, gripping article on the disappearance of the young ladies and the events leading up to it, closing with an appeal to Gilles, or anyone who knew of this mysterious piper, to contact city hall in Eagletown, please.

Four hours later, Mike answered a ringing telephone. The caller introduced himself in heavily accented English as Kommissar Gaet, a police inspector from Hamelin, in Germany. Mike assured Gaet he had a wrong number and started to hang up. Gaet said he was calling in regards to the mysterious, colorful piper called Gilles, and Mike perked up. They conversed at length, with Mike doing most of the listening. Finally, Mike thanked Gaet for calling and said if anything came up, he'd be in touch.

Mike was in deep thought for a long while. Apparently, 700 or so years ago, the townspeople of Hamelin had refused to pay a colorful piper for removing a pestilence, and he had lured their children away in retaliation. The children were never seen again, nor was the mysterious piper. Hamelin had never forgotten this, and had followed up on it. Throughout the years the colorful piper had removed roaches in Japan, rats in Argentina, rats again in Capetown, bedbugs in London, and wolves in Russia, to name a few. He seemed to reappear every forty or so years. The Kommissar, Gaet, had cautioned Mike that if perchance Gilles should reestablish contact, Mike must negotiate fairly with this gentleman, or the imperiled young ladies would possibly never be seen again.

A week went by in a very quiet, sober Eagletown. Wednesday rolled around and no one even seemed to want to read the TALON. Mike went to his office and Dawn told him a caller had left a number for him to call, and then had hung up rather abruptly. She said she thought it had been Gilles, and Mike's heart leaped.

Dawn followed Mike in, helped him remove his coat, brought him a cup of coffee, and waited patiently. Mike seemed lost in thought, drumming his fingers on the desk. Finally, he dialed the number. It was the piper, Gilles!

Gilles seemed terribly agitated, and wasn't making much sense. Apparently the captive ladies were driving him out of his mind. He said he had released them from their spell several times but they wouldn't leave. Mike was trying to find out why, but Gilles was almost incoherent. He was now pleading with Mike to take the ladies back, but why?

Mike was finally getting a handle on all this. These six were simply too much for Gilles. They ate like little pigs, he said, and he was getting low on money for food. Always wanting to go shopping, constantly quarreling, and always complaining about something. It was obvious they were more than he could handle.

Gilles finally regained enough composure to tell Mike that it was the accursed magic fife. He loved to play on his fife, and whenever he played it the young ladies would approach him, rubbing against him and hugging and kissing him, even removing clothing, forcing him to stop playing. Gilles' notes from the fife were apparently an aphrodisiac to the sexy young ladies and they would never leave the fife. He was stuck with them whether he liked it or not, and he didn't like it. He wanted out and he was willing to strike a deal.

Mike was just devious enough to think he might be able to get the best of a very distraught, desperate Gillis, and his brain was churning. Finally he interrupted Gilles.

Mike told Gilles Eagletown could accept the young ladies back, but they wouldn't remain. They would just leave with Gilles again, as he had the fife. He offered Gilles $150 to make up for the shortage in the envelope that Jojo had borrowed. and he would purchase a fife for Gilles from the Emporium to exchange for the magic fife, which would remain in Eagletown, at least until the young ladies had rehabilitated.

Suddenly Gilles was no longer incoherent and rambling. He pointed out that he had removed thousands of vermin in good faith, and he had been cheated. He asked also for the remaining $350 in the original contract, plus $500 for the magic fife. Only then would he return the ladies and make the fife swap. In one year he would return to regain his magic fife.

Mike thought this was a good deal for the city, but he wanted to bargain some more. He told Gillis the city could only pay $250 for the fife, but would release it in 6 months instead of a year.

Gilles jumped at this, as his fife was his livelihood. He agreed, but added he would keep one young lady for the six months as collateral for the return of the fife. For some reason, Gilles really liked Lisa and Jojo and wanted to keep one of them, but only one.

Mike thought and thought. Damn! Why couldn't it have been that trouble-maker, Karen, or Stella? He finally told Gilles it was no deal, unless he took Karen. Mike could almost feel Gilles shudder over the phone. Gilles wanted no part of the mischevious, capricious Karen, nor the voluptuous, but conniving Stella, but he would accept Lilly as collateral. Mike told Gilles no, regarding Lilly, but if he would drop the $250 for the fife, he could take the lovely, but unpredictable Ros. Gilles said no, he'd rather have the money. Mike then told him no, all the young ladies must remain in Eagletown.

Grumbling, Gilles finally agreed, saying he would be at city hall at noon tomorrow with the young ladies.

After hanging up, Mike felt a bit triumphant. He told Dawn to call Lanita at the paper with the good news, and to arrange a council meeting for tomorrow at eleven AM. Then he dialed Kommissar Gaet in Hamelin to relate the good news.

When Mike told Kommissar Gaet he had just spoken with the piper and negotiated for the young ladies' return, Gaet insisted on the details. Mike related the conversation and told the Kommissar he felt Gilles had been reasonable and that he seemed satisfied with the outcome.

Gaet replied that the colorful piper would not have called unless he wanted something. But what? The money wasn't really that much. He advised Mike to be very careful tomorrow, and to give Gilles anything else he asked for, or there could be dire consequences. Gaet said, "The piper is merciless. He wants something in your village and he will get it."

Mike was a bit shaken up over the conversation with the Kommissar, and he hung up the phone slowly. What more could the scoundrel want? He had taken the beautiful young ladies, was unhappy with that, and now he was getting the money on his own terms. Mike shrugged. We shall see, he thought.

Jim had cleaned all the Dairy Queen debris from Jojo's new convertible and stored the car in his garage. He had driven it to town and had parked it for Jojo right at the steps leading up to City Hall. Then he had joined the others in the council chambers, where they were awaiting the piper.

There were very few townspeople in the chamber. Most were in awe and a bit afraid of the colorful piper, and had remained in their locked homes.

Suddenly a few notes from the dreaded fife wafted through the open windows. Gilles, as promised, had arrived. Mike felt his heart in his throat.

Gilles had stopped piping at the steps leading up to City Hall. The young ladies were now milling about. Jojo and Ros climbed into her car to have a cigarette, as Jojo had some in the glove compartment. The alluring Dawn had come outside to greet and give everyone a hug. Lisa and Lilly entered City Hall with Gilles, and Karen and Stella headed for Mike's bar to cadge drinks.

Lilly and Lisa were greeted warmly by the council, and they seemed to be happy to be home at last. Gilles entered the chamber, and he, if possible, was even more colorful than before. His trousers had one red leg and one white leg, and his shirt was blue on one side and white on the other, giving him a sort of checkerboard look. He wore the same multi-colored tasseled cap as before.

The piper approached Mike and Mike handed him the envelope with his money. Gilles counted it carefully and tucked it inside his shirt. Mike then proffered the Emporium bag containing the fife, and Gilles revoved the magic fife from inside his shirt. They then exchanged fifes.

Gilles placed his new fife to his lips and produced some melodious tones. God! He was good! Suddenly he produced a discordant note, then continued with the melody. Looking around as if to see if anything was following him, he moved around the room, producing amazing melody with an occasional terrible note. Finally, satisfied he no longer had a magic fife, he left the council chamber, tootling happily away.

They all ran to the windows as Gilles left. He went down the steps to the street, both hands on his fife as he tootled away. As he passed the group around and in the convertible, he hit a terrible note, then moved on southward. His knees were pumping high now as he had assumed that peculiar marching motion. Dawn, as though in a trance, was suddenly following Gilles, now with her knees rising high as she strode to keep up. Suddenly, both Gilles and Dawn magically disappeared. As the Kommissar had said, Gilles will take what he wants.

Good choice, huh?

THE END

CHRISTMAS FUN

PART I

Dear Santa:

Santa, I'm sorry I haven't written in years, but time flies. Bet it's cold up there at the Pole. Probably almost as cold as Canada. Europe got hit with a cold snap, too, but it's fine here in Texas. Hope all the elves and reindeer are fine, as well as Mrs. Claus. Santa, I need your help, as I have a few needy friends. I am still playing in Eagles league and a few of the players are in need. I thank you for helping in advance, and I now will begin my list.

One of my neediest friends is Karen. She's really a nice, gracious person. Very little foul language, and sometimes acts like a lady. An Angel, really—sort of. She always needs batteries. You will know what kind and what for. I have no idea, myself. Also, Santa, she needs time off. She says so constantly. We give her time off and she stays and complains of no time off. Keep her away for awhile. The longer, the better.

My friend, Dawn, is needy also. she has become uncommunicative and her game is slipping. If you can find time, give her more fives and aces in her cribbage hands. She'll know how to use them, believe me. Give her enough fives and aces, and she's the most vicious player on the planet. Also, if you would, leave a few shrimp cocktails on the hearth. She loves them and they bring a rosy glow that makes her quite attractive.

My friend, Lena, needs to win more games, Santa. I hardly ever play against her because she gets eliminated so soon. Maybe you could give her a few more double runs every game so she can advance through the brackets. She also needs new shoes or a new coat, maybe, but I forgot which.

My friend, Crissie, has this paranoia about playing lowball, yet she keeps playing it. I thought maybe you could give her some new movies to watch during lowball tournaments. She loves movies and she needs to have something done about this love-hate relationship with lowball. It's kind of like hating hand grenades, yet keep pulling the pin.

My friend, Scott, who is really a good kid, has a rather rough exterior, although a lot of that is misunderstanding him. He really tries to be good, but things seem to work against him. Maybe if you can keep Karen away long enough and away from him, he may straighten out. He is very imitative and seems to "pick up" on the wrong things. His mother loves him, I think.

My friend, Lilly, is doing fine. She needs to ease up a bit on her Hi-Low game, though, or no one is going to play against her. Think she's either won or placed second in the last 25 tournaments. If you happen by her house, you might drop her off a few pounds of coffee, and some doggie treats. She loves coffee, and Pookie is an adorable little pooch.

Tricia is a problem for me, Santa, as she seems to think she's a dog. She sluuurrps and walks on all fours. You might leave her a wheelbarrow to get her to walking erectly. She's a good friend, and happy, but it's embarrassing to be licked on all the time.

Nece is a good friend of mine, and she is just now learning how to get a bit a bit assertive. She has a lot of talent, but she thinks of herself as a Wingnut first, and a talent secondly. Most of her talent is wasted touting the Wingnuts, and they are only a second—tier team, despite the fact that they're usually in first place and no one can beat them.

Ros, a good friend of mine, has a current problem in that she is losing a lot of games. She blames her partner, Neil, for these losses, and she is in need of a reality check. Can you do those?

Georgia is another good friend who seems to be doing well. She has been acting strangely lately, though, and I'm afraid that since they moved near DC she may be getting into politics. Hope so. this woman could run the Oval Office AND the Pentagon and still skin a caribou.

Pup

The last friend I will mention now is Lisa. Lisa is a fine person and a real lady. Her problem is getting dates for Date Night. Maybe you could drop off a couple of dates for Lisa on Christmas Eve. It would give her a choice for a change, as she, herself, is usually the last choice.

Thank you, Santa
Merry Christmas
Pup

PART II

Telephone ringing: "ring—ring—ring." Finally— "This is the Pup residence. Oh, Hi, Santa." (Pup listens)

Pup: "I know, Santa, but—."
(Pup listens after Santa interrupts)
Pup: "Karen's not really that bad. Just two years ago, she almost—."
(Pup listening)
Pup: "What does your list have to do with it? I told you she was needy."
(Pup now listening to Santa)
Pup: "Maybe we can get her some batteries through the Salvation Army, Thank you, anyway, Santa."
(Santa talking)

Pup: "Gaet is always good, Santa. I just didn't think he was needy enough to mention—"
(Santa interrupts and talking now)
Pup: "Nice of you, Santa, you think of everything, Prime example, you say? You sure have an accurate list."
(Pup now listening to Santa)

Pup: "I agree. Reward the good guys. Peanuts are the perfect gift. Leave him a lot, will you. Gaet loves nuts."
(Santa talking to Pup again)

Pup: "I knew you'd get around to Scott. I know you have rules, but—."
(Pup listens—sound from phone growing angry)
Pup: "Every time I've been around him he's been too dam bad, but—."
(Pup listening to Santa)
Pup:"I forgot they had to be on your list, Santa. I—"
(Pup nervously listening to Santa)
Pup: "Any way he can get on the list?"
(Santa answering loudly now)
Pup: "I was afraid of that. A bad apple spoils the lot, you say?"
(Pup listening to Santa again)
Pup: "Yes, of course. I've seen it happen in the lobby. Well, I tried."
(Santa raising voice now, chastising Pup)

Pup: "I didn't think it was that ridiculous. I was just asking about it."
(Santa explaining)
Pup: "But, Santa, how was I to know Ros's tremendous ego would resist a reality check?"
(Pup listens to Santa)
Pup: "Any way you can pick up Neil's game a notch or two?"
(Santa talking to Pup)
Pup: "OK, Santa, scratch that one, too. Thanks for trying."
(Pup again listening to Santa)

Pup: "She did? Dawn really did that? Good Lord! I can't believe it, Santa."
(Santa explaining to Pup)
Pup: "Wow! And I thought Dawn was a saint. Thanks for finding this out, Santa."
(Pup listening to Santa)
Pup: "You have to do what you have to do, Santa. We can probably get a local deli to deliver her a few shrimp cocktails, Sure figured she was on your list, though."
(Pup now listening again)

Pup: "But I was sure Chrissie was on your list. Such a quiet, caring person. I had no idea—"
(Santa interrupts Pup)
Pup: "She does? She actully loves lowball? Something fishy going on here."
(Santa talking)
Pup: "It's good to know she almost made your list. She's sure made a lot of lists here in Eagles."
(Santa's turn to talk).

Pup: "Nece is very clever, and an excellent poet, but everything she writes is about the Wingnuts, and everyone is sick and tired of getting beaten by the Wingnuts."
(Santa now talking)
Pup: "No, no, no, Santa, Not Nece. Nece has never done anything like that in her life."
(Santa getting loud again)
Pup: Wow, Santa. I just lost all faith in human nature. Nece, of all people—"
(Santa interrupts). Pup-changes subject.

Pup: "Nice to see you're going along with me for Lilly and Lena. They are really sweet people, and good friends of mine. I appreciate it, and—"
(Santa interrupts again)

Pup: "She did? Tricia actually asked you for Milk Bones for Christmas? What are you going to do?"
(Santa now talking)
Pup: "I figured she was probably on your list. Good idea, Santa. Chocolate may just do it. Weaning her over to people's food just might do the trick. Never knew she had written you."
(Pup listening to Santa now)

Pup: "But I never asked for anything for Georgia." I thought you'd know what she wants,"
(Santa excitedly talking to Pup)
Pup: "You're wrong there, Santa. She has to be on your list."
(Santa is almost snarling now)
Pup: "Good Lord!. She did run for office? And she was elected? I figured she'd would, living near those guys, but I never figured on this. But why did you remove her?"
(Santa explaining to Pup)
Pup: "Well, I certainly agree. I wouldn't have a Klu Klux Klan Grand Wizard on mine, either."
(Santa changes subject to last request from Pup)

Pup: "It might do the trick, Santa. Actually a good idea. You've had cases like Lisa's before?"
(Santa talking to Pup)

Pup: "I wholeheartedly agree. A bit more confidence, and the case of cosmetics and the five garter belts for Christmas from you should make her somewhat dateable."

Phone: Chattering at Pup:
Pup: "Thanks for the call, Santa. Nice to hear from you. It's been 75 years. Bye."

The End

.

DAYCARE FUN

CHAPTER I

The first day care center in Eagletown opened in the spring of 1954. Eagletown had a population of nearly 13,000 now, and with inflation and the graduated income tax, more mothers were now working, with the two-wage household becoming the norm. Licensed by the state, and spanking new, the LITTLE DARLINGS nursery was opening early Monday morning. Marc, the local reporter from the TALON, had been interviewing the owner-operator, Georgia, for most of the morning.

Her first customer was Marie, who worked at an insurance office. Marie had a pre-schooler named Doo, who was 3-years old. They signed the agreement, Marie told Georgia that Doo was an orderly, obedient child, and they were to call her (Marie) if they had any problems at all. The only possible problem that Doo had, according to her mother, was that she "slipped" once in a while, when excited. She promised she would bring extra underwear to the center with her. Doo was on no medication.

Ed, a real estate agent and notary, was interviewed next. He had two little ones—Lisa was 3 1/2 and Carol was just over 2. Ed said they were good, healthy kids, and no medication involved. Lisa was a chatterbox, but harmless, and Carol was almost "potty trained". Ed also requested it would be best if the girls ate nothing with sugar in it

Lena, the merchant, had one young one, Anneke. She was confident Anneke would be very little trouble. In fact, Anneke was very gifted four-year old child. She could read already, but could get a bit "noisy"at times.

Mike, who owned the Eagletown tavern, had a 3 1/2 year old kid named Pup. Mike assured her that Pup was very quiet, well behaved, and was "potty trained". No medications. Mike's only admonition was that Pup was very fast for his age, and to keep an eye on him because if he got out, they'd never catch him.

Monica, operator of the hotel, registered her pre-schooler, Mariska, who was 4. She said that Mariska played well with other children, and was very good at doing coloring books. Mariska also knew the alphabet.

Dawn, who worked at the hospital, brought her two young ones with her to register. Ros and Karen were twins. Three years and a few months old, and going on fourteen. Georgia looked at these two precious little girls and felt like she should pay Dawn for leaving them. (She was in for a shock, indeed)

Paul, the town dentist, registered his 4 1/2 year old son, Bill. Bill was a neat, sort of handsome kid, a little big for his age, No medications, and Paul was sure little Billie would be no trouble whatsoever.

Bonnie, who worked at the hotel registered her 4-year old. Dan was a good kid, she said, but he didn't like being "made fun of", No pottie problems and no meds.

Debbie, the town pastor, brought and registered her 4-year old daughter, Lilly. Lilly was an adorable little 4 1/2 year old blonde girl, and Debbie always kept her neat and well-dressed. Georgia felt very fortunate to have such clean, well-behaved and intelligent children registered.

The last children registered for the opening day were Chrissie,5, and Tammy, 3. Their father was Doug, who just hung around the tavern, playing cards and pool. Georgia looked at these two kids and made a mental note to keep the insurance paid up, and no sugar for these two, either.

In addition to these thirteen charges set to arrive on opening day, the LITTLE DARLINGS nursery had two under two years, and three under one year. These five were too young to play outside with the others, and were assigned cribs in the nursery section.

LITTLE DARLINGS was a beehive until about 7:30AM. parents arriving and leaving kids and instructions. The thirteen older kids were getting acquainted with one another, and having some milk.

For their first assignment Georgia gave them the option of coloring with crayons or modeling with clay. The first "incident" occurred when Mariska grabbed little Tammy's coloring book, telling her she was "too little" for that book, and she wanted it as she was good at coloring. Chrissie immediately grabbed Mariska and retrieved her sister's book. Lisa and Doo, both born tattlers, were screaming and pointing at Mariska, telling Georgia "She started it". Georgia sort of let Mariska and Chrissie know that this type of behavior was not allowed.

The kids playing with clay were having a great time. Billy had formed some sort of weird-looking creature with legs, arms, and some other appendages. Ros asked him what it was, and Billy looked around and finally pointed to Karen, saying it was "her". Karen was upset, and said it wasn't her because she didn't have one of "those", pointing to a certain obvious appendage. Then she said, "See," pulling her shorts down. Sure enough, she didn't. Ros pulled down her own shorts. It wasn't Ros. Then Ros pulled Lilly's shorts down. It wasn't Lilly, and Lilly pulled her shorts back up and punched Ros. Pup pulled Lilly's shorts back down and ran off, giggling. Georgia broke it up.

Time to play outside. This was going to be a bit sticky, Georgia thought. Her equipment was all state-of-the-art and safe for toddlers. A lot of plastic stuff, a very safe not-too-high slide, monkey bars, swings that couldn't go very high, and a sand-box. Georgia turned them all loose, and they ran whooping to their favorites. She could see right away that four swings were maybe not enough. Chrissie, Mariska, Bill, and Dan had the swings already, and they just happened to be some of the biggest kids. There was a line at the slide too. Doo apparently wasn't a good slider, and she was stuck halfway down, with Karen and Lisa hung up behind her. Pup and Ros at the sandbox had little Carol screaming her head off because they were trying to fill her underpants with sand Carol had happily filled her little bucket with her little shovel, and Pup had her shorts pulled back, with Ros dumping the bucket. Anneke and Lilly and Tammy were at the monkey bars behaving themselves.

Chrissie had left her swing and disappeared. Georgia panicked, and just then Chrissie came around the corner of the house. She had a garden hose that was streaming water full-blast, and every kid in the playground was soaked before Georgia could get it away from her. Georgia decided it was enough play—time. Now it was "dry off" time, and time for a nap. She was really looking forward to this bunch taking a nap.

That evening Georgia decided she needed more help, especially during the playground period. It was impossible to keep an eye on thirteen kids who never stopped moving. Someone always had to be inside to answer the phone and to care for the small ones in the cribs. Two people just simply weren't enough. Her prayers were answered within the hour, when the telephone rang. The caller was a newcomer to Eagletown named Rose, who would teach High School when school started in September. She had a 3-year old daughter, Nece, and, until school started, she would be glad to donate a few hours a day to help out She would be over in the morning with Nece, get Nece enrolled, and help out for awhile. Georgia insisted on paying her and hung up the phone, breathing a sigh of relief.

Rose was an attractive, business-like lady, and Nece was a very pretty little 4-year old girl. Georgia introduced Nece to the others, and it was milk time. Georgia and Rose were showing them something new—water colors. Each child had a paper cup of water and a small palette. The kids thought making colors with water and a brush was the greatest thing ever. Giggling and laughing, they were creating hundreds of different colors and showing them to each other. Suddenly Tammy brushed some paint on Dan's arm, giggling and calling attention to it. Dan looked at his arm, looked at Tammy, took his finger and smeared paint all overTammy's face. Instantly, every kid there was painting another kid. Rose rushed in and she and Georgia managed to get the paints put up, but all the kids were a mess. The clean-up took almost an hour. That was just bodies. Their clothing was a mess.

CHAPTER II

Rewards for Good Behavior

Rose being a school teacher was a boon to Georgia, but by the end of the first week, they were both nervous wrecks. These kids were holy terrors. Besides peeing their pants and constantly taking their clothes off, they were, in general, completely unmanageable. Rose admitted to Georgia that even Nece was getting to be a pain. Nece was a natural copy-cat, and she learned fast. Discussing it, they decided to try an honor system. If a child behaved, they would be rewarded, and if a child misbehaved, some sort of mild punishment could be figured out.

Monday morning the "fearless fourteen" had their milk and their morning chatter, which usually amounted to who was threatening to "get" whom, and then they were seated at the big table. Georgia and Rose had made up a big chart. From top to bottom, on the left side it had the name of each child, with rows of squares running to the right. She was explaining how it worked. The kids were fascinated by the chart and very quiet.

Carol's name was at the top, and she had three gold stars for last week to the right of her name. This was because she had been "good" three days last week. This started a buzz. Little Carol proudly said she was "always good", and some others were saying Carol was never "good", she was just "little". Lilly's name was next to the top and she also had 3 gold stars for last week. More boos. Tammy, Anneke, Nece, Bill and Mariska had 2. Dan, Lisa, Doo, and Karen each had one gold star. Chrissie, Pup, and Roz didn't have any gold stars, and all three were pretty upset. There was an instantaneous uproar of agreement (with finger pointing) that they shouldn't have any stars because they were "bad". Georgia explained that every two weeks a nice prize would be given to the child with the most stars.

The kids were a bit better that day than they had been, all trying for a gold star. The problem started when the kids went home. The first phone call was from an irate Dawn who wanted to know why they were picking on her Ros. There wasn't a better child in town than Ros, she said. Georgia, a bit taken aback, told her they were working on the problem, she was sure Ros would respond, and things were fine. Dawn growled that they'd better be, and hung up. Immediately, Bonnie was on the phone wanting to know if they had a problem with her little Dan, who would never misbehave. Debbie called and said that if they had any problems with her darling Lilly it was because of all those "heathen" kids being there. Mike called and said his little Pup was pretty upset because they had too many "teacher's pets" there.

Ed called and said it just might be a good idea if the other kids stopped picking on Lisa. Georgia was trembling when the phones finally stopped ringing.

Kids are sort of funny in that they seem to know who was the "toughest". No real fights had broken out largely because no one had figured out where they were in the pecking order. Bill was the biggest, but Bill was not a fighter. He was basically just a big, friendly kid. Chrissie was the one they worried about. She was big, well built, and hard to "read". Mariska was the other "dark horse". She was a pretty girl, big for her age, and she never took other kids into her confidence. Another problem was that Pup wasn't afraid of any of the others. He was so elusive, and could run so fast no one could do anything to him, and he, notwithstanding the mischevious Ros, was probably the "worst" kid of the lot.

Tuesday morning, over milk, the kids were all so excited to see who would get gold stars today. Seated quietly at the table, they cheered as Georgia got out the chart. Before Georgia said anything, she studied the kids, one by one, and they all looked so innocent, almost angelic. Carol got another gold star!!! A groan went up. "Teacher's pet" was screamed by several, and little Carol was so proud of herself she just beamed and clapped her chubby little hands. Lilly got another gold star, and the kids were starting to grumble. Doo even said that she "had seen" Lilly being bad yesterday. Georgia went down the line, issuing praise and gold stars. When she got to Chrissie, the kids were holding their breath. No star for Chrissie! She had taken a swing away from Lisa, leaving her screaming and in tears. A big cheer went up from the kids, and they looked at Chrissy disdainfully. No star for Pup. More cheers and dirty looks. Running around the playground with a bucket of sand and throwing it all over everyone was a no-no. No star for Ros, either. She had crayoned a bad word in Tammy's coloring book. Georgia wondered where she had learned the word, and how to write it.

Pup was half-scared of Georgia, but he wasn't afraid of Rose. As they ran whooping to their favorite, the playground, Rose felt someone tugging at her pants leg. Looking down, it was Pup, with a serious look on his face, telling her that he was going to be "real good" today. It wasn't five minutes later that Doo, ever excitable, "wet" her pants on the slide, making it unslidable, and kids hung up behind her again. Pup got there first, pulled Doo down, and helped dry the slide so the others could use it. Georgia was dumbfounded. She made it a point to tell everyone how "good" Pup had been, telling them that is how you get stars; by being good. Pup was strutting around like a little peacock. He strutted by Chrissie, who grabbed him, and pulled his shorts down. Pup was swinging his little arms, pulling his shorts up, and cussing Chrissie.

Ros and Nece were getting chummy, and Rose noticed it. She was a bit worried because she could see that Ros was a bit "old" for her age. Ros didn't have "anything" yet, but Rose knew she'd be a hellion when she did. When Ros got around any of the boys, Rose kept a close eye on her. Nece was starting to ask her questions she didn't want to answer just yet, and she felt Ros was at the bottom of it.

Little Tammy and Carol loved the sandbox. They'd just sit there busily filling their little buckets, chatting away. It had rained the night before and the sand was wet, making it a bit cohesive, and they found out they could dump their buckets and leave a bucket-shaped lump, so they decided to build a wall out of "bucket-blocks". Tammy and Carol did it! They had a row of nice blocks spaced just right, and were starting a second tier. Dan and Ros had come over to watch, and they were getting interested. Tammy let Dan dump a second-tier bucket, and Ros wanted to do one. Carol handed her the full bucket, and Ros dumped it perfectly. These two little girls were the center of attention, and they were shovelling like mad. Dan and Ros were dumping ever so carefully, and the wall was rising. Every kid on the grounds was watching and giving advice. Ros dumped the first bucket successfully on the third tier, and everyone cheered. Dan made it, and everyone cheered again. Georgia and Rose let them continue long after their normal nap time, and everyone was so happy and proud of their wall.

CHAPTER III
Gold Stars and Teamwork

The next morning over milk they were unusually excited. Each and every one would kill to get in the sand box right now. Seated at the table, it was all they could talk about. A big cheer when Georgia got out the chart. Georgia told them she was extremely proud of them. Everyone gets a gold star for the first time! Instead of a big cheer, she got a lot of angry feedback, kids pointing st each other and making accusations. Ros and Chrissie and Pup had gotten their first gold stars, and the other kids were furious.

She finally got them refocused and told them that the wall they had built in the sand box was a great piece of work, and it shows how people can get things done when they work together. She told them this was called "teamwork". She had a "teamwork" project for them today. A fun project, and they were to pay attention.

She got seven kids on each side of the table, and got out scissors, rulers, pencils, colored construction paper, and paste. The kids were fascinated by these new items, impatient to start whatever it was. Rose showed them how to make a colorful "chain" out of the paper, using the paste and paper strips. The kids were squirming with excitement. Wow!! This was just simply going to be the most fun they'd ever had. Three things had to be done—outline the strips using the ruler and pencil, cut the strips out with the scissors, and paste the strips into little interlocking rings forming a chain.

Rose had one team and Georgia the other. Each team had two kids to trace around the little rulers, three kids with scissors, and two pasters. An assembly line process, passing the items to their "teammates". Each child was shown how to do their "job". Anneke, Mariska, Lillly, and Chrissie had made chains before. They told the others it was really fun, and were raring to go. At first, it looked as if Georgia's team was going to walk away with this one. Chrissie and Lisa could outline like the wind, and were starting to pile up papers in front of the cutters. Doo was good with the scissors, but when she started getting behind, she stressed out and wet herself. No time outs. The line on that side faltered a bit as little Tammy (an assigned paster) had to start cutting. Bill and Nece were fast cutters, though, and the remaining paster, Ros, was happily pasting and making a chain. Rose's team was getting the hang of it, though, and chain was forming on both sides. The chatter was constant, most of it being one side or the other calling the other side "cheaters", and urging their comrades to go faster.

The cutting took the most time and Rose had chosen well. She had Anneke, Lilly, and Dan cutting, and they were almost keeping up with her two outliners, Karen and Mariska. Her pasters were Pup and Carol, who were having a problem keeping their hands clean enough to make the required loops, press them together, and release them. Doo was back in action, chatting away with her little scissors flashing. Georgia's pasters were Tammy and Ros, and they, too, were having a problem with sticky fingers.

Chrissie was a born schemer with no scruples whatsoever, and she always knew what was going on. She was across the table from Mariska, and Mariska had laid her pencil down for a moment to get a drink of water, Chrissie broke the lead off her pencil and quickly swapped pencils with Mariska. When Mariska came back she couldn't write. A big wail went up. Mariska was screaming bloody murder and glaring around. Rose gave her another pencil, wondering what had happened. Chrissie was looking so innocent and tracing away. Chrissie scowled at Mariska and told her she sure was a "cry baby".

The outliners only had a few sheets of paper left, meaning the "race" was nearing a conclusion. Pup just couldn't paste anymore because his hands were too sticky, but suddenly he had a plan. He whispered something to Carol, and Carol nodded her head "no". Pup whispered to her again and showed her his hands. Carol nodded "yes" this time, and Pup dashed to the boy's room. Carol and Tammy were both so little they had to paste standing up. As soon as Pup dashed off, Carol got under the table, crawled across, yanked Tammy's shorts down, and hung on. Tammy felt her shorts going down, and saw it was Carol. She started screaming and kicking, trying to get her shorts back up. Ros was kicking at Carol to make her let go, and little Carol was hanging on for dear life. It took ten or fifteen seconds to get Carol loose, and Pup came running back and started pasting. Ros walked around the table and pulled Pup's shorts down. Karen pulled Lisa's shorts down, and kids were tugging on shorts all over the place. The construction site was permanently shut down.

The playground, the ensuing fight over the sand box, which was placed "off limits", an early nap, and this day from hell was over, Georgia thought Oh, no!!!! The phones again. Mike wanted to know how he could send Pup in so clean every morning, and Pup come home so dirty and "messed" up every afternoon. He asked her if she was running a "glue" factory down there, and hung up. Dawn called and said Ros had told her that they were really having fun until some kid had started pulling everyone's pants down. Well, her Ros and Karen didn't pull pants down, and they'd better not get their pants pulled down, and she hung up. Doug was pretty upset because Chrissy had told him that one of those little perverts had pulled his little Tammy's pants down. Didn't they have anything better to do down there? "Get 'em some marbles or something," he said, and hung up. Ed called and said if his Lisa ever got "pantsed" again, he'd see her (Georgia) in court. Debbie, the preacher, called and told Georgia it was a shame that Lilly had to wear a "hot" dress from now on in the middle of summer, all because of those little "infidel over-sexed" sinners down there.

Monday morning the "fearless fourteen" had a new member. Tricia was a 4-year old child who had been around a bit. Her father, Gaet, was an engineer with the Transportation Department, and they were resurfacing the highway through Eagletown. He had enrolled his "darling" little daughter for one month only. Over milk, the kids were chatting, threatening each other, and eying the newcomer, who was eying them back. Tricia took an immediate liking to Dan, and she wasn't bashful, either.

CHAPTER IV
The Visit

Mike was having a slow morning at the tavern. Doug was there, trying to hustle a pool game or two, and Ed was having a drink with them. They got on the subject of the day care center and decided they'd take a stroll over there this afternoon. Ed jokingly told Mike not to pull any pants down, and Mike said he wouldn't mind pulling some of those adult pants down over there, All three laughed.

The morning was uneventful so far at the day care center, but things were building up. Tricia had been "stalking" Dan all morning, never getting over a foot away from him. He knew it, too, and was getting a bit tired of it. Most of the girls were chatting away and coloring with crayons, showing their work to each other. The boys had a big pile of blocks they were stacking and arranging. Anneke and Mariska and Lilly were really good with crayons and some of the others would just watch them, give advice, and ooh and ahhh. Bill was a great block stacker, and he was sort of imaginative. He'd build something and show it off, and then build something else and show

Pup

it off. Pup was getting upset. He couldn't think of anything to build, so he just quit and pouted. Dan was a better sport, and he and Bill were having a great time.

Playground time. Georgia had had a good day so far, and Rose was there to help now. The kids whooped out to the yard, and, first come, first served, grabbed their favorites. Dan and Chrissie had swings already, and Tricia was headed for Dan. Karen and Ros, the twins, were good on the monkey bars, as was Lilly. Doo, Lisa, Nece and Anneke loved the slide. Pup was still pouting, Bill had a swing, and the others were at the sand box.

Lilly was hard to beat on the bars. She was especially good at hanging by her knees and swinging. Most of the others would just fall if they tried. Lilly was all over the bars with Ros and Karen, when suddenly she hooked her knees and was swinging away, upside down. Wearing a dress, her skirt came down over her face and she couldn't see to get down. All the kids were running to the monkey bars to see Lilly when the three gentlemen from the tavern arrived. Seeing the crowd of kids all around the monkey bars, they went over to see what the attraction was. They got there about the same time as Georgia and Rose. The kids were all cheering Lilly, and a red-faced Georgia pulled her down.

Georgia assured the gentlemen she could explain everything. This was not a normal occurrence here.

Would they like to see some of the work these talented children have done? Having said this, she hoped she could find Mariska's coloring book. Most of the others looked like hen scratchings.

The three gentlemen were gracious enough to say nothing, but they were starting to wonder about this place. Near naked kids hanging upside down and all. Looking at the swings, they noticed Dan and Tricia on the same swing, and she had her arms around his neck. Doug pointed, and told Georgia she sure started them out "young" here.

Georgia went over and yanked Tricia off Dan, and set her down hard. Tammy was so excited to see her daddy there that she had wet herself Rose was explaining some things to the parents when all hell broke out at the sand box.

Monica and Bonnie had left the hotel to pay LITTLE DARLINGS a visit shortly after lunch. Walking leisurely along and enjoying the bright summer day, they met up with, and joined Dawn and Marie, also on a surprise visit. They chatted as they walked along, bragging on their wonderful and talented children.

When Tammy wet herself at the sand box, Carol was so upset she dumped a bucket on Tammy's head, and Chrissie had grabbed a screaming Carol and wouldn't put her down. Lisa pulled Chrissie's shorts down, and shorts were coming down all over the sand box area. just as the other four parents made thair entrance. These little kids were active and didn't have a problem with pulling shorts down. They loved it, and with parents there, they wanted to show off. Ros and Karen had Tricia's shorts pulled down and Tricia was screaming bloody murder when she introduced something new to these "innocent" kids. The "finger". Tricia was good at it, making upward jabbing motions with her little hand. Every kid there learned how to do the "finger" in a heartbeat. Instantly, around a dozen "birds" were being flipped. They didn't know what it meant, but it sure was fun to do. Dawn looked as though she were having a heart attack, and Marie was searching for her little Doo, who was in the sand box with her shorts around her ankles flipping the "bird" at something.

Mike sort of thought this was great, until his kid, Pup, tried to pull Monica's shorts down. Pup was still in a foul mood anyway and Mariska kept giving him the "finger". There was a crowd around Marie in the sand box, and her shorts almost came down. Dawn was hanging on to her shorts with both hands. Chrissie and Karen were hanging on to Mike's shorts, but his belt saved him. Bonnie was swatting kids and trying to keep her shorts up.

Georgia came back out with a cleaned up Tammy and couldn't believe her eyes. Rose had just given up. With Georgia back, things gradually got back to normal, except for a lot of "bird" flipping.

From that day on, these parents never visited the day care center. What these had seen was never revealed to the remaining parents. At the end of the summer session, Debbie, the pastor, called Georgia, thanking her for the excellent care her little Lilly had received at LITTLE DARLINGS, and, yes, she would reccommend it to her congregation.

They say Dawn took to drinking, and her twins became pole dancers. Marie did not appear in public for over a month, and even on the hottest days always wore a dress and a veil. Doo graduated with honors and became a college professor. Lisa joined the Air Force and attained the rank of Colonel. Dan and Bill were athletic stars, both getting good scholarships. Rose taught high school in Eagletown until the first of these kids got to high school age, then inexplicably resigned her tenure, leaving Eagletown. Pup joined the Navy and spent a lot of his time in the brig. Chrissie won a big lottery and moved away. Tammy became an actress. Lilly became a political activist, lobbying for women's rights. Anneke got into the hotel business, and eventually became a tycoon. Mariska went out west at an early age and became a rodeo star. Nece became a famous author of children's books, although some critics felt they were a bit risque. Carol married, but chose not to have children, Tricia only spent a month in Eagletown, so no history on her.

After her first very successful season, Georgia was well established in the day care center. Overnight, it became LITTLE DEVIL'S day care. With this very successful business in Eagletown, she had opened two other branches in neighboring areas. Her slogan was "LITTLE DEVIL'S makes LITTLE ANGELS"

THE END

SOFTBALL FUN

CHAPTER I

The Lady Eagles were the darlings of Eagletown. They had won the summer Intercities softball league, and to date were undefeated. The Ladies' coach, Dawn, was being besieged with offers to coach elsewhere, but her loyalties were to Eagletown and her Lady Eagles.

When the Ladies brought the trophy home, Eagletown had held a huge celebration, and it was decided that to top off their winningest season ever, they would play the Eagletown men one game for the "City Championship".

Mike, the men's coach, had had a dismal season in that all summer long they had only won one game, Their only win was against Toraville, which only had a population of fifty-four, and that was by only one run, 10-9.

At first, Dawn was reluctant to schedule the game because of her distrust of Mike, the men's coach, who could be a bit (ahem) devious at times. Tammy, the Mayor, who was also the right-fielder on the Ladies' team, knowing the city's revenue from this one-time event would be substantial, finally talked her into it, promising that they would go over the rules carefully with Mike, making sure there were no shenanigans. Dawn finally agreed, saying she wanted primarily to be sure Mike would use eligible players.

The two coaches met in city hall with the mayor and the city parks director, Gilles, who would also be the home plate official. Gilles was known for his honesty, and was a great official. He had had extra seating brought in to the largest municipal diamond in Eagletown, and was prepared for a large group of spectators.

Dawn, who took few wooden nickles, studied Mike's roster intently:
Scott first base Michael shortstop Ken center field Bill third base Gaet catcher Ed second base Chuck left field David right field Dan, Doug, and Larry were listed as pitchers. Pup and Harold were listed as the only two substitutes.

Dawn was familiar with Mike's team, but Larry was a mystery. To her knowledge he hadn't been on Mike's team before, and she asked Gilles to get a clarification on his eligibility. The three conversed, and Mike said Larry had recently moved to Eagletown and joined the team, and he probably wouldn't use him anyway. Dawn smelled a rat here, but initialled Mike's roster. Pup made her a bit nervous, also, as he was a speed demon on the bases, and just might mess up a good game if he ever got on base.

Dawn's roster read as follows:
Ros shortstop Bonnie centerfield Georgia first base Nina third base Chrissie catcher Lisa second base Tricia left field Tammy right field. Karen, Monica, and Doo listed as pitchers. Subs were Anneke Nece Jojo Debbie Lena

Mike initialled Dawn's lineup, and the game was scheduled for Sunday afternoon at 2PM. The game was advertised on the local radio and flyers were distributed all over and around Eagletown. It was going to be a huge success. Tickets were selling like hotcakes and people from miles around phoning in for more.

It was Saturday. Tomorrow was the big game, and Dawn had cut the practice short, given a short pep talk, and let the Ladies off early. The men were a huge underdog, but Mike had them practicing intensely, and the newspaper reported them looking much better than they had all season. The Ladies were just simply a smooth unit. Dawn was a good coach of fundamentals and she had a lot of talent and speed on the team. Chrissie and Nina, her two power hitters had over thirty home runs already this season, and her team was at its peak right now. Dawn had a nagging worry, though, and that was Mike. She'd heard he had been placing bets on the men to win, and she knew Mike wasn't one to throw money down the drain. She also knew Mike didn't believe in miracles. The sleaze always made his own miracles.

Sunday was a beautiful day for a ball game. Not a cloud in the sky, and a slight breeze. The stands were almost filled two hours before game time, and hot dogs, peanuts, beer, and soda were a big seller right now. The Ladies were on the field taking infield practice as the men arrived. Mike ran the men through a few exercises and then they hit some long fly balls and played catch. The men had new red and black uniforms, and they looked sharp going through their drills.

The Ladies wore their blue and gold jerseys, gold hot-pants, and knee pads to protect their legs, and they were really getting the whistles and the attention. The men took the infield now. It was 20 minutes until game time, and the fans were beginning to get noisy. The men looked sharp during their infield warm-up, and Dawn was starting to get a bit more nervous. They hadn't been this good all season. She shook it off. Mike simply didn't have a pitcher good enough to beat her Ladies. This was a cupcake game.

Josee, a former Lady Eagle, and now Municipal judge, would throw out the first ball in exactly ten minutes, and Dawn finally got a glimpse of Larry, Mike's new player. He arrived in uniform and made a few warm-up throws. Dawn's face paled. Having coached for many years in the area, She recognized him instantly, The smooth, effortless delivery, and the powerful upward flight of the ball as it approached the plate. She had forgotten his last name. but she knew his history as a player, and also knew that he and Mike were old friends.

Larry had been a softball pitcher for many years for a team called the Navigators, They were located somewhere over in the Norlite area of Case's County, and had won almost all their games for years. Three or four years ago Larry had left, having signed as a professional to pitch for some major-league team in Ohio. Dawn couldn't believe that even Mike could stoop so low as to bring such an obvious ringer into this game.

The two coaches met with Gillis and Judge Josee, who would be the on field official, to discuss the matter. Gillis was about as honest and fair as a man can get, and he was a bit disappointed in Mike. Apparently, Larry had leased Mike's enclosed gazebo and rented a Post Office box in Eagletown, making him, ostensibly. a resident of Eagletown, and eligible to play on the team. Dawn said if Larry played, she would pull her team out, so Gilles and Josee conferred in private for a while.

Gilles and Josee had arrived at what they thought was a fair agreement. Dawn's team could play the game under protest, and Larry, the professional pitcher, could only pitch to three batters; not necessarily in a row, but to three batters total. Dawn and Mike agreed, and the game was on. The two teams had agreed to an 8-man batting order. No pitchers would bat.

Mike entered the dugout and swore. That Dawn wouldn't trust her own mother, he thought. He only got Larry on the team to even things up a little. Mike had a few hundred riding on this game, and he wasn't giving out any free passes.

The Ladies were home team, and Monica took the mound. Monica was a rather unconventional pitcher in that she wasn't necessarily fast. She had a windup that was unbelievable. She was left-handed, and would go into motion, waving that left arm around every which way, and at some point in time would release the ball. The batters had to be careful not to miss when she actually threw, as the "windup" would continue. She struck Scott out, smirked, and faced Michael. Michael seldom struck out and had good power. He never even saw the first pitch, then swung late on the second, and popped up to Ros at short. Mike was upset already, and had complained that Monica's delivery was illegal. Ken was the men's best hitter for average, and he concentrated on the ball well enough to hit a screamer to Nina at third base. The athletic Nina knocked it down and threw to Georgia for the out, ending the inning.

Mike started Dan, his big righthander. Dan was a conventional hurler, throwing with the smooth underhand motion that caused the ball to rise slightly. If Dan had a problem it was control, but he walked few batters, working into a lot of long counts. Ros, Dawn's leadoff hitter, seldom struck out, and she was a terrific base-runner. On the sixth pitch, Ros hit a sort of soft high liner to Ed, at second base. One out. Bonnie, the speedy center fielder, singled to center field, and the lanky left-handed Georgia was facing Dan. There was something about Georgia that always left respect. Maybe it was her straight imposing posture. Anyway, Dan walked her, and Mike had a problem. Nina, Chrissie, and Lisa were the next three batters. They were all sluggers, and all three were difficult to pitch to. Mike couldn't use Larry yet, and Dan had already thrown about twenty erratic pitches.

Doug took the mound and warmed up. Doug was a power pitcher, and fairly accurate. Very little windup. One pump, and the ball went screaming to the plate, off his hip. Nina stepped up to the plate, and it got a bit quiet in the stadium. On the third pitch, Nina lofted a long drive to left that was foul by a foot or so, and then struck out looking. Chrissie leaned over the plate, her powerful body coiled to strike, and she did! Dead center field and over the fence. Ladies 3 men 0. Mike was white-faced as Lisa grounded out to end the inning.

CHAPTER II

Dawn was a bit more relaxed now. She should have known this would happen. Larry was no threat as he could only face three batters, and Pup, even if he did get on base, could only score once, and Mike would have to take him out, as he was a terrible fielder. The Ladie's dugout was a happy bunch right now. Lisa and Tricia, who were always "wound up" were hugging and slapping everyone. Even Lena and Georgia, normally very reserved, appeared lively and excited. Ros, her "trash-talker", was at the railing verbally baiting the men, as the powerful Bill selected a bat and approached the plate.

Bill, an excellent fielder, was also probably Mike's best overall batter, and was also captain of the team. A good, well-liked field leader. Mike had made a good choice. Monica was tiring a bit from all the antics and smirking, but she was fired up. Bill was a bit undecided as to when to swing as the first pitch just floated over the plate. Chrissie gloved it before Bill even knew it was thrown. Monica smirked, went into that endless, gyrating windup of hers and it was strike two on Bill, who was shaking his head in disbelief. Smirking at Bill, Monica went into her motion, and Bill hit a high, long fly to left field. it came down just inside the fence with Tricia making a great running catch. Tricia was a show-off of the first water. The press loved her, and she was a willowy, pretty, rather curvaceous young lady, and loved to perform. Holding both arms outward and upward in front of her, Tricia faced the stands and swayed her hips, brandishing the ball. The fans loved it, and the press, already in the left field area, were popping flash bulbs like crazy. Josee finally made her throw the ball in, and the game resumed.

Mike, watching Tricia make that great catch, muttered under his breath. That damned Dawn's got 'em on steroids, he thought. All the excitement was getting to Monica. she was starting to miss the plate, and was tiring rapidly., She walked Gaet, who was told not to swing at anything. Dawn walked to the mound, consulting with Chrissie, Monica, and Georgia. Finally, she signalled to the bullpen, summoning Karen to the mound.

Gaet, the runner, was very fast, but it would be impossible to steal second, especially against Chrissie, who could throw a "closeline" to second from the crouching position. With a runner on, Mike needed a break, and he needed it bad. His mind was racing. Dawn was getting tense again as she watched Karen warm up. She needed some good innings from Karen before she put her ace and closer, Doo, into the game.

Ed, the second baseman, was not the best batter alive, but he was a good man to have up in the clutch. Karen was an orthodox pitcher with good control and uncanny accuracy. She threw few pitches simply beause she threw strikes. Almost no windup, and she fired them straight from her well-rounded hip. On an 0-2 pitch, Ed singled to right field and Tammy momentarily bobbled the ball. Gaet seized the opportunity, and made it into third after the catch.

Chuck, the left fielder, spat on his hands and got over the plate. Chuck was not a power hitter, but he was difficult to pitch to, as he sort of "crowded" the plate and hunched over. Karen decided to pitch low, and, with the count 1-1, Chuck hit a long fly ball to center field, and Gaet scored after the catch. A few cheers and a lot of groans went up from the stands. The Ladies were an obvious fan favorite here. Karen struck David out on three pitches, retiring the side. Ladies 3-Men 1.

Doug was warmed up now and he was just getting ready to throw the first pitch to Tricia. Tricia was fast and loved to bunt and scamper to first base. Mike had the infield drawn in closer to home plate. Tricia stuck the bat out in front of the ball, made contact, dropped the bat, and fled for first base. Ed covered first base, and Scott, the first baseman threw her out by a hair. One pitch, one away.

There was a lot of chatter in the infield as Tammy, the right fielder, stepped into the box. This was an important out for Mike, as the top of Dawn's batting order was coming up, and he didn't want anyone on base. Tammy had a good eye, and a "good" body, and she took a nice, long cut with great follow through. She was rather callipygous (look it up) and the press was en masse behind home plate. Doug simply just blazed the first pitch through the swinging bat and all the flash bulbs. Strike one. On the second pitch Tammy swung from her heels, and hit a ball straight up that twisted every which way, and finally started down. It was foul and behind home plate. Gaet was twisting and turning with the ball, flash bulbs were going off, and he finally made the difficult catch. Two away.

Ros, the leadoff hitter, was "endowed" in a lot of ways I won't mention here, and she was an excellent batter. Let it suffice to say that the photogs were still behind home plate. Mike was thinking that with two out, he could walk Ros, Bonnie, and Georgia, and have Larry come in and strike out Nina to end the inning. He glanced over at Nina, but there was something about the way her jaw was set that made him shudder. On the third pitch Ros, who had a lot of power, hit a long drive to right center, sure to clear the fence, but Ken, the fastest player on the team, excluding Pup, made a spectacular streaking catch to retire the side.

Top of the third, and Karen was really firing now. Nece had replaced Tammy in right field, as Tammy had pulled a back muscle on that powerful swing. Scott, the leadoff hitter, stepped up to the plate.

Scott had a good eye for the ball, and a classic swing. On the third pitch, he singled to center field, and Michael was up. Michael hit Karen's first pitch, a sharp grounder to Ros at short. The smooth, quick Ros threw Scott out at second, and Lisa made a beautiful pivot and throw to first, but the fleet Michael beat it out. Ken, with the highest batting average on the team, walked. Bill singled up the middle and the fleet Michael went to third. Gaet, a very careful and powerful hitter, flied out deep to Nece in right field, and her throw to home was too late, Michael scoring. Ed, another careful hitter, walked. Then Karen, bearing down, struck Chuck out on four pitches

Dawn had a 3-2 lead now, and her heavy hitters were coming up. Doug seemed to be getting sharper on every pitch now. Bonnie strode to the plate. Bonnie was a spectacular looking woman—tall, well proportioned, and a tremendous athlete. She covered center field like a blanket, and she had a good eye. She fouled off two pitches, and hit a line drive to the fence in center field. holding at second with a double. The fans were getting noisy now, sensing a big inning here.

Mike was very agitated right now. Doug was pitching as well as he'd ever seen, and still having a problem with these hopped-up women. Georgia, methodical as usual, worked into a 3-2 count, and lined to Michael at short. One down. A very determined Nina stepped up to the plate, spat on her hands, and singled between short and second, scoring Bonnie. Lisa, another of Dawn's "centerfold" type players, was a hard swinger, but she struck out a lot. When Lisa swung the bat, the very air whistled and flash bulbs popped. Doug kept the ball down, though, and she finally hit a hard one-hopper to the mound, and Doug alertly threw Nina out at second, Lisa to first. Two out, and one on.

Chrissie strode to the plate and Mike strode to the mound, beckoning Gaet to join him. Mike wasn't about to let Chrissie bat. He told Doug to walk her, and make sure nothing came even near the plate. He felt they could get Tricia out and end the inning.

Dawn knew exactly what Mike was going to do, and she had plans of her own. The best contact hitter she had was Lena. Lena was a clutch hitter, and this was "crunch" time.

Doug intentionally walked Chrissie, and Dawn substituted Lena as a pinch-hitter. Jojo would replace Tricia in left field. The fans were very quiet now, as they sensed a bit of drama here. Lena slammed Doug's first pitch high and long over the right field field fence, foul by a scant yard. Doug was getting a bit unsettled now, and Mike called time, going to the mound again. A short conversation and Larry was in to pitch to Lena. Dawn protested, as Lena already had one strike on her. Gilles explained that he couldn't deny the legal substitution and Larry made a few warm-up pitches.

Lena was a very smart player, and she had an eye for the ball. Larry went into that smooth windup, and Lena really dug in. The ball was just a blur going to the plate, and Lena hit it dead away to the center field fence. Ken leaped and made another spectacular one-handed catch to end the inning. Ladies 4—Men 2.

CHAPTER III

The 8-man batting order had been agreed upon prior to the game, as Mike was very short on extra players. Justin had shown up in uniform about the second inning, and Dawn agreed that he was eligible to play. Dawn figured if he played, he'd probably pitch, and she knew her Ladies would tee off on him. Mike had another problem. Larry could only pitch to two more batters, and pitching to Lena had sort of shaken Larry up. She'd have homered if Ken hadn't leaped and caught it at the fence. Scheduled for six innings, they had three to play, and Mike was getting short on manpower.

In the fourth inning Karen struck David out on three pitches. She was bearing down now. Scott flied out to Nece in right center field, and Michael, the shortstop, singled to left. Mike wanted to put Pup in as a pinch-runner, but not for Michael. Michael was too good on defense. Ken walked after fouling off about six pitches, and Karen was beginning to tire a bit. Bill fouled off a few, and popped up to Ros at short. Three out.

It was top of the batting order for the Ladies, and Ros was facing Doug. Doug struck her out swinging, flash bulbs going off all over the place. Doug walked Bonnie, and Georgia hit a dribbler to Doug. Doug tried to get Bonnie at second, but she was just too fast, and Georgia was on at first. Two on and one out, just like that. Mike was livid. Looking across the field and glaring, he went to the mound to talk to Doug. Doug still had his stuff, but these souped-up Amazons were just too fast and too strong. Nina hit a screamer to Bill at third base, and he doubled Bonnie at second to retire the side. Mike had just gotten a big break, and he knew it.

Top of the fifth. Ladies 4 Men 2. Time was growing short for Mike. Doo was now on the mound for the Ladies, and she was almost impossible to hit. She had a mean wind-up. Her her arm went out and up, twisted around, then swung down and in. The ball would release off her hip like a bullet, and she had uncanny control. In addition her long fingers gave her a bit of a curve when she needed it. Debbie was now in at third base for Nina, as she was a bit better fielder. Dawn was going for defense now, protecting her lead. Anneke, her remaining sub, was a terrific hitter, and Dawn was saving her for just the right spot in case she was needed,

Mike told Gaet just to hit the ball somehow and hope for a break. Two straight blazing strikes, and Gaet hit a slow dribbler to third. Debbie, racing in, grabbed it and threw to first, and it looked as though Gaet was out, but Josee signalled him safe. Dawn was on the field in a heartbeat, contesting the call. Josee said that Georgia had moved her foot off the base to catch the throw, and that Gaet was safe. By now, everyone on the field was miling around first base, and Gilles and Josee were conferring. Gilles finally asked Georgia if her foot had left the bag, and she honestly replied that it had. Gilles ruled Gaet safe at first, and to "play ball". Dawn glared at Josee, Gillis, Georgia, and Mike and stalked to the dugout.

It took Mike about one second to get Pup in as a pinch runner. Harold would replace Gaet as catcher. Mike's last sub was Justin, who was primarily a pitcher. Dawn was getting a bit red in the face. She felt a two-run lead was a good margin, but somehow she also knew they'd have to keep Pup from scoring.

Doo struck Ed out on three pitches that looked more like blurs, and Pup had stolen second on the second pitch. One out, and Chuck was in the batter's box. Chuck was hard to pitch to, even for Doo. He stood so close and all hunched over. Chuck hit the first pitch, a one-hopper to Ros at short. She started to throw to first, but Pup had broken for third and had already passed her. She quickly threw to third and they had Pup trapped. Pup was too fast to run down, so Ros and Debbie just kept him going back and forth.

Pup seemed to know he was losing the battle, and finally made a dash at Debbie, who was protecting third.

Ros threw to Debbie and Pup quickly headed back toward Ros. Debbie quickly threw to Ros, and Pup faked a turn, ran right through Debbie and slid into third base safely under Ros's throw to Chrissie, who was covering.

Mike knew just how fast Pup really was, but he wanted to be sure Pup didn't mess up. He replaced Bill as third base coach, and told Pup to scoot for home on anything that was hit. David was choked so far up on the bat he had more handle sticking out than he had bat. With two quick strikes on him, he popped up to Lisa at second. She caught it about eight or ten feet behind and to the right of the bag, and Pup broke for home! Lisa made a great throw to Chrissie, in front of the plate, and Chrissie tried to swipe the flying Pup with the ball, but missed. Dawn was white as a sheet. Nobody can run that fast! That dam Mike has all those idiots on steroids, and she was playing fair. Doo fanned Scott to retire the side and end the inning.

Bottom of the fifth. Ladies 4 Men 3. Mike had substituted Pup for Bill at third base, making Pup the second batter in the sixth inning and Justin was in for David. Switching Pup and Justin, he had Justin on third and Pup in right field, and Ken was playing a sort of right-center field to cover Pup as best he could. Dawn had figured the shady Mike would keep Pup in the lineup somehow, and Ken was just fast enough it might work. She inserted her best left-handed hitter, Annneke, for Lisa, and Anneke would be the new second baseman.

Anneke was facing a tiring Doug. Mike was really pacing now. Chrissie was up next, and he didn't want any runners on. Anneke did just exactly as Dawn had hoped. She was strong and she hit a hard liner right at Pup in right field. Pup never even had to move. He got his glove up, and the hard-hit ball went right through his glove, imbedding itself in his abdomen. Pup fell over backwards with the wind knocked out of him, the ball still buried in the pit of his stomach.

Anneke was already rounding first as Ken raced over and grabbed the ball. As soon as Ken had the ball Josee signalled that the batter was out. Dawn was screaming, wanting an explanation. Josee explained that the ball imbedded in Pup was officially still in the air. It had to touch ground to be a base-hit, and it hadn't. When Ken picked up the ball, in actuality, he, Ken, had made the catch, and Anneke was out on a fly ball. One out, and Chrissie coming up.

Dr. Dan, always at the games, was checking Pup. He said Pup would be okay. No broken ribs. He would assist Pup off the field and the game could resume. Mike said Pup wasn't leaving no damn field. He was the right fielder and he was staying in right field. Mike had no more substitutes, and he desperately needed Pup in the game. He told Gilles just to let Pup lie there and get his wind back. The Doc says he's okay, and Ken can see to it that no ants crawl on him, and no more balls hit him. Gilles agreed, but said if Pup was unable to continue Mike would forfeit the game.

Dawn was feeling a lot better now. She had Mike over the barrel. If Pup did get his wind back, he'd be slowed down a bit. Mike wasn't so happy. He'd gotten a break on the play, as he was lucky Pup fell over backwards. Now, how to handle Chrissie? Walking her with one out was an option, and Larry pitching to her was another. Suddenly, he had an idea.

Chrissie was rubbing dirt into her hands and waving that big bat when Mike went to the mound. He told Doug exactly what he planned to do, and Doug nodded. Chrissie was walked on four pitches, and Justin went to the mound. Doug took over at third and play resumed.

Justin was a slow-pitch hurler and he had an uncanny ability to get the ball high in the air and down into the strike zone. Mike knew Jojo wore bifocals and would never be able to hit the ball well with her head raised. It worked. Justin struck Jojo out on four pitches. Two away, and Nece in the batter's box. Nece was a greedy hitter. She'd clobber one of these soft pitches into the next county. She dug in, sneered at Justin, and fouled off the first pitch. Nece dug in again, fouling off the second pitch. She was getting a bit upset with herself, and Justin threw a high pitch that was way outside. Nece, in her eagerness, went for it, and popped up to Scott at first. Side retired.

Pup was standing now, and moving around. When the inning ended Ken had helped a very woozy Pup to the dugout. Mike always had a flask hidden somewhere, and he got Pup where Gilles couldn't see, and made him down a big belt. Pup gagged and almost choked, but the color came back into his face.

Doo didn't waste any time. Ken grounded out to first, and Pup was up. Dawn studied him closely. He seemed normal. Gilles asked him a few questions and looked into his eyes, and declared he could play. Pup was the world's worst batter, but he was fast, and Dawn knew Mike would have him bunt and scoot. She pulled her entire infield way in, and told Doo to just blow them past him if she could. Mike told Pup to bunt and run like a wounded deer. Doo quickly had two strikes on Pup, and he hadn't even attempted a bunt. Mike was getting a bit upset and kept hollering at Pup. Doo went into her windup and Pup swung!

He hit a weak little fly ball that came down about ten feet to the right of second base, but no one was there. Anneke was covering first for the bunt, and all the others were near home plate. Pup never even slowed down at first, taking second base with a double. Dawn was pulling her hair. That had to be the luckiest hit ever made in the history of softball. Harold was the next batter, and on the second pitch, Pup stole third. Dawn was livid by now. Pup was acting like he was drunk or something. Harold struck out and Ed was Mike's last chance to tie the game. He was tempted to have Pup get into another rundown between third and home, but Pup was sort of dumb, and you can only get lucky so many times.

Ed was a good man to have up, but Doo was just too fast. The first pitch was tipped, and the second was a blazing strike. When Chrissie tossed the ball back to the mound, Pup broke for home! Pup was just a blur as Doo rifled the ball back to Chrissie, and there was a big cloud of dust at home plate. Gilles was right on top of it, but had made no signal. It appeared as though Pup had made it to home plate, and it was evident that Crissie had tagged him, but which came first? Gilles told Chrissie to carefully get off Pup so he could see where he was. Pup was about two inches short of home plate, and Gilles signalled he was out. The game was over. Ladies, 4-3, final score.

Dawn breathed a deep sigh of relief. Her heart had been pounding so hard it was difficult to breathe. Mike was still at home plate claiming that animal, Chrissie, had blocked Pup. Ken, still watching out for Pup, got him to his feet and to the dugout and away from Mike. Pup headed for the hidden flask, had another big snort, and lay down on the bench, tuckered out, but feeling no pain.

The press had abandoned the normal "exposure" targets and had Chrissie surrounded. Chrissie was then awarded game ball as MVP. Tammy, the mayor, gave a short speech, lauding both coaches and teams for excellent play and unusually good sportsmanship in the tradition of Eagletown, handing the winged GOLDEN EAGLE Cup to Dawn.

THE END

WORLD WAR FUN

CHAPTER I

In 1914 some dissident assassinated an Archduke named Ferdinand in Austria. He was a second-cousin twice removed, or something, to the Prussian king of Germany, Kaiser Wilhelm. Old Kaiser Bill was already upset with France for grabbing some land he thought was his and this assassination was an excuse for him to raise a little hell in Europe and maybe get his some of his land back. The German war machine was formidable, and war broke out all over Europe. The French, hit the hardest, held out, and the war there ended up being a standoff in the trenches, mud, and barbed wire of no-man's-land.

Nation sided with nation. The British siding with the European Union, namely France and it's allies. The German, French, and British fighter planes began harassing their enemy's trenches constantly and inneffectually, ending in another stalemate. This resulted in more and more aerial warfare over the English Channel in an attempt to gain air superiority. The Americans had now sided with the British and the French and were sending an Expeditionary Force to the continent. Many Americans were already fighting with their allies. Our story begins here.

Who was to say who had the better fighter pilots? Many famous aces on each side. This is a story of some of the more famous aces.

The RAF was forming an elite fighter squadron, as the number of German kills over the channel was rising. Three of these aces were American. Flight Lieutenalt Lilly, Squadron leader Debbie, and Wing Commander Chrissie. Lilly was from New England, was already an ace with 25 kills, and she flew and loved her pale blue Sopwith Camel, a very maneuverable and deadly fighter plane. Debbie was from North Carolina and was an ace with 32 kills. She was trigger-happy, (one reason she was flight leader) and ran out of ammo a lot. She flew a French Spad. The French-built Spad was a faster, newer plane than the Camel, but not as maneuverable. Chrissie was from New England also, and Chrissie? Well, Chrissie just liked to fight. She had been banned from the base officers club. She was an ace with 28 kills, and flew an orange Nieuport, also a later, faster craft than the Camel.

The other three pilots chosen were all British. Flight Lieutenant Cathy, Wing Commander Karen, and Group Captain Mike, a British-Canadian. Lt. Cathy, an ace with 24 kills flew a Spad, and was just simply a tough, what—the—hell, seat-of-the-pants type fighter pilot. Her motto was "You can only fall so hard". Commander Karen was considered the ace of the RAF with 41 kills, and counting. She loved dogfighting, and had turned down promotion to flight instructor to remain in combat. She flew a purple Spad. Mike was a sort of devil—may-care type flier who wasn't quite an ace yet. He had 12 kills, flew a red Camel, and was a deadly competitor who was always eager to go into combat.

The elite squadron of the RAF began giving the German air force more than it could handle. Generaloberst Don ordered his top aces from Spain and the Balkans home to Berlin, and formed an elite squadron of his own.

The second leading German ace at that time was Hauptmann Monica, a Dutch pilot. Holland was neutral, but a lot of the Dutch were siding with the German cause. Monica had 39 kills, the most of any ace in the northern front. She flew an orange Albatros; a fast, very agile biplane. She was selected to lead the squadron. Two other foreign pilots were selected. Oberleutnant Anneke, another Dutch ace, had 33 kills, flew a pink Albatros, and when not flying was a lady much chased after by the male pilots, Major Tony was an Italian-born ace, recalled from Spain, where he had recorded 33 kills. He flew a new sparkling-white Fokker D.VII, to date, the most agile aircraft in the war. Tony was a flamboyant, handsome sort, and was loved by all the ladies.

The other three aces assigned were all Germans. Obersleutnant Lena was from Stuttgart, and she had been a scholar. An ace with 24 kills, she flew a deadly Fokker D.VII, and was a merciless hunter The youngest member of the squadron was Hauptman Tammy, recalled from the Russian front. Not quite an ace with 14 kills, she was a renowned aviatrix, Born a von Zeppelin, she was a flier from birth, and she had political clout. The last member was recalled from the Balkan front. A super-ace with 54 kills, Baron von Pup flew a bright red Fokker triplane. The latest German innovation, the triplane was the most maneuverable of all aircraft to date, and the Baron was a relentless master of the aircraft.

It is probably inevitable that these two squadrons will meet in mortal combat over the channel. The ensuing dogfight would be one from hell.

Saturday night was a big one at the RAF officers club. Mike had quickly attained ace status, and the pilots were celebrating. Wing Commander Crissie was even allowed in, She had promised not to fight tonight, but she was allowed to arm wrestle if she liked. The ale and wine were flowing. Mike was being hugged and congratulated. He had quickly gone to 21 kills, fighting alongside the aces. They had a great time telling war stories and getting swacked. Morale was good, and spirits were high.

Across the channel, Baron Pup and Obersleutnant Anneke were playing cribbage at their club, and Anneke was winning. The Baron couldn't peg on her, and he was getting upset. Tony and Monica kept kibitzing, and the Baron finally just gave up and left in a huff. Morale was good, though, and their first sortie over the channel as a group was tomorrow at dawn.

The German squadron attained altitide, Monica flying lead. The channel was covered with morning fog, and they flew over it, searching for targets. If none appeared soon, they'd strafe an RAF airfield, and go home. The range of these planes was very limited, and whatever they did, it had to be done quickly. Nothing showed for several minutes, so Monica headed for the white cliffs of England. They neared the British airfield, climbed, and swarmed down. Two British fighter planes, both Spads aloft for surveillance, were quickly disposed of, and the strafing began. The British pilots would quickly be aloft, and the Germans, short of ammunition, would be in peril. Several RAF aircraft were damaged on the ground, some engufed in flames, as the German pilots fled for home.

The RAF squadron had just gotten over the channel. It was a cold, clear morning, and they were itching for a fight. Nothing in sight, Debbie led them eastward and they soon encountered about a dozen Fokkers apparently headed for England. The ensuing battle cost the Germans dearly. Eight more kills for the aces. The Brits had lost their gunslinger, though. Debbie had headed home for more ammo and fuel, and her landing gear had collapsed She had crash-landed, and fractured her wrist. A terrible blow to the squadron.

Her replacement was a pilot instructor, who had been assigned to a base in Scotland. Wing Commander Dawn had no kills, having never been in combat. She was to take over as lead pilot for Debbie. She flew a green Spad with a yellow shrimp painted on the fuselage., She could fly, and she was as mean as a cornered rattlesnake.

The German squadron also had a replacement. Obersleutnant Anneke had been assigned to lead an additional team of super-haupts. Aces were getting scarce, and Anneke's replacement was a friend of the Baron's, Hauptmann Deni. Deni had been in combat for about 6 weeks in southern France, and had 9 kills. An excellent fighter pilot who flew a yellow Albatros.

Baron von Pup had 64 kills now, leading all aces. He was a skilful, tricky flier, and knew his aircraft. However, much of his success was due to the German technology that had made it possible to fire his Spandau machine guns thru the propellor. This gave the pilot better aim as the guns were right in front of the pilot and not on top of the wings. and the pilot could usually unjam them if necessary. In addition, a drum of ammo could be reloaded while in flight. The Baron was the only pilot with this advantage as his triplane was a prototype.

The RAF squadron missed their cowboy leader, but Dawn was a capable replacement. She had 8 kills within a week. The RAF pilots were hearing more and more of the destructive German squad, and they were itching for a fight. Small friendly bets were placed on who would "get" the Red Baron. Lilly and Karen were the favorites here.

One morning, clear and cold, the RAF squad finally spotted the Germans. Six planes in perfect formation, and the sun gleaming off the red fuselage of the dreaded Fokker.

Monica noticed it at once. the multi-colored RAF planes had to be the ones they had been seeking. This was going to be the day. She motioned upward, and the Germans attempted to gain an altitude advantage. The Brits, still in formation started upward also. Soon the planes converged, and the battle began.

Miraculously, not a plane was shot down. These pilots were so skilled at protecting each other that very few shots were even fired. Lilly had Tammy in her sights once but had to peel off to save herself from Deni. Even the Baron couldn't get a burst off. This went on until fuel was low and they had to give up.

Two weeks later, these two squadrons met again over the channel. The Brits had surprised the Germans from behind, and the battle was on. The Baron, climbing instantly, spun out, dove on the Brits, spraying bullets in an attempt to demoralize them. Dawn, or possibly Lilly had already shot Deni down. She was picked up in the channel and returned safely, Tony had damaged Chrissie's aircraft, and she was cussing, trying to get aim with a crippled aircraft. She put a few rounds into Lilly's Camel before she had to bail out. Mike had had a terrible time, but had finally evaded Monica enough to look for prey. Karen, deadly and all business as usual, had finally managed to get Tammy off her tail, and the tables were turned. Tammy went down, to be rescued in the channel.

Mike and the Baron were mixing it up, and the Baron was making sure of the kill when Cathy came flying in to assist Mike. The Baron made a couple of moves they'd never seen before, and Cathy's smoking plane went down, her parachute billowing out above it.

Monica and Dawn were maneuvering all over the place when Tony, free for a moment, shot down Dawn's bright green Spad. Tony's guns had now jammed, and he had to head home. Baron Pup was still after Mike, and finally attained a height advantage, Mike, desperate for altitude, slowed just enough for Lena to blow him from the sky. Lilly and Karen were no match for the remaining Fokkers, and were forced to head home, low on fuel and ammunition.

The Red Baron was never seen over the channel after that day. Some say that, low on fuel, he never made it home, and, out of fuel, crashed in the channel. A crude wooden cross bearing the inscription, DAS ADLER (the Eagle), erected on the Normandy beach, was soon washed away by the tide.

Monica survived he war, and returned to her native Holland. Lilly became a barnstormer in midwest America. Mike returned to Canada, and became a Naval pilot. Dawn, Tony, Karen, Cathy, and Anneke disappeared from history. The titled Tammy became a German industrialist, Deni emigrated to America, and became an actress on Broadway. Debbie, the gunslinger, went home to No, Carolina, and became a state Senator. Lena became a college professor in Munich.

The End

OPERATIC FUN

CHAPTER I

In the elite world of opera singers, there have been few really famous tenors, and possibly even fewer really famous sopranos The soprano voice is rare because the vocal chords, coordinated with extraordinary lung power must be able to produce and hold notes several octaves above middle C, an extraordinary feat. The few divas who possess these powerful voices are in great demand, simply because of their rarity. This is a story of one famous soprano from Europe who made an American tour in the year 1896.

Dawn was hot, cranky, tired, hungry, and extremely disagreeable. The train was creeping along slowly, and she wasn't looking forward to the night at all. They would be in a small town named Eagletown for the night, resuming the trip to St. Louis tomorow. She hated small towns. Dawn was used to the spotlight, and she loved it. Well, it was only for the one night. No spotlight in this burg, for sure. She was traveling with her agent, Mike, who was a rather devious character, but knew his way around the operatic world well. He had good contacts, and he didn't come cheap. Her other two companions were Ros, a fellow Brit, who was her voice coach and sort of handmaiden, Ros had been with Dawn for years, and was a dependable, loyal assistant. The fourth member of her retinue was her body-guard, Bill, who had also been with her for years,. Bll was a big, pleasant-looking man, always polite and charming. No one even touched Dawn in public without Bill allowing it. He was good at his job.

There were two reporters on the train also. Nece was with the London Globe and would follow the troupe throughout the American tour, Nece was a pest, but Dawn liked her basically, and Nece always flattered her in print. The other reporter was from New York. Well-known on Broadway, Paul was one of the top entertainment experts of his era. They were both enamored of Dawn, because of her ability and her fame.

Standing on the platform after detraining, Dawn was surprised. This was not what she'd expected at all. Eagletown was a very clean, interesting, colorful small town, and almost everyone in town was there to get a glimpse of the famous diva. Actually, she almost felt flattered, The mayor, Tammy, a very attractive youthful-appearing lady presented her with the traditional "Key to the City", and welcomed her to Eagletown. The Eagletown reporter was a gentleman named Marc, who insisted on a photo. She graciously complied, and answered a few questions from him.

The troupe and the two out-of-town reporters were all being checked into Chrissie's hotel, the nicest of the two in Eagletown. The clerk at Chrissie's was a rather handsome woman who seemed to smirk when she spoke. It unnerved Dawn a bit, but Monica was very efficient and assigned rooms quickly, much to Dawn's delight. Monica also offered her services as concierge should they need anything. Chrissie, an imposing, attractive lady, welcomed them to her hotel, gave them menus to the dining room, and wished them a pleasant stay. Dawn was actually impressed with Eagletown so far.

Their bellhop was a small, rather ratty-looking fellow, who easily handled their big bags. Dawn and Ros shared an airy, colorful, and comfortable room with a good view of a very pretty and rustic Main Street. Pup set the baggage down, opened a window, and stood patiently. Dawn knew he wanted a tip, but, although a very wealthy woman, she seldom carried money, leaving all that up to Ros. She turned her back on Pup, and Ros, who was almost as stingy as Dawn, finally gave him fifteen cents and shooed him out.

Two hours later, The four headed for the dining room. Chrissie's had a large dining room with a really large stage for a town this small. Debbie, their attractive, blond hostess, quickly had them seated at a spacious table, telling them the show would start in about forty-five minutes, to enjoy themselves, and introduced their waitress, a willowy, very pretty young lady named Lisa. Lisa took their order for drinks, and they all ordered wines. Lisa explained that all they had in spirits was beer and whiskey. Dawn and Ros were a bit upset, but politely ordered a bottle of whiskey and a round of beers for the four.

Lisa was an experienced, quick attendant, and they were soon sipping beer and whiskey, chatting, relaxing, and enjoying themselves when the show began.

The curtain went up, and the big dining room became silent. There was a piano on the right side of the stage, and a tall, very pretty, slender young lady, introduced as Doo, came on stage, Dawn noticed that one of Doo's arms hung a bit lower than the other. An odd deformity, possibly a childhood accident. Doo seated herself, flexed her long fingers, and started playing, As she played, the speed and intensity of her playing increased. To the trained musical ear of Dawn it seemed impossible to play like this. It must be the heady whiskey, she thought. Crescendo after crescendo, faster and faster she played. Dawn was shocked, This was the best piano playing she had ever heard and she had worked with the best in Europe for years. Automatically, her lips parted, she cleared her throat, almost breaking into song. She restrained herself just in time. Ros and Mike were speechless also. They glanced at each other knowingly. They had a prodigy here!

Needless to say, Paul and Nece, the big city reporters, were also a bit worked up over this performance. They were animatedly discussing it and pointing at the stage. Mike, watching, knew it would be all over the national press in a matter of days. Maybe he could figure a way to get Doo under some kind of contract without Dawn knowing. Damn those two reporters for being here!

Doo stood, bowed, and left the stage. Chrissie announced a ten minute recess, and the noise level had risen in the room again. Mike was trying to figure out some way to get away from Dawn and get to Doo somehow.

The curtain rose for the second time, and Doo seated herself at the piano. Chrissie had merely announced the next performer as Lilly, a local singer. Dawn thought this would be interesting. A local untrained singer in accompaniment with this outstanding pianist, Doo began slowly and, as before, worked into some amazing notes. Lilly, a pretty young lady with long blond hair, broke into song. She was soprano, and had an incredible voice range, her voice unquavering and powerful. Dawn was shocked. Shivers ran down her spine. This young lady was good! Doo was really playing fast now, and Lilly's powerful voice was staying with her. Suddenly several goblets in the room shattered and Lilly and Doo shut it down. The townspeople had expected this, and broke into applause. Lilly and Doo bowed and left the stage.

Chrissie, the imposing owner, appeared on stage ten minutes or so later and announced the last performance of the evening. It would be the famous

Act III, scene 3 of Lohengrin, composed by Wagner, and first shown in Riga in 1855. Chrissie presented Nina, portraying Elsa, and Gaet, who would portray Lohengrin. Dawn's ears perked up. She had played Elsa many times in her career, and it was a difficult role, even for a soprano as accomplished as she was. Why isn't Lilly doing it, she thought? Lilly was just good enough to maybe accomplish it, she believed, Something just wasn't right here. The role of Lohengrin had to be performed by an excellent, experienced tenor, also. What was going on here?

The curtain rose for the third time. Doo was at the piano flexing those long fingers. Softly at first, she began playing. Gaet, in costume, came onstage with a perfect accompaniment, and in maybe the most perfect tenor Dawn could recall. A reply from offstage came in the smoothest soprano voice Dawn had ever heard, and Nina joined Gaet onstage. A stunning performance followed: possibly the finest she'd ever heard. The audience was standing and applauding. Bows were taken, and the curtain lowered.

CHAPTER II

Paul was in a quandary, He needed to interview some people as soon as possible and get to the telegraph office. This had to be the scoop of the century in the entertainment field, and he lacked enough information for a story. Nece had disappeared, and he wondered what she was up to.

When Paul arrived at the stage entrance Nece and Mike were already there demanding entrance. Karen, who always allowed or disallowed entrance to the dressing rooms, was no one to fool around with. Mike had tried a fifty-dollar bill, and had been denied. Nece's press credentials had also failed. Karen protected her people from any outside interference very well. In the past, she had even had to show a few "who was boss". She, along with Cathy, who was the bouncer in the hotel casino-bar, were the two best street-fighters in Eagletown.

Bill and a very disappointed, but still scheming Mike, had retired to their room, as had Dawn and Ros. A bit tipsy from the drinks, and still awed by the performances they'd seen, the ladies discussed it. Dawn knew she couldn't leave Eagletown at this time. For one thing, she just HAD to sing to the piano music that Doo had played. She also had to know if the two sopranos she'd heard tonight were as good as she was. It worried her. She had never doubted her talents before.

Pup, the bellhop, also cleaned off the tables in the dining room, and then he would help Bonnie, the dishwasher, clean and restock them. He could hear Chrissie and Monica saying how honored and happy they were to have a famous singer staying at the hotel, and they sure hoped Dawn had liked their little small-town performance.

Whether Dawn liked it or not, she was to stay for another week. Dawn and Ros breakfasted alone. Immediately after her after breakfast coffee, Ros set out to the telegraph office, wiring St. Louis to cancel their appearances, due to illness. Dawn renewed their room for another week, and inquired of the smirking Monica how she might get in touch with the hotel performers. Monica was more than glad to tell her, and Dawn went back upstairs.

Paul had come downstairs, and when he heard this, his mind went into action. Now he had a whole week of grace. Word of the prodigies probably wouldn't be out for another week, unless— hmm, that confounded Nece. He must get to her and tell her the good news. He also wired his office, telling them he would be in

Eagletown another week. Unknown to Paul, the word WAS out. Ros had unwittingly sent it.

The editor of the St. Louis Dispatch had sent his best reporter to Eagletown on the first train out. There was something suspicious about this "illness" thing. Dawn had never been sick a day in her famous life. He smelled big-time news here, and Ed was just the person to dig it out. The editor was not alone. In a few hours no less than fifty people would be converging on Eagletown to get to the bottom of this cancellation.

That evening Chrissie's dining room was jammed with people standing, and people waiting to get in. Mike knew several of the newcomers, as did Paul, The evening Eagletown TALON had mentioned the cancellation in St. Louis and they knew the newcomers were greedy for a scoop. Debbie, the hostess, had handled the extra people very efficiently.

Dawn and her party were seated, and Bill was doing a great job of giving Dawn her privacy. Lisa, pretty as ever, had attended to them, and they were chatting over whiskey and beer

The curtain went up for the night's entertainment. Doo was seated at the piano, flexing those long fingers. This was a dance number introducing two young local dancers, Lena and Jo. A good performance, really, for a small town week night. Applause. Two more mundane skits, applause, and the show was over for the night. Dawn was puzzled, A turkey-in-the-straw performance, but why? All that talent, all these experts to watch it, and the prodigies nowhere to be seen.

Ed, the St.Louis reporter, and Paul were old friends, and trusted one another. Paul told Ed of the performance he'd seen. It sounded incredible to Ed. Two world-class sopranos, a world-class tenor, and an accomplished pianist all here in this small town. He knew Paul well enough to know there was a story here, somewhere

Tammy, the youthful, attractive mayor of Eagletown, had never seen a situation like this. Every passenger train that stopped here seemed to have dozens of people getting off, and it was getting out of hand. Eagletown had become the show business capitol of the world. Dawn refused to leave until she got what she wanted, and the little town was inundated with reporters, music critics, theatrical agents, and fans of the famous continental diva. Both hotels were jammed, as was every spare room in town. The telegraph office had put on three more operators, and the lines to get in there were still long. Don, the Police chief, had had to install twenty-four hour patrols on Main Street just so traffic could flow. No real problems yet, but they were inevitable, so Tammy called a meeting at Town Hall for ten o'clock Thursday morning.

Lilly answered the knock on her door. She couldn't believe her eyes. It was Monica, and she had brought the famous Dawn with her! Bill, always at

Dawn's side, was the third party. Awestricken, she invited them in, extending her hand to Dawn. Dawn igored Lilly's hand and instead gave the young lady a big, warm hug. Dawn explained why they were here. She had been impressed with Lilly as a singer, and wanted to meet and get to know her better. Also Dawn wanted to take to the stage in Eagletown with Lilly, Doo, and possibly the two who had performed the opera scene. Lilly, of course, was flattered, but said that would depend on Chrissie, as her hotel held the only two large stages in town.

Dawn also mentioned that it seemed unusual to her that last night, with all the big-named national critics in town, Lilly and the others hadn't performed for them. Monica explained that she and Chrissie held auditions for all Chrissie's shows, and that almost all shows were local talent, maybe not the best, but the best locally. It was a lot of fun, and the townspeople here disliked opera, really. They loved the local talent. The musical show Dawn had seen had been staged just to try to have a show that she (Dawn) would enjoy. Monica said something could probably be worked out with Chrissie, Most of the visitors to Eagletown would eagerly attend. They then chatted over coffee, as Lilly begged Dawn for more and more about Europe and her career.

Mike knew all was lost here. There were about thirty or so agents in town, and most of them were a lot more mercenary than he was. It was a cutthroat profession, at best. He almost wished he were still a tout at the race-track.

With the news from Eagletown spread all over the world, Nece finally got an article off to her London paper. She had accidently met Doo and sort of interviewed her. Doo had had no formal training in music, and to her knowledge, no one in Eagletown even gave piano lessons. She had thought about it, but not many in Eagletown liked piano music. Besides, she loved her job at the bank.

The meeting was called to order by Tammy. Marc was the only reporter there. A lot of merchants in town were making a lot of money here, and were loath to end this prosperity, but they all knew as long as Dawn was in town the congestion would only get worse. Chrissie was a council member and was in attendance. She said that Dawn was one of the most gracious guests she had ever had, but her fame was just causing too many problems. The town was almost out of beer and cigarettes, and people were grumbling. Monica probably knew Dawn better than anyone here, as she had escorted her around town many times. She explained that Dawn was simply an artist and wanted to get onstage with Doo, Lilly, and, if possible, Nina and Gaet. Maybe, once all these show business people in town saw the performance, they would leave.

Later that afternoon, Bonnie and Pup were putting up posters all over town, There was to be a special show tomorrow afternoon at three PM on the big stage in the hotel saloon featuring the famous soprano, Dawn. The town buzzed, and the telegraph office went crazy.

By noon Friday, Eagletown's population was about that of Pittsburgh. People everywhere, and the big casino could only seat about two hundred. All available tickets had been sold, and some resold already

Pup and Bonnie had finished sweeping, cleaning, and polishing in the saloon, and were setting out more folding chairs. Bonnie was a good worker, but Pup was a little lazy, and Chrissie and Monica had to keep getting after him to do his share. The big theater was almost ready. Three hours to go.

Ros had had 24 hours or so to put together a show for the foremost music critics and reporters in America. She had one professional, no script, three amateurs, and a piano that had seen better days. Apparently, Gaet had left town a few days ago to visit someone. Ros was a pro, though, and the three Eagletown musicians were quick learners. Doo, with no formal training whatsoever, had remarkable retention. She could replay anything she had ever heard. Ros, an accomplished pianist herself, played a demanding piece from Chopin, the great Polish pianist. Doo easily duplicated it and actually may have improved on it.

Training Lilly, Nina, and Dawn to sing in unison was also easier than she thought it would be. Hearing all three at the same time was a bit eerie; it was as though there were only one powerful voice. Ros and the talented artists had (she hoped) come up with three short but entertaining musical performances.

Pup and Bonnie were getting tired. The midnight Express had delivered kegs of beer, cases of whiskey, and countless tins of tobacco and cigarettes, and they had been sent to unload the baggage car at the depot, and restock the items for Chrissie. Bonnie handled mostly the heavier beer kegs and Pup the tobacco and cigarettes.

CHAPTER III

Chrissie was finalizing things in the saloon-casino theatre, and Monica had assigned Bonnie to make and sack popcorn, as well as bag peanuts. A lot of snacks would be needed during the performance. She had kept Pup at the desk to carry flowers upstairs, as they were pouring in. The Eagletown Florist Shop was sold out and had closed. Pup had a few more loads to carry upstairs and then he had to go help Bonnie. Dawn's room was full of flowers now, so he was just dumping them in the hall. Dawn was in a dressing room backstage, and Ros was in the hotel room trying to get dressed, She'd gotten tired of Pup barging in with flowers, finally giving him twenty-five cents and telling him to leave them in the hallway outside.

Chrissie had it set up so the entrance to the theater would be through the dining room, where popcorn, nuts and other refreshments would be sold. Entering the theater, the patrons would pass the length of the long bar, where they could obtain drinks. They would then they would be in the seating area.

Karen and Cathy had been taking tickets at the dining-room door off the hotel lobby. The theater was filling up early, and Debbie was trying to seat people to their tastes. The area near the stage filled first. Lisa and the two pretty dancers, Lena and Jo, were serving drinks up at a fantastic rate. Some of these out-of-towners were big flirts, too. The three young ladies were having a good time and raking in the tips.

Paul and Nece had gotten good seats, side by side, and wondered about all this. Both knew the enormous amount of time needed to prepare, rehearse, and deliver even a short show.

Mike had tried to get Dawn to let him backstage, but she refused. She knew he'd make these young people promises and offers, and she needed them to stay focused, Everything was going fine so far. Ros had joined, and was probably the most nervous of the lot. The only person backstage who wasn't a performer was Bill, and his job was to keep it that way. Chrissie, also backstage, would be the Master of Ceremonies.

Dawn showed the two young singers how to use an atomizer to moisten the throat. They giggled, thinking it was the "neatest" thing. They were relaxed, and it was looking good. Doo, always flexing her fingers and wanting to play, said she was going to get into that bottle of whiskey they had right after the show. They all laughed.

Dawn had liked the format of the piano, followed by two singing performances, and had decided to follow it. Ros had agreed.

At exactly one minute after three PM Chrissie parted the curtains and adressed the now quiet audience. She welcomed them to Eagletown, to her theater, and apologized for not having time to print programs. She announced three performances. Doo, the first performer, would play a Chopin piece they all recognized as extremely difficult. A buzz went up. Chrissie raised her hand for silence, announcing the second performance would be the aria "Ave Maria" from Act IV of "Otello" by Verdi. It would be sung by Lilly, Nina, and the famous Dawn. The crowd was almost on its feet. Three people singing an aria was unheard of. Arias are for soloists. Waiting for quiet, Chrissie then announced the third performance would also be an aria from "La Traviata" Act III, also by Verdi, and would also be performed by all three singers. The audience wondered what was going on here, No unknown piano player can play Chopin, and no one but a trained soloist can do a difficult aria.

The acoustics in Chrissie's theater were really quite good and sound carried well and clear. The curtain came up and Doo bowed. Then, sitting at the piano, her long fingers strayed over the keys. Faster and faster they flew, and suddenly the learned audience realized what she actually was playing one of Chopin's most difficult, and she was playing it amazingly fast! It seemed different somehow, but it was all there, and it was beautiful. Doo closed with a flourish, and the applause was deafening.

Only moments after Doo's performance, a few opportunistic "earlybirds" were pounding on the stage-entrance door. Bill was just big enough and good enough that none got in, but he was glad to see the police chief, Don, come around the corner. Don assured Bill he would get several officers to help out here, and Bill thanked him.

There was a pretty good buzz in the theater as the curtain went up for the second performance The audience then got so quiet you could hear a pin drop. Nina was to the left side of the stage, Lilly was near the piano on the right, and the famous soprano, Dawn, was center-stage. They wore identical white gowns with bright blue wide, tight waist sashes, giving them a full-figured and voluptuous appearance. The aria opened as Nina broke into song. Her perfect soprano voice rose and swelled with power. The aria continued and suddenly they were realizing that with no break in the perfect deliverance, Nina was no longer singing. The incomparable Dawn was now perfectly continuing the narrative of the aria. Suddenly, again with no break in sequence, Lilly was now singing it. Again a perfect, powerful, and beautiful soprano voice. It was as though it were only one singer. This incredible performance continued back and forth on the stage, and you could close your eyes and picture the singer pacing the stage while singing.

When the performance began, Monica had Pup and Bonnie clean and mop the large lobby floor as it had gotten dusty. They were almost finished as the curtain went down on the second act, and she told them they could come watch the rest from the dining entrance with her if they liked. Then she changed her mind and sent them to the linen room to do bedding and towels.

The telegraph ofice was like an ant hill already. Probably twenty or more reporters had left after the second performance, knowing they'd be in line for hours, and were scuffling for position to get their messages sent.

There were a few empty seats now, and Ed joined Paul and Nece. They knew they'd be hours getting their reports to their papers, but they wanted to see the final performance. The three agreed that this was certainly an unprecedented and magnificent performance so far.

The curtain rose for the final performance. The three singers were in the same positions for this more demanding aria. The only change being that they had tight bright red sashes now. As before, Nina began the aria, or did she? No, she and Lilly were both singing in perfect unison! Dawn joined in, almost unnoticed, as Nina dropped out, and Lilly and Dawn were singing. Taking turns, two at a time, they sang this aria pefectly. It was an awesome experience to hear two powerful, identical, perfectly synchronized voices simultaneously. Coming to a patrticularly high, demanding part late in this magnificent aria, Dawn and Nina were joined by Lilly, all three pushing their voices higher and higher. Suddenly the crescendo became too much. A window shattered, the music stopped, and the big curtain came down.

Silence for a few moments, then standing applause, and people running toward the stage. Karen and Cathy had all they could handle, but they handled the crowd well. People were rushing out to either the telegraph office or to the stage door, which was off-limits to all.

The three singers and Doo, still on stage. were hugging each other and a very happy Ros. Bill had gone to the apron to assist the two bouncers with crowd control.

Chrissie came onstage with Tammy and Marc, the only reporter allowed to interview here. Not being into opera, the townspeople wondered what the fuss was all about, really. Tammy did know that Lilly, Nina, and Doo would have to leave Eagletown, temporarily at least, for it to assume some degree of normalcy.

Dawn had a plan. She could take the three with her to Denver, her next stop. It would give Eagletown a respite, and should be a nice trip for them. Denver was a beautiful city, and none had been there before. An adventure, really. Whether they performed was up to each of them. Doo automatically flexed those long fingers

Pup and Bonnie had finished the linens and Monica had them diligently painting one of the rooms. Pup was working hard to finish, He wanted to bellhop again before Ros left, as she was a big tipper.

THE END

Author's note: I think there may be a lesson here. Let us assume that the renowned Dawn had been infatuated with herself, disdainful, jealous of other talents, or extremely haughty. She could have cruelly crushed these younger, possibly lesser talents who adored her. Think about it.

FUN IN THE 'HOOD

CHAPTER I

Prohibition was one of the biggest mistakes our government ever made. It was largely uninforced, people drank more than ever, and it helped spawn organized crime An odd piece of trivia for you: The wealthy New England Kennedy family got their "start" largely from "rum running". Our story begins in the year 1937, a few years after Prohibition was repealed.

Lilly was one of the happiest people on earth. She was an accomplished seamstress and tailor by trade. By saving her money, she had purchased a large two-story bulding on Main Street in Eagletown, and operated a thriving dressmaking and tailoring enterprise on the ground floor. Her unique garments were always in demand. She had three expert tailor-seamstresses in her employ. Monica was a Dutch immigrant who had worked in Paris, the fashion capitol, for years. Her close friend and countryman, Anneke, also worked for Lilly, as did Dawn, a British immigrant. Dawn claimed she had tailored some garments for the Royal family.

Lilly had also hired a sort of down-and-out fellow named Pup, who worked in the back room. His job was primarily to press garments and he was also general handyman.

Lilly leased the other half of the ground floor to a gentleman named Mike, who had opened a tavern there shortly after the repeal of Prohibition. Mike and his wife, Vicky, lived over their bar, as did Lilly over her shop. The remainder of the upper floor was leased by an attorney, Lena, and a dentist named Chuck. Dr. Chuck, as he was called, was a humanitarian type professional, and did an enormous amount of work for little or no pay. Lena, adversely, would charge her own mother top dollar for counsel.

Mike seldom left his office. His two managers, Deni after 6pm, and Karen, who opened up in the mornings, basically ran his business. He also sold food and had a wonderful cook named Georgia, who had been with him since he opened. His bouncer, who came on at 8 pm, was a British—born American named Cathy, who had a short fuse. Actually, a rather genteel, well-managed, and quiet establishment. A place you could take your children.

Across Main Street from Lilly's shop, two barbers, Doug and Bill, did a great business. They always seemed to know what was going on in Eagletown, and loved spreading the dirt. Just south of their barber shop, Katie and her partner, Doo, operated a delicatessen and grocery store. Their butcher was an amiable gentleman named Vern, who usually gave the poorer customers an extra bit of meat.

Just south of the deli was a gun shop. Debbie and her husband had moved to Eagletown and opened their shop about a year ago. Her husband was a gunsmith and a gun trader. They also sold ammunition, new guns, and various outdoor supplies. Debbie herself was a renowned marksman and had the trophies to prove it. Her weapon was a lever-action Winchester.30-30, and she could snuff a candle at 60 yards. There were other businesses along Main Street, but these are the focus of our story.

Deni noticed the three men as soon as they entered. A bit too flashily well-dressed, and, somehow, seemingly ominous. Very out of place here. They approached her, and asked to see the owner. Deni said he had retired, but they could address her. After they were assured she had the authority, they told her she was going to need some "protection" for the establishment, which they could provide. It would cost $150 per week, starting Friday. Deni told them she didn't need any damned protection, and to get the hell out, or get thrown out. These men were tough as nails, and were just about to demonstrate to this woman why she needed protection, when Chrissie, the bartender, came out swinging with the baseball bat she kept under the counter. Caught by surprise, two hoods went down immediately. Cathy, the bouncer, and a few customers appeared at Chrissie's side, and they threw the three gangsters out.

Pup

Word of this incident spread through the tight-knit group of business owners. Were they to become victims of the mobsters as had merchants in New York and Chicago? Chief Don of the Eagletown Police Department called a meeting of the merchants at two o'clock the next afternoon.

Don explained why he just couldn't arrest these people. They'd have a high-priced attorney get them out in a matter of hours, and they would seek revenge. Apparently, the Gotti family had moved into the area, and were taking it over a bit at a time. But Don had a plan. He was in touch with an insurance company that could insure them against "protection". Don said that he had met with them, and he believed these people could do the job. He advised them the agents would be here sometime tomorrow to sign them up. They would show their business cards. The cards would have a red wing on them, with the name of the agent.

Word spread quickly on Main Street. The insurance agents were at Mike's Place accepting policyholders. Mike had already joined by the time Lilly arrived, and Debbie was signing now. This was not what she had expected. These people sure didn't look like insurance agents. Young, businesslike, energetic, handsome people. The agents had their business cards on the table and she took some. The three at her table were named Gaet, Lisa, and Marc. The insurance was almost free. Three dollars a month. She couldn't believe it, really. The head agent was a gentleman named Ed, and as soon as everyone had signed on, he told them that any malicious damage to any of their businesses was covered, with no deductible, and not to worry about a thing. Everyone wanted to know how they could do this, but the Redwings weren't answering questions. Chief Don was there, and reassured everyone they were in good hands.

Unknown to the residents of Eagletown, late that night a dark car crept down Main Street and slowed for a second in front of Mike's tavern. Two men leaned out of the car. One threw a brick at Lilly's plate glass window, and the other threw a brick at the plate glass window of the deli across the street. The car then sped away, not knowing that on each side of the street a dark figure had emerged from the shadows and caught the bricks.

At ten o'clock the next morning the gangsters arrived to get their protection money. To their surprise, no damage could be seen. Entering the deli, they were met by a very pretty young lady with a meat cleaver in her hand, and another clutching a long, curved butcher knife. Off to the side, they saw a blonde, attractive lady sitting in a rocking chair with an old lever-action carbine across her lap. Weird people in this little burg. Doo was fighting mad, and was waving Vern's meat cleaver. Katie told the men she had had no damage and wasn't giving them any money. One of the hoods casually walked to Vern's meat display, removed an automatic weapon known as a "Tommy gun" from inside his coat, and broke the display glass with the butt of the weapon.

The leader of the Mafiosa pointed to the damage and explained that is why they needed to pay protection. This could happen a lot. There was a loud, prolonged, ominous clicking sound as Debbie chambered and pointed the carbine. Just then two formidable-looking gentlemen holding straight razors strolled into the deli, along with Chief Don and Lt. Tammy of the Eagletown police force.

The store seemed suddenly full of people. Three well-dressed young ladies walked into the store, observed the damage, and approached Katie. They displayed business cards to the mobsters, and politely introduced themselves as Rose, Jojo, and Nece. Nece explained that they were insurers of the establishment, and they (the Redwing Insurance Company) owed Katie and Doo for the damage to their display case. Jojo then explained to the mobsters that malicious damage such as this was always appraised at a minimum of five-thousand dollars, and she instructed Rose to issue a check to Katie for that amount. Then she told the mobsters they were responsible to the Redwing Insurance Company for that amount plus expenses, and it was due and payable. Mobsters usually carry a lot of cash, and, surrounded, the bewildered hoods had no choice but to pay up. Nece politely gave them a receipt, and Chief Don told them to leave their weapons behind as they left. One hood threw his Tommy gun to the floor in disgust. Jojo examined the floor, then advised Rose to issue another five-thousand dollar check for damage to Katie's floor. The unarmed hoods paid up again, and very cautiously left the deli.

Across the street the other Mafiosa had smashed Lilly's cash register, demanding that she pay up. Monica and Dawn had come up front with large scissors in their hands, and suddenly Mike, from next door came in. He always carried this thing he called his "cosh" in his pocket. It was in his hand now. Lena came in, as did Chuck the dentist, carrying a large hypodermic needle. The place was filling up fast. Chrissie was swinging her bat and scowling as Sgt. Carol and Patrolman Willow entered. Karen was face-to-face with one gangster, her hands on her hips, daring him to make the first move. Suddenly, three well-dressed young people entered and passed out business cards, introducing themselves as Bonnie, Lisa, and Marc, representatives of Lilly's insurance company. After extracting five thousand dollars plus expenses for the damage, they allowed the disarmed Mafiosa to leave. Chrissie and Karen escorted them to their car. God, they wanted to fight. The gangsters were more than glad to leave Eagletown.

CHAPTER II

In Defense of the 'Hood

Don Gotti was mad as a hornet. He'd sent some of his best "soldiers" out to this hick town to generate a little bit of protection revenue, and they come back empty-handed. Two had banged-up legs and they're short about twenty thousand dollars. On top of all this crap, they didn't make much sense telling what happened. Women with Wild West rifles, ball bats, scissors, and meat cleavers. Men with blackjacks, razors, and needles. An insurance company that makes you pay for the damage, plus expenses. What gives with this little burg, anyway? He'd been tearing up businesses for over fifteen years, and he sure as hell wasn't paying any insurance companies. Well, he was going to pay this little dump a visit himself.

Lt. Tammy of the Eagletown Police Force was parked at the north end of Main St. in the shadows. Patrolman Willow had just finished her doughnut, and they were watching the incoming traffic. Chief Don and Sgt. Carol were at the south end. It was a few minutes before ten pm when Tammy signalled Don that the two vehicles were on Main Street.

Old Don Gotti sniffed, What a burg! It was a shame they had to even mess with the hicks in these little towns. The two cars pulled up and parked in front of Mike's saloon. Might as well have a drink before knocking off these hillbillies. He noticed a blond lady across the street in a rocking chair with an old rifle on her lap. He snorted. Who the hell is that? Annie Oakley? He chuckled to himself.

The Mafiosa went into Mike's and ordered. Two tables were joined to accommodate the eight, and they sipped their drinks. Soon, one of the hoods went over to the jukebox, put in a coin, cursed, took a length of pipe from inside his coat and smashed in the front of the jukebox. Surprisingly, no one at Mike's seemed to notice. Several people were coming in now. Four unusually attractive ladies sat at the table next to theirs and ordered drinks. They each had a large pair of scissors sticking out of their purse, which they removed and placed on their table. Two gentlemen sat down at the table on the other side of them, and both laid huge straight razors on the table. The Don was getting a bit nervous Surely, by now these yokels must know we mean business, he thought. More people were coming in. A sleazy looking fellow even came in with a heavy metal SAD iron in his hand and sat right behind them. A formidable looking man appeared out of nowhere with a blackjack in his hand, ordered, and sat near them at the bar. Weird people, the Don thought.

Chrissie, the bartender, refreshed their drinks, The Don had never seen anyone with a baseball bat in her apron before. He laughed. Two more pretty ladies came in and ordered drinks, joining the seamstresses at their table. One had a meat cleaver sticking out of her purse and the other had a long butcher knife stuck in her belt. Another rather large gentleman entered, joined Mike at the bar, laying a huge hypodermic needle filled with a brownish fluid on the countertop. The Don was getting a little nervous. Too many weirdos in here. Suddenly, one of the gangsters stood, picked up his chair, and smashed it on the floor. No one even seemed to notice. Deni quietly replaced his broken chair with a smile. In exasperation, the old Don drew his pistol and shot a hole in the ceiling to get attention.

Almost immediately, four well-dressed young people entered, looked around, and the leader, Ed, went straight to Mike, sitting at the bar. The others amiably went to the other patrons showing their business cards, and introducing themselves as Dan, Gaet, and Lisa. Ed was still talking to Mike at the bar, The Don noticed the blond lady with the old rifle was now standing just inside the front door. Suddenly the crowd somehow seemed closer. Yes! These stupid nuts had stood, and had them surrounded. One of the hoods immediately reached under his coat, but Lilliy poked the back of his neck rather sharply with those big scissors. A second gangster started to reach into his coat, and out of the corner of his eye he saw Bill's shiny razor almost at his throat. God! The Don realized they had a serious problem here. Now the cops were here! Chief Don and Carol were behind the counter blocking the rear exit, and Tammy and Willow were at the front entrance alongside Debbie and her rifle.

Lisa came to their table, presented her business card, smiled, and told them she represented the Redwing insurance Company, Mike's insurer. Gaet had examined the broken jukebox and Dan was picking up and examining the broken chair. Nece, another Redwing agent, came in from outside and said something to Ed and Mike, pointing outside.

Finally, Ed came over to the table. He told the mobsters politely that he had instructed Dan to issue Mike a check in the amount of twenty-five thousand dollars for malicious damages to his establishment. He told the Mafiosa since they had done the damage they were liable to the Redwing Insurance Company for thirty thousand dollars, which included the damage and all expenses.

The Don felt helpless. He had a very angry Doo right behind him who held a big meat cleaver over his head, and now this! Ed was listing the insured damage Jukebox, chair, floor damage from chair, bullet hole in ceiling, and tire damage to curb in front. Apparently, they'd parked against the curb and Nece had noticed it. Five items at five thousand dollars each came to twenty-five thousand dollars total claim paid to Mike.

The old Don hated banks, and he carried a big bundle, but he didn't want to pay up. Don and Tammy had come over to the table by now. Don told him how it stood. Pay up or do heavy time for malicious destruction of private property. The old Don knew he could beat a murder rap anytime, but malicious destruction of property was a gray legal area he wasn't sure of. It was clear that the mobster was trapped, so he asked who he was dealing with here. Ed told him he was dealing with the Redwing Insurance company as they had paid Mike's claim. The Don asked why so much for so little damage? Ed told them there was an attorney here, and would he like her to explain Mike's policy? The old Don jumped at the chance, knowing he needed an attorney, and bad. Lena, who was now sitting at the bar, said she would be glad to examine the policy. Mike quickly produced it. Mike was a sort of conservative guy who took few chances. He kept his insurance policy, his liquor license, and one one-thousand dollar bill taped to his chest. You never knew what's gonna happen, he always said.

Lena studied Mike's policy with the very nervous Don Gotti watching closely. Finally, she cleared her throat and addressed the assemblage. She stated that this was a legal document, drawn up between the insurer, Redwing, and the insured, Mike, the owner of the establishment. The terms of the policy were a minimum of five thousand dollars in damages for each malicious incident and that the amount was correct. The Don gave up. What a stupid insurance company! They'd be broke in no time!. He told Don and Tammy that it was a stupid policy, but he would pay up, and he reached inside his coat very slowly. He could feel a meat cleaver blade barely brush his head as he produced a huge bundle of bills, and he carefully paid the claim. The charming Lisa gave him a receipt for the money with a smile, and Chief Don told them they were free to leave, as soon as they turned in their weapons. Don and Tammy supervised the disarming, and Ed intervened once more. He told the old Don that Lena, the attorney also held a policy with Redwing that guaranteed her payment for counselling, and that Dan had just issued her a check for five thousand dollars.

Redwing got their last five grand out of a very shaken old Mafiosa Don, plus a grand for expenses. Then Don and Tammy allowed the unarmed racketeers to leave. They left very cautiously, careful not to disturb anything.

Old Don Gotti never had another good night's sleep. Razors, scissors, baseball bats, that damned rifle, and most of all that terrible meat cleaver haunted his dreams He got his 'family" out of the protection business the day after the Eagletown incident, saying it was too "unprofitable". He cancelled all his insurance and it was noticed that he would go around the block rather than pass by an insurance office.

The Redwings cancelled all the Eagletown policies as they should never need them again and moved on. Their services were needed elsewere, and they rode off into the sunset.

As a result of the Eagletown incident, the Mafia pretty much phased out of the risky "protection" business, going into mostly gambling, narcotics, prostitution, and labor-racketeering.

THE END

GLORIOUS FUN

CHAPTER I

"The Glory that was Greece" is an often heard phrase. Edgar Allen Poe is reputed to have penned, "The Glory that was Greece; The Grandeur that was Rome". Did he coin it or repeat it? The Roman Empire "Grandeur", however, was not to come until five centuries after the "Glory" Athens enjoyed.

Around 480 BC Athens was overrun, sacked, and virtually destroyed by Persian invaders. The Athenians were not really a warlike people. They had a scholarly bent, and learning was very important to them. Athens was also one of the earliest democracies. They had developed an excellent alphabet that would survive even into modern times, and could communicate with written words, rather than with pictures and symbols. This helped enable them to attain, for that period in time, an extraordinary amount of learning. This story is of some of the remarkable people who completed the rebuilding of the City-State of Athens. The year is 435 BC, and the city is still rebuilding.

The three architects were huddled over the blueprints. The Athenian King, Georgia, had summoned them to Athens to rebuild on the Acropolis, a huge mesa of rock in the center of the city. Georgia was a devout follower of the godess Athena, and she wanted the large temple rebuilt on the Acropolis where Athena could be properly worshipped. The architect Tammy, born in Peloponnesus to the south, had expatriated to Athens as had many scholars and scientists. Tammy was a structural engineer, possibly the finest of her time. Her job was to make the structures as strong and durable as possible. The second architect, Lena, was from Thessaly, to the north of Athens, and her love and specialty was adornment. Her job was to make them beautiful. Almost all of the massive marble and bronze work would be performed under her supervision.

Gaet, a native Athenian and the third architect, was nearing the end of his preliminary project, preparing the site for construction. After many years of toil, his minions, mostly slaves, had completed the first phase of the restoration. Gaet had superbly supervised the clean-up and removal of the rubble, burying most of it onsite. The site had been smoothed, and some of history's most incredible and beautiful structures were beginning to take form. (and countless priceles artifacts would be buried beneath them).

The Temple of Athena (for whom Athens was named) was later called the Parthenon. Parthenon loosely means something like "virgin lady". Not as large as the Pantheon in Rome was to be, but the

Athenian scholars, 500 years or so earlier, had a good knowledge of geometry, and the Athenian sculptors were equal to, or maybe even surpassed their Roman followers, One such dedicated artisan was Karen, who was in charge of the construction of the massive statue of Athena, the protector and Goddess of the city, inside the structure. Karen was a very talented and prominent sculptor, much respected and admired, and her students were the best. She had selected an unmarried Athenian beauty named Ros to model for the statue, and work had begun on the massive piece of statuary. The Greek word for bonny, or beautiful is "iraios", possibly coined for the hundreds of hours Ros had spent posing for this work of art.

Lilly, a native Athenian, was a famous mathematician, which, in Athens, made you automatically a teacher. Her students were all over the Acropolis assisting the architects with computations. Geometry was her specialty, and working on the Acropolis was a mathematician's dream. The famous Greek teachers sort of picked their own students, and only tutored a handful at a time. Almost all students were of the aristocracy.

Lilly's contemporary was Chrissie, another famous mathematician. Chrissie, unlike most Athenians was a worshipper of Poseidon, another powerful god, who, in their mythology (religion), had had differences with Athena, and they were still at odds. Freedom of religion was pretty much allowed in the democratic Athens, and Chrissie was not alone. There were many in

Athens, even among the aristocracy, who worshipped Poseidon, who was also God of the Sea.

Georgia. the King, loved to visit the site. She was a high-born member in the aristocracy, and ruled over the Council, also usually highly-born people. She spent most of her time with Lena, making suggestions. It was Georgia who suggested a sculpt of both Poseidon and Athena on the west wall of the Parthenon facing one another (a gesture of peace, or further hostility?) Georgia's body-guard and loyal follower, Dan, was always at her side. Dan was also a strategos (full general) in the Athenian arny, and, physically, an extremely powerful man. The Greek word dynatos translates into "powerful". Possibly coined from Dan ?

This massive construction project used an enormous amount of alabaster, a beautiful white, semi-opaque marble, that was quarried near Corinth and hauled by ox-cart to the Acropolis, about 15 miles away. Nece and Bill, two mathematicians, were in charge of this challenging operation. Bill was in charge of the quarry, and Nece would accompany the shipments of the huge slabs to the Acropolis, where they were shaped and worked into the architecture. Bill, a native Athenian, had an innate ability for calculation, and he was thrifty. Very little of the precious marble went to waste. Nece, born in Sparta, was a perfect "wagon boss". Her whip was ever ready to keep a slave or an ox moving, but she kept her slaves and oxen well-fed and healthy as a rule, and her deliveries were almost always on schedule.

The head Athenian magistrate was Monica. Incredibly wise, and a teacher of philosophy, she answered only to the Council or the King. Philosophy was very important in Athens, because of their desire for learning, and their ethical nature. The ancient Greek philen-(love) and the ancient soph-(wisdom), gives us our modern word. Athenian ethics were strict, but not restrictive, and Monica spent a lot more time in the classroom than she did on the bench. She also spent a lot of time with Lena, the architect, helping to keep the statuary and ornamentation as authentic as possible, yet beautiful.

The treasury and the mint, where the bronze and gold coins were minted, was to be moved to the unfinished temple basement, but were now in downtown Athens. Most streets in Athens were unnamed, ant the mint was unofficially on Chrimata Poicos,(Money Street). Dawn was the treasurer and banker of Athens, and she was usually referred to as the "Lady of Chrimata Poicos", Born in Epirus, to the Northwest, she was shrewd, but fairly honest, and she was highly respected. She was also very wealthy, and an influence to be reckoned with. Pup and Bonnie, both Athenians by birth, were her chief engravers, and their talents were often needed at the Acropolis to do some of the more intricate work on the statues and other adornments.

The upper surface of the Acropolis was only three hectares in area (about 7 1/2 acres). The temples to the various gods all had other functions, and a spacious government and courts building was also planned. Streets, squares, and access had to be carefully laid out on this small plot. This is where Nina and Paul excelled. Athens had fine paved roads as a result of their expertise, and under Gaet's supervision, they now had the roads almost all in place, allowing the heavy materials to be brought on site. Construction was moving along as per schedule. Nina and Paul were also well-known for their preparation of the Olympics surfaces where the popular games were played.

Tammy sent a runner to summon Lena to the temple. The last huge crossbeam had been raised and put into place, and it was almost 1/2 meter short. Bill, at the quarry, had never made a mistake like this before. Lena arrived and the two architects together studied the inscriptions on the massive piece. It was indeed intended to be the last beam of the temple. It could be fitted, filled in, and would suffice, but both architects felt it would fail within a few centuries, and opted to reject it. Ordering and obtaining a new one would take around 4 months, but the delay was inevitable. They decided to lower it, reshape it, and use it as a beam on a smaller building, cancelling the order for that beam. Sending a runner to the quarry with the exact specifications for the beam, and the message to Bill, they resumed operations.

The most famous, and probably the most accurate Oracle in Athens was a rather mysterious young lady named Lisa. There was no doubt she had psychic powers, and if the Gods spoke, it would be through her. She wielded enormous power, and when the

Gods "spoke" through Lisa, Georgia listened. Lisa had been troubled with dreams of an impending plague, and the King was nervous. What had they done to the Gods to deserve this?

Although progressing well, the project had occurring problems. Ros, the model for the statue of Athena, had "gotten with child", and it was starting to show. Sculpting was usually from the top down, but in this case Karen had the "middle" done first, and then worked up and down from there. Athenian ingenuity was unsurpassed.

The Athenians ate well. The mountainous terrain was perfect for goats, and goatherding was not looked down upon. The sea was an endless source of food, and a wealthy farmer to the west, Mike, supplied various fruits and vegetables, including the fabulous wine grapes and the wine that was always in demand. Mike seldom came to Athens, but when he did, after completing his business with the methodical banker, Dawn, who usually cheated him a little, he would go "on the town". He was a playboy, buying drinks for everyone, and the ladies loved him. Leaving, he would always take a few young ladies with him to "help in the vineyards". These ladies would be returned on his next visit, when he would abscond with some different ones.

The seer, Lisa, had been a student of Chrissy's but dropped out to become a student of philosophy under Monica, but left there, also, after she started having her "visions". A very attractive maiden, on her first trip to the Acropolis, she had been "stricken" by the imposing, handsome architect, Gaet. A persistent young woman, she started hanging around the site, and it was becoming disruptive. Monica and Georgia were helpless to do anything, as Lisa said the Gods had ordained she and Gaet be together. Who can find fault with the Gods?

The smaller temple in honor of Zeus was almost completed about the time the last cross-beam of the Parthenon arrived and was installed. The project was in its final phases.

Most of the fortifications of Athens were to the east, as the dreaded and warlike Persians and Ottomans would occasionally attack from that direction. There were rumblings from Sparta, to the south, but The Athenian diplomats had almost always avoided conflict. The famous Athenian diplomat, Doo, had studied rhetoric for years under Monica, Except for possibly Monica, herself, Doo was the fastest talker in Athens, and seldom lost a battle in "the war of words".

Nece always rode near the head of the caravan. She was cursing and barking orders. It was always something! A broken axle on a loaded cart would take many hours to repair. She sent a runner ahead to inform Athens. The road at this point wasn't wide enough to send the other wagons ahead, as they couldn't get by. She signalled the caravan to stop. Where was Elaine? Elaine was second in command here, and usually rode about four carts back. She had probably spotted a unicorn and was pursuing the elusive creature. Well, luck to her! No one had ever caught one to her knowledge. Elaine, born in Crete, was always chasing something, usually a man. Nece swore under her breath and resumed barking orders.

CHAPTER II

Mike, the wealthy farmer, was paying Athens his periodic visit for money and fun, and Lena and Tammy had ceased operations for the day. The fun-loving, free-spending farmer-vintner was treating the town, as usual, and most of the workers had left to join in the fun. When the flamboyant Mike came to Athens, it was a holiday. Most of the work in progress at this time was merely adornment anyway. The marble shipments had dried up, and a court hearing would begin tomorrow, when the Magistrate, Monica, and a picked jury would try the case.

Marc, the Corinthian owner of the quarry, had a contract with the city of Athens, and billed the city by the cubic meter for marble removed. Bill's mathematicians would record the measurements meticulously, calculate the amount, and send the invoices periodically to Dawn, the Athenian treasurer, along with the bills for labor and other expenses. Dawn would then ship the required amount of drachmas to Bill, and he and Nece would pay the bills. Marc had said the last payment was too low, sending her a higher bill. Dawn, the penurious treasurer and banker, had balked at the last request for funding, and work on the nearly-finished structures on the Acropolis was in limbo. Dawn, under pressure, had petitioned Monica for a magistrate's ruling, and a court hearing was set.

Monica was seated at the head of the forum. The raised throne-like seat directly behind her was where Georgia, the King, would soon be seated. The King loved the courts. Georgia was the only person who could legally overrule Monica, as she had Supreme power. She, in her wisdom, had never done so. Chrissie, Lilly and a few of their students were seated at a marble-topped table, poring over and auditing the records and measurements of the period in question. The beloved King Georgia entered, followed by the powerful Dan, and seated herself.

A five-man jury had been impanelled and seated. Doo, attorney and diplomat, would examine (question) on behalf of Athens, and Tricia, a fast talker from Corinth, was her opponent. Marc and his mathematicians were seated to the left, and Bill, Nece, and their two mathematicians to the right, along with Dawn, the treasurer.

Lilly approached the bench, informing Monica the audit was complete, and the trial commenced. Lilly, the first witness, said the audit indicated no evidence of wrongdoing. All calculations were correct, and that the disparity was in the volume of marble shipped to Athens during the period. Doo and Tricia both declined questioning, and Bill was called.

There was a brief interruption as Ros's baby girl began wailing, and Ros was escorted to the anteroom. Bill, seated, was being examined by Tricia. Bill stated that, Yes, the two mathematicians at his table were the two who had measured the marble in question. Tricia asked if he had any reason to think either of them would falsify a measurement, and Bill replied, "Absolutely not." Tricia sat, and Doo asked Bll how long the two had been with him in Corinth, and Bill replied, "Over 5 years." Doo asked if either had brought their metraios with them to court, and Bill assured her they both had. Doo asked Bill to explain to the jury what a metraio was. Bill explained that almost all mathematicians ended up in the building trade or surveying, and that accurate measurement was of the utmost importance. Therefore, each mathematician usually had a personal metraio. A metraio being an object exactly one meter in length, and graduated into one-hundredths. Most were wooden, well crafted, even sometimes ornately adorned. Just call it a Grecian yardstick, if you like.

Nece was not called, and Marc took the stand. Tricia ascertained through Marc that Athens had been purchasing some marble from him for over 30 years, with no previous problems. He billed Athens by the number of cubic meters quarried at the going rate, and that was the final price. Yes, the two mathematicians with him had taken his measurements. Marc always had the shipments measured and calculated, also, for verification. The two were identified as Ed, who had been with Marc for over 10 years, and Carol, whom he had hired about 5 months ago upon her graduation. Tricia immediately requested that the four measuring standards be brought to the bench. Monica stood the four on end, placed them together, and selected one. This was a very expensive and ornate piece of equipment. It proved to be Carol's, and it was almost 1 1/2 centimeters short.

Carol had been a disciple of Chrissie's, and her very expensive metraio had been presented by her family as a graduation gift. This was confirmed by Chrissie, who had been present at the graduation.

Carol, an excellent young mathematician, purchased a new metraio and kept her job. The jury was paid and dismissed, and Marc was satisfied that he had been paid the exact and proper amount for the marble. Most importantly, the marble shipments to the Acropolis were resumed.

The Acropolis displayed what was probably the last big project using the classical Doric architectural order, The stately Doric columns gave way to the more popular Corinthian. The colums are not solid pieces, as they appear. They are hollow, fitted together, and the cavity is filled, usually with wax.

Georgia was a little nervous with Lisa not being in Athens. Very God-fearing and dedicated to her subjects, she was nervous with her" link to the heavens" away. Lisa was in Olympia with Gaet, who was finishing a project. Georgia resisted the impulse to send a runner to Gaet ordering him to Athens.

Lilly and Chrissie were both obssessed with the idea that man could fly, and had made countless drawings and models, all failing so far. Lilly knew that somehow they needed to get some type of power into the craft, and all they had to work with was fire. Chrissie posed the idea that if they could heat air and contain it somehow they would have a lighter—than-air craft. Both were working on this concept and weren't far from making a hot-air balloon two thousand years or so before one was actually made.

Pup and Bonnie were at the Acropolis almost daily now. The year was 431BC, and they were doing some final intricate engraving on several works of art. Pup was fast but he was careless, and Bonnie was always busy touching up Pup's mistakes. The mint and treasury were on the "hill" now, and most of the government had been moved. The huge statue of Athena was nearly complete, No longer needed, Ros had left, and Karen was personally finishing up the majestic sculpture.

Visitors to Athens were so impressed with the completed Acropolis, especially the Temple of Athena, that many high-born citizens from other cities were now sending their offspring to Athens to study architecture under Lena or Tammy.

Athens suffered a terrible plague in 430BC, one year later. Lisa had periodically warned of this, yet they were unprepared for the most part Llittle was known about pestilence even though the Athenian physicians were among the finest in the world. Athens survived.

We have met the beloved and wise King, Georgia—the perfect leader, really. She had good citizenry, and she protected more than she ruled, with the powerful Athenian general, Dan, always protective and at her side. The two learned architects, Tammy and Lena, who's dedication made them refuse to use a less-than-perfect beam, although they knew it would cause a critical delay. Gaet, the handsome architect, and his able assistants, Nina and Paul, ever willing to build another superb surface.

We have met Karen, the sculptor and artisan, who helped make the Temple of Athena (Parthenon) one of the most ornate and stately structures in the world. Ros, the patient and beautiful model, who, even through childbirth posed for countless days until she was no longer needed. Lilly and Chrissie, the two mathematicians, who almost discovered flight thousands of years in advance of the technology required to do so.

We have met Dawn, the methodical treasurer and banker, who refused to see Athens cheated, and oversaw the financing of probably the largest construction project of the era. Pup, the speedy but careless engraver, and Bonnie, who cleaned up after him. Bill, the dedicated overseer at the quarry, who lived and worked in the dust, heat, and cold for many years. Nece, the persistent and capable supplier who was almost always on schedule, and the adventurous Elaine, her second in command.

We have met Mike, the devil-may-care wealthy supplier of provender who was always a welcome sight in Athens, where he would be paid and then party with the citizens until his departure. The psychic oracle, Lisa, whose troubled prophetic dreams were heeded by the King, herself, and her passionate attraction to the handsome architect, Gaet.

We have met the learned magistrate and philosopher, Monica, whose desire for truth, and not for power, influenced her decisions. Doo, her disciple, who could prevent armed conflict with wise words Tricia, the thorough Corinthian attorney. Marc, the Corinthian who sold them the precious, beautiful marble, who had made an honest mistake. Ed and Carol, two great Corinthian mathematicians.

This handful of people, in a period of 25 years or so, were directly or indirectly involved in the completion of a Grecian Monument that was destined to live forever.

At this point of time in history, Athens was moving into it's heyday. Within one hundred years most of Greece would be under one rule, and it's magnificent Capitol would be in Athens. Of course, there were the inevitable conflicts in between. Corinth, Sparta, and many others would have or had had their brief moments of glory, but Athens and Greece were to have five centuries or so of it.

THE END

HIGH SCHOOL FUN

CHAPTER I

The faculty at Eagletown High School was arguably the best in the state. An inordinate number of alumni had attained higher education, left their small hometown, and had become renowned in their field. The state Board of Education had sent Dr. Caro and Dr. Dale, two eminent educators who sat on the Board, to Eagletown for a few months to sit in at the school and attempt to discover why so many "super-grads" were coming from this particular high school. On the train, they had jokingly agreed that with "today's kids" it had to be the "water".

Arriving on Sunday, they were surprised to see what a clean, colorful, and peaceful small town Eagletown really was. They checked in at the Eagletown Hotel, the town's finest. At four stories, the hotel seemed out of place in this small town, and they were pleasantly surprised with the service there. A very pretty young lady with a name tag that identified her as "Lisa" quickly assigned them adjoining rooms and rang for assistance with the luggage. Lisa and a handsome young fellow with a name tag that said

"Dan" escorted them to their rooms and opened the windows, giving them menus to the dining room, and showing them where everything was.

Dale tipped Dan as he was leaving and casually asked Dan if he had gone to High School in Eagletown. Dan politely replied that he was currently a senior at EHS, and worked at the hotel after school and some weekends. Inquiring as to Lisa's status, Dan said Lisa also was a senior at EHS.

The Eagletown Hotel Dining room was a bit large to be cozy, but it was so quaint and clean it seemed so. The linen covered tables were very inviting. Caro and Dale entered and were met by a young, attractive, blond maiden who seated them to their choice. On a hunch, Dr. Dale asked the young hostess, Debbie (on her name tag) if she had attended EHS, and she smiled, replying that she was in her senior year.

Midway through their meal, a table adjoining theirs emptied and a rather large, muscular young busboy came out and was efficiently clearing the vacated table. Dr. Caro was intrigued by all this, and asked the young man (Ric) if he attended EHS. Ric stated politely and proudly he was a senior this year. Jokingly, Caro said, "I'll bet you play football." Ric answered, "Right tackle."

The two Doctors wanted to be at the High School early and were a bit tired from the trip, but decided to have a nightcap at the bar before retiring. They were both a bit intrigued by the fact that so many high schoolers here were seemed to hold jobs, and they discussed it over their drinks. They had certainly been impressed by the polite, capable students they had met so far, and were anxious to set foot in Eagletown High.

The two visiting educators shook hands with Lena, the attractive, youthful appearing Superintendent of Eagletown High School, and with Mike, the ruggedly handsome principal. Arriving at EHS they had been surprised at how small the school building was. Maybe fifty by eighty feet square, two stories high, and red brick, it appeared much too small for a modern High School.

Made comfortable, and seated, they were chatting with the two school officials. Dr. Caro had extended plaudits for the past results of the school, and Dr. Dale had remarked that in "these" times it was a difficult to find an institution with a record as impeccable as this. He added that they were here to analyze Eagletown's approach to education and to determine if some aspects could possibly be adopted statewide to improve badly needed overall student performance.

Lena folded her hands, cleared her throat, and said it just might be class size. They had 23 seniors this year, about normal. Mike, the principal, added that it might be the discipline. They had strict discipline here. Dr. Dale inquired as to the faculty. "You must have a very large, dedicated, experienced faculty here to graduate so many to major universities".

Lena spoke up, "An enormous amount of our learning here is in Study Hall. The introduction and lecturing is done in the classroom, and the work is done in Study Hall, where Tammy and the students work together on any weaknesses. Occasionally a classroom teacher will be summoned to Study Hall to assist."

Dr. Caro was a bit puzzled over this, but said nothing. Instead, she asked, "How many classroom teachers do you have?"

"Mike teaches two math classes daily as well as being football coach, and I teach two English classes and one Latin class daily. In addition, Georgia teaches Latin and English full time. Lanita and Stella are history teachers. In addition. Lanita teaches one English class, and Stella is also our basketball coach. Our other math teachers are Jojo and Dawn, who is also the tennis coach. Including Tammy, eight in all."

The Administration desk and office was on the second floor center, and was quite small. One quite attractive lady introduced as Donna seemed to handle all the office business quite efficiently. They had just met the entire administrative staff of EHS.

A strikingly pretty young lady entered and went to the counter overlooking Donna's desk. Lena informed the visitors this was a senior named Jean, and she was checking in late because she worked at the local coffee shop until nearly eleven. Jean had one morning class, and that was English IV with Georgia from eleven until lunch.

Dr. Caro wanted to see this Study Hall, and Dr. Dale wanted to sit in on English IV.

Lena introduced Caro to Tammy, the Study Hall teacher. Tammy seemed young to be a teacher, really. Extremely pretty and very lively, she greeted Dr. Caro warmly, and said she was at her disposal.

Seated at Tammy's raised desk, Caro surveyed the room. About twice the size of a normal classroom, the interior wall was lined floor to ceiling with books. Opposite the library was a bank of personal computers, all occupied by students, and there were five elongated tables in the center that could each seat up to ten students. Three of these were partially covered with textbooks, and occupied, with the students conversing animatedly. The fourth table had three sitting students, and one standing over them, seemingly explaining something. The fifth table was unoccupied.

A hand went up at a computer and Tammy excused herself. Whatever problem the very pretty young lady at the computer had was soon solved, and Tammy returned, with the young lady typing away again.

Tammy seated herself and smiled at Dr. Caro. "Before you ask, that young lady is Ros, one of our fine sophomores. She is very meticulous and had come upon a mistake in the material she was typing. Eagletown High does not offer a typing course. However, almost no one graduates from here without the ability to type at least fifty words per minute. Most of our seniors can type well over sixty and with ease. They learn it here in Study Hall on the computers with some formal assistance and the use of Gregg manuals. It saves the District money and makes it fun for them. We hold speed competitions occasionally and it brings out the best in the kids."

Tammy continued, "The three busy tables you see are where the studying is being done. There are almost always Sophomores, Juniors, and Seniors at each table. The nearest table is the Math table. The next table is the English and Latin table, and the far table is the History and (unofficially) Geography table. The study of History involves Geography intensely, but we need no Geography classes at this level. It is taught in grades 5 through 7 here."

Dr. Caro pointed to the fourth table, and Tammy continued, "That is our remedial table. Students who are difficult to teach, or, you might say, are slow to learn, use that table to receive remedial tutoring by upperclassmen, and on some occasions, faculty. These students almost always respond. If not, in time they go to the fifth table. Chrissie, the senior you see lecturing there, has completed with honors all we at EHS have to offer, and is assisting the faculty. This gives her experience as a leader, good review on the subject, practice in public speaking, and a sense of pride when a student responds. She is also a forward on our basketball team."

"We weed them out early." Tammy paused a moment, then pointed, "The three students at table four, Scott, Karen, and Pup are all sophomores. All effort will be made to keep them abreast of the others, but if we fail they will be at table five. "

Dr. Caro wanted to know more about the empty table five, but the bell rang, signalling noon recess.

CHAPTER II

Dr. Caro asked Tammy how to get to the school cafeteria, and Tammy blushed slightly. "Eagletown High has no cafeteria. Eagletown is so small most students can easily walk or bicycle home for lunch. A few bring their own, and the eight rural students we bus usually bring their own lunches. I'm going to Monica's Cafe for a salad and you're welcome to join me. Monica's is only a block away. She's a sweetheart, and her food is delicious."

Just then, Dr. Dale and a rather tall, imposing woman, introduced as Georgia, entered. They chatted a few minutes, then the four set off on foot for Monica's Cafe.

Monica's Cafe wasn't a hole-in-the-wall. Clean, roomy, and modern, it contained around eight tables, a long, low counter with stools, and around twenty diners when the four arrived. The hostess, Monica, was a handsome, well-dressed and efficient person. Tammy introduced her to the two visiting educators, and Monica graciously remarked that she was surprised. She had flatteringly thought them to be "new students".

Discussion at the table was underway immediately. Dr. Dale remarked that the state mandated High School Cafeterias, and he thought the Federal Department of Education did also. Georgia looked at Tammy knowingly, smiled, and replied," Dr. Dale. we could care less here in Eagletown what the Feds mandate. We accept no Federal money, and pray we never have to do so. As to the state mandate, we fall under the clause that exempts schools under 125 enrollment."

"We have a cafeteria in our elementary school, and, by our standards, it is a failure. It is expensive, and too much food is wasted. Children eat what they like to eat, not what we force upon them. We are considering closing it."

Caro changed the subject, remarking that EHS appeared to be a low-budget school, having no unecessary faculty, and almost no administrative staff. Was it patterned after charter schools, possibly?

Tammy answered. "The Eagletown School Board is very conscious of the School District's financial impact upon the community, and, yes, we try not to waste resources. However, our primary concern is educating children, not saving money. With small class sizes and virtually no minority enrollment, we haven't had to adopt any of the many expensive, inneffective, and wasteful programs the inner city schools are forced into. No one on the faculty here is even a union member."

Dr. Dale glanced up just as Mike entered the lunchroom. Mike was accompanied by the most stunning, callipygous woman he had ever seen. Mike approached, introduced Stella, pulled up two more chairs, and he and Stella joined the group. Mike knew almost everyone in Eagletown, as he had been mayor for years. He told Monica he wanted a "Mike" burger, winking at her. Stella ordered a BLT and iced tea.

Lena and Donna were 'brown-baggers", almost always bringing their own lunches. Sitting at Donna's desk, chatting, suddenly the phone rang. Donna picked up the phone, "Eagletown High School, this is Donna." Listening, she made a notation on her calendar. "It will be fine. Thank you for calling." Lena looked questioningly at Donna. "Lilly?" Donna giggled. "Bridge day at the east forty."

Eagletown and environs had about ten really good contract bridge players, and Lilly, Cliff's mother, was probably the best of the lot. They would assemble every other Tuesday afternoon and "battle" it out, rain, shine, or sickness notwithstanding. Lilly would invariably call the school to get permission for her son, Cliff, a High School Junior, to drive to school that day, as she needed some "errands" taken care of and he could run them after school. Cliff was president of the Junior class, very popular, and an excellent student. Living on a large farm east of town and off the bus route, Lilly normally drove him in and picked him up.

EHS did not normally allow students to drive to school. Too many problems. They could walk, be dropped off, or bicycle. The school district operated one full-sized bus for the grade school children and two for the nearer surrounding rural children.

Dr. Dale went to study hall, and Dr. Caro had been escorted to Dawn's Math classroom on the first floor. Dawn was a trim, well-tanned, attractive, and athletic appearing woman. Caro recognized Pup and Karen, two sophomores from study hall, and Dan, the efficient bellhop at the hotel. This class was Plane Geometry, and Caro could tell by the opened textbooks they were nearing the end of the course.

Dawn introduced Dr. Caro, from the State Board of Education, and a murmur arose in the classroom. Dawn explained to Caro that all students here were sophomores, except Dan. Dan was a senior, had excelled in both Plane and Solid Geometry, and was here to assist for part of the period.

Dawn just turned the class over to Dan, and, turning to Dr. Caro, she stood and smiled, saying, "Now, we tutor for about forty-five minutes."

Introducing the students as Karen, Bill, Pup, and Sarah, she sat down with them at the rear of the classroom and went into the most intense session of tutoring Dr. Caro had ever seen. Dawn begged them to ask questions. "How can I help you learn if you don't tell me what you don't understand?" seemed to be her approach to teaching, and it seemed to work. Dawn loved communication between student and teacher. It let the teacher know what the child needed better than any test result ever could. Dawn could seem complimentary, critical, and helpful all at the same time. The kids loved her, and were responding.

It was obvious to Caro that Dawn was a very dedicated classroom teacher, and her objective was not just teaching Geometry to these kids. It was to make sure they understood it. She would be relentless on a point until she was assured they understood it completely.

Dr. Dale in Study Hall was enjoying chatting with the always exuberant, vivacious Tammy. She was informative and knowledgeable, and, it seemed to Dale, did very little actual work. Occasionally a hand would go up, or a student would approach Tammy with a question or a request.

Dr. Dale had a few things bothering him. He turned to Tammy, "It seems odd that your school offers only three subjects, Math, Language, and History. Doesn't that seem a bit too basic for a High School Diploma?"

"Dr. Dale, may I ask you a question? In retrospect, when you attended High School, what three High School subjects did you enroll in that helped you the most in forming your esteemed career as an educator?"

Dale thought a moment, finally replying, "Good question, Tammy. A good command of English is necessary, of course. Some Math is imperative, even in everyday life. Thirdly, History, I suppose. I agree that knowledge of history has far more importance later in life than most students realize."

Tammy added, "We offer General Science (basic Physics) in grades 8 and 9. English begins in earnest in Grade 6 and never lets up. Health habits in grades 5 and 6. Geography in grades 5 through 7. Home economics is taught in the home. We could offer it, but the young ladies would still learn more from their mothers. As you can see, typing is almost mandatory. Lena wants to add Physics to the curriculum next year, and the School Board has been receptive. Jojo is tutoring some students now in Physics."

By Friday the two Doctors were acquainted with more than a few students, were familiar with all the classrooms, and were on a first name basis with all faculty. Something was nagging both. It seemed to be related to a lack of teaching resulting in a plethora of learning. All the faculty seemed to spend the majority of their time tutoring only those few students who needed help. In addition, Dr. Dale had secured a Friday dinner date with the alluring history teacher, Stella.

CHAPTER III

Lena, Dawn, and Lanita were to pick up Dr. Caro in the hotel lobby Saturday at 10:30 for some shopping at the Emporium and a light lunch at Monica's. Then they planned to go to the Eagletown annual Chile Cookoff at the fairgrounds. Dr. Caro had just awakened and shut off her alarm, when she thought she heard Dr. Dale's door close.

Opening her door slightly, she could see Dale headed for the stairs, wearing jeans and a button-down shirt. Probably going to the hotel coffee shop for breakfast. She would wish him good morning on the way out. She had no idea what his plans were for the day. He might even want to join her group.

The Eagletown Emporium was a shopper's paradise. Quality goods at quality prices. Everyone in the huge store seemed to know the three teachers, and Caro was introduced to several parents of high schoolers she knew. The parents seemed to have a very good relationship with the school, and the teachers seemed well-liked and respected.

Lanita was sort of a fitness oriented person, and she wanted to go to the Sporting Goods section, She was an expert archer and wanted to browse some new equipment. When they entered, there was a very trim, well-dressed, classy blonde lady at the counter conversing with the young man there. Greetings were exchanged, and Dr. Caro met Lilly, Cliff's mother, and Gaet, a rather handsome, well-mannered high school senior.

Lilly had just purchased a large beverage cooler which she was going to fill with soft drinks and ice to take to the Cookoff. Lilly was a very wealthy farmer, and it seemed she was always donating something to whatever event was happening. The proceeds from the Cookoff were usually used by the Chamber of Commerce to finance yet another event. Eagletown loved its "get-togethers". Lilly was also a judge in the Cookoff and was eager to get to the fairgrounds.

Lena and Dawn and Caro watched Lanita expertly fire an arrow into just about the center of a bullseye target about 15 yards away backed by several bales of straw. Placing four more arrows on the bale next to her, she smiled at them and went into action. Swish! Swish! Less than ten seconds later, the center of the target was covered with arrows. Lanita told Gaet to place the bow and a dozen arrows on her account, and wrap them up.

Gaet was a salesman nonpareil. On the Saturdays he worked, Gilles, the store manager, usually

assigned him to the department where he assumed
they'd have the most traffic. Gaet was fast, and he
was a relentless salesman. Dawn told Caro that
Gilles loved to tell the story about the fussy lady in
the Shoe Department.

Gaet had tried about a dozen pairs of shoes on her,
and she was still undecided. He was starting to run
out of her size, and wanted to make a sale. Gaet
approached the lady with yet one more shoe box.
Looking around nervously, Gaet finally sat on the
stool in front of her, opening the box. Looking at her
admiringly, Gaet remarked, "I can see that you really
know shoes. You will be the first lady in Eagletown
to see these shoes." Looking furtively around again,
Gaet removed one shoe from the box. "I can't sell
these, but I wanted you to see them," he said. The
lady was intrigued by now, and asked Gaet why he
couldn't sell them. Gaet was really getting "nervous"
now, and glancing around. "Because once they've
been seen, we will have orders for hundreds of
pairs, and the shipment has not arrived. It may be a
month or so yet."

The lady was so fascinated by these "new" shoes,
that she insisted Gaet sell them to her now. He
finally told her that if she bought two other pairs
also, he could probably let her buy them now and
still keep his job. The lady proudly left the Emporium
with three new pairs of shoes.

Dr. Caro loved Monica already, and her clean eatery
was almost a daily "must". Monica had already gone

to the fairgrounds to supervise the preparation of her Cookoff entry. Dawn loved chili and remarked that Monica's Cookoff chile was even better than the delicious bowl here at the Cafe. Donna had now joined the group and they all decided on iced tea, saving their appetites for the Cookoff.

The chatter finally got around to education, as usual, and Caro asked if the students who worked after school and on weekend days did so out of need.

Lena answered, "A need, yes, but not a necessarily a monetary need. We have found that when it comes to learning, some students are a bit (ahem) lazy. Learning is work for some students and if those students won't work, they won't learn. We try to find those students a job. This teaches them to work, and the proceeds from the work gives them a bit of independence. Their grades rebound almost immediately as they realize, now being in the work force, that education has its blessings later in life. Most importantly, they have learned to work."

The early May day was warm and sunny. The Eagletown fairgrounds was located in a wooded area at the northwest edge of town. Tents had been set up, and the Cookoff was in full swing when the ladies arrived.

Admission was free, and when they entered, they spied Mike at a bank of beer kegs. Mike waved them over, and poured each a large plastic cup of the cold liquid. It appeared that Mike had had a few.

He was enjoying himself. The beer was free, with a "donations" basket, now filling with money, on a table beside the kegs.

Dr. Dale appeared out of nowhere with three empty cups which Mike refilled. Stopping to chat, Dr. Dale said that he loved chili and had his own recipe. When he had heard of the Cookoff, he had told Stella, and she had entered him in the contest, insisting on helping with the preparation. He had arisen early, gone to the market, and then on to the fairgrounds. Stella had met him there, along with Georgia, the English teacher, who had always wanted to "learn how to make good chile". Dale was a bit inebriated as this was about his fifth beer and was confident his chili would win the cookoff.

The "chile" tents were across the compound from the beer tent and the vendor tents, and the ladies strolled across, following Dale to his assigned tent. There were seven tents. Six were for entrants and the center tent was the judges tent. Each tent had a long table and a dozen or so chairs.

The aroma of the delicious cooking was getting to Dr. Caro, having foregone lunch. Nothing bashful about Dawn. She just picked up a bowl, handing it to Stella to fill. Several people were in the tent sampling the chile already, and apparently it was very good chile. Georgia handed Caro a small bowlful along with a white plastic spoon, telling her that there was "more where that came from". Dale liked a lot of suet in his chile, a mixture of coarsely ground beef and pork, and he liked a lot of peppers and garlic, carefully minced. It was really more of a "green" chile, and he served it with hot, buttered tortillas.

Caro looked down at this reddish-green oily looking concoction with little green and red and white things floating around in it, and she started to push the bowl away. She was surprised it smelled so good. She glanced across the table at Lanita and Donna. Donna was going after it like a wolf, fanning her mouth and chasing it with beer and buttered tortilla. Lanita had picked up her bowl and was almost drinking it. Sighing, the hungry Caro tore off a chunk of tortilla, buttered it, dipped in the bowl, and put it in her mouth. Wow!!! The pungent, salted, heavily spiced broth was delicious with the tortilla. Now, the heat was getting to her. Not enough to burn her lips or tongue: actually very pleasant. Dawn was already on her third bowl when Caro finished hers and handed it to Stella for a refill.

It was crunch time now. Cliff came in from the judges' tent with a tray and three small bowls. Their samples would now go to the judges for evaluation. Dr. Caro had had three delicious bowls, and actually could have had another. She thought to herself, "If Dale's chile doesn't win, there is some damned good chile being made here in Eagletown."

The three judges were Lilly, the farmer, Tammy, the study hall teacher, and Chuck, the reporter from the TALON. They, like Dr. Caro, had never eaten green chile before, and consumed it with the tortilla and beer chasers. Lilly was first to speak." It's absolutely delicious, but is it chile?" Chuck had sweat running down his nose, and said, "If it isn't, it oughta be." Tammy, who could eat fire, said, jokingly, fanning her mouth with her hands, "Needs more peppers."

Dr. Dale's entry won the cookoff and had introduced Eagletown to "green" chili. The ensuing mob at his tent quickly wiped out his remaining supply and the cookoff was over. Monica had placed second and was graciously begging Dale for his recipe.

By Wednesday, Monica had added "Dale's Chile" to her menu, and by Friday, Dr. Dale was a sort of hero in Eagletown.

CHAPTER IV

The Eagletown High School building was much larger than it appeared from the front. A subterranean gymnasiun had been added to the rear of the building with an auditorium above it. The large auditorium stage was also used for band instrument practice. Dr. Dale and Mike had just finished a handball session, showered, and Dr. Dale was in the office with Donna, going over some transcripts. It was Monday, and basically the last day of school. A few remaining tests would be taken for two days, then Thursday and Friday would basically end things for this term.

Dale had to admit to himself that he had never seen such high marks. Four B's, one B-, and one C, all sophomores, and all other marks were B+ or higher. That C belonged to Pup, who had an IQ of over 125, and the work habits of a grasshopper. Donna said all these lower marks would improve immeasurably in the following two years. They always did under the intense tutoring the kids received here. Mike and Lena were relentless in finding the weak points in a poor student, and then focusing on that. Mike, and many times Lena or Dawn had had many "heart-to-heart" talks with parents, telling them their child was going to learn whether they helped or not.

They looked up as there was a tapping sound in the doorway. It was the voluptuous Stella, beckoning with her finger and pointing to her wrist watch. Dale looked at Donna. "Excuse me.", and meekly followed the shapely, tightly-clothed figure down the hallway. Donna giggled and went back to her transcripts.

Dr. Caro was in Lanita's History class, listening to today's story unfold. Lanita loved History, the story of the world, and she taught it that way. She knew the story well all the way from the Neanderthal to today's news, and she was a walking encyclopedia. In addition, she was a magnificent speaker, making it interesting for her students. They loved her class and hung onto every word.

Stopping occasionally and looking at her students, she would ask a few questions. Then, if satisfied with the response, she would continue with the story. She was a rapid but clear speaker, slowing occasionally to stress an event, or a name, and then continuing. Dr. Caro, in about twenty-five minutes, had heard the best chronologically perfect synopsis of the Italian Renaissance she could ever hope to hear, presented almost romantically. She thought to herself, "This should be a teacher's college, not a High School."

Dr, Caro had accompanied Stella to Study Hall, as she was helping out there this period, and she wanted him present. Study Hall was almost full. It appeared almost all the seniors were there. He noticed Georgia at the English table and Jojo was at the math table. Tammy was at a crowded table four, along with Mike and Dawn and six or so students. Despite the crowded conditions, table 5 was unoccupied.

At EHS, the faculty spent most of their time in Study Hall during the last few days of a term. Their Seniors were forgotten now. They had done all they could for them, and they were as good as gone. The Faculty was already focusing on the next term, and the Study Hall was perfect for a cram session on any weaknesses. A little summer work was recommended, but not required.

Stella joined Lanita at the History table, and Dr. Caro seated himself. Stella took over on one end of the table, Standing, she seemed to know what every student there knew, and what they didn't. She didn't lecture. She went from student to student with eye contact and no notes whatever, and told them what they might want to read or watch (on television) this summer. She issued some praise, and she issued some criticism, mostly for lack of effort. Then she just visited with the kids, asking what plans they had for vacation.

Dr. Dale excused himself and went to the math table, joining Dr. Caro, where Jojo was winding up her session with the kids. She ended her short lecture by telling them that they would love Algebra, and even Geometry once they understood it better, and she would do all she could to help them. Jojo was a rather tall, willowy lady, with long legs, and it was hard (probably) for some of the older boys to concentrate in her classes. She ended by saying she was looking forward to working with them next term. Then, they just chatted, mostly about what they were planning on doing this summer.

The intercom from the central office came on, and after a pause, Superintendent Lena's voice came over: "Attention! All students, except table 5, are dismissed for the day. The remaining classes will resume tomorrow at ten AM. All table 5 students report to Study Hall within fifteen minutes, please." There was a big cheer for the late start tomorrow, and then students were filing from Study Hall. Dr. Dale looked at Dr. Caro questioningly, and she just shrugged. Then he looked at his watch. it was 2:45PM. They were both intrigued by however table 5 figured in all this, and were not about to leave Study Hall.

A few minutes later, Lena and Mike reentered and approached. "You're welcome to sit in on this, if you like", Lena said, smiling. "You'll find it a bit (ahem) extracurricular." Dr. Caro replied, "I'm sure Dr. Dale will agree that we're both anticipating it."

The table was filling now. Tammy was with the two state educators within easy earshot of table five, and was explaining a bit of this. Pup, Karen, and Scott were told to sit together at one end of the table facing Lena and Mike. The others were allowed to sit at random. Soon the table was full, and Tammy was asked to close the door.

Mike took over the meeting by asking Chrissie, in attendance, how much she had earned from her work at EHS this semester. Chrissie replied that the school had paid her a little over $600 for the semester for her ten or so hours weekly tutoring underclassmen. She told Mike she had saved about half of it, and intended to work while attending the State Teachers College next year. Chrissie was a born teacher and she was the EHS valedictorian. She said her commencement speech was concering the benefits of work.

Jean was next. Jean was a straight A student despite putting in around twenty hours weekly at the Coffee Shop. She had made around $1250 the last semester and had saved some for next year at the university. She had worked up to cashier and loved her job. She, too, would continue working.

Dan, this year's Salutatorian, had worked two jobs. He had made, counting tips, around $500 at the hotel, and about $250 at EHS. Sadly, he was almost broke now, but still employed at the hotel. However, with some help from his father, he had the newest, shiniest motorcycle in Eagletown. Dan was going to Duke next year, and intended to find a job near the University.

The Study Hall door opened and Donna came in with Gaet. Gaet went to Tammy, handing her a bundle of papers wrapped in a rubber band, telling her something. Tammy went to her desk and removed a calculator from a drawer, putting on her glasses. Gaet sat at the table, and Donna joined Caro and Dale.

The bubbly, pretty Lisa was next. Seemingly always happy, she said she loved her job, and she had made almost $700 dollars at the hotel, and had saved most for her summer and freshman college year. She said she was looking forward to working full-time there for the next few months.

The big, powerful Ric was next. He said he had made almost $450 in the hotel dining room, and had quit yesterday. He had received a full scholarship from the State University, and was leaving next week, as he needed to engage in football tryouts. He added, smiling, that he just wasn't into washing any more dishes right now.

Dr. Dale was beginning to see the reasoning behind all these testimonials. They were all being made for the benefit of the three underachieving sophomores, who were partially in awe of these popular seniors.

Debbie was next, saying she had worked up to hostess in the dining room at the hotel, and had made a little over $800 plus maybe another $100 in tips this semester. She "sort of" liked her work, and would stay on at the hotel for another six weeks or so to defray the expense of getting settled in at the University.

There was a pause then, and Mike went over and sat with Tammy. The kids at the table were just chatting away, waiting on Mike to return. Lena had joined Mike and Tammy, and suddenly all three became animated, looking at each other, as Tammy handed them a final figure on whatever she'd been doing. Mike and Lena returned to table 5 and asked Gaet about his job at the Emporium.

Gaet said he was a salesman at the Emporium, working Saturday and a few afternoons during the week. Gaet added that he loved sales work. He didn't know how much he'd made, but he added he'd spent a lot of it. Lena interrupted here, "Gaet does not get an hourly wage. He is paid a commission on his sales only. No sales, no money. It seems Gaet did quite well." Looking at the paper in her hand, Lena continued, "Since January, Gaet has sold over $120,000 in goods from the Emporium." Pause, then continuing, "His commissions totaled almost $14,000. In addition Gaet received sales incentive income of over $600, and two achievement bonuses of $250. Gaet made a total of over $15,000 in less than five months." A loud murmur went up, and everyone was staring at Gaet in awe. Gaet said he had no idea he'd made this much, but said he'd stay on at the Emporium for a few months into the summer, adding that his boss, Gilles, seemed to really like him.

There was a pause, as everyone was trying to talk to Gaet at the same time. Mike then took over. "A few more questions and we can let you seniors leave. First of all, we faculty here at the High School commend each and every one of you, You have been excellent students, and, speaking with your employers, exemplary employees. Now, any seniors who have sat here at table 5 before, please raise your hand."

All hands went up, except Chrissie's. Mike said, "If it was at the end of your sophomore year, raise your hand again." The hands stayed up. Lena dismissed the seniors, saying that EHS was proud of each and every one of them.

Now, Mike got down to some serious business, telling the three sophomores he and the school would appreciate it if they worked a few hours a week during their vacation this summer. After the success stories they had just heard, and knowing that all those fabulous seniors had at one time been at this table had really impressed them.

Mike had a list of all the businesses needing part-time help this summer, and passed the list around. Karen decided to apply at the Eagletown Drug Store. They needed a soda fountain employee, and she joked she'd like being a "jerk". Scott, the dreamer, wanted to go to the Emporium, as there was a stocking position open. Pup was to apply at the local creamery where he would help unload shipments and stock the coolers, as well as assist in deliveries to the local stores and restaurants. Mike and Lena wished them luck and assured them that should any problems arise, the school was here to help.

The kids were dismissed for the day, and Caro and Dale joined the group at the table. They were to leave Eagletown on the morning train tomorrow, and both were really a bit loath to leave. Eagletown was such a clean, orderly, and friendly town

Mike smiled at Dale and Caro. "Well, you have seen our table five, used one time per term. What would you call this table?" Dale finally answered. "Well, Mike, i can see where just the mystery of it would be a boon to discipline, and, frankly, I had no idea what to expect. To me it is sort of an "if all else fails" table." Dr. Caro said, laughingly,'" Seems like a "this is how it is" table to me." They all laughed.

Lena said they referred to it as the "Careers" table, as it had launched a few young people into the work force, letting them know that nothing should be free. It should be earned. Tammy laughingly added that she referred to it as the "dusty" table.

THE END

BAVARIAN FUN

CHAPTER I

The Castle

Deep in the dark hills of Bavaria, the gloomy, dark Frankenstein Castle was built into (or out of) a sheer cliff of solid granite. Adlerdorf, the small village a mile or so below the foreboding structure, was separated from the ominous castle above by a sheer, high rock wall constructed by the superstitious villagers many years ago because of the belief of a monster having been resurrected from the dead by the Castle's owner, Baron Dr. Frankenstein.

Many years later, the granddaughter of the infamous Baron, the wealthy Baroness Lisa Frankenstein had moved into the old deserted castle and the villagers had grudgingly installed a gate in the wall for access to her castle. Our story begins here, as the villagers are becoming once again a bit concerned that bizarre occurrences are going on inside the bowels of the ancient castle.

Since tha arrival of the Baroness Lisa and her entourage, many workmen had been summoned to the dreaded castle to perform remodeling and repair to the massive, ancient structure. The workmen always made sure to leave the dreaded castle area well before nightfall, and strange tales were being circulated by these tradesmen. The work had been completed weeks ago. The massive old structure was now much brighter with colorful paint, and was well-lit, even at night. A magnificent sight from the village, and the villagers were actually beginning to be proud of the beautiful, towering edifice. More and more tourists were arriving to view it, and the village was prospering.

The Baroness was never seen in Adlerdorf. To their knowledge she had not left the castle since her arrival. Her housekeeper, Dawn, a very stern, proper, attractive, and aloof woman, had always conducted her business in the village. Now accompanied by the dwarf hunchback, Pup, Dawn, always dressed in black, would purchase supplies and food for the staff at the castle, while their carriage driver, Gaet, would frequent Das Gasthaus, the village alehouse. Finished shopping, they would summon Gaet, load the carriage, and leave for the castle. The villagers were familiar with the little hunchback, Pup, as he had been the sole occupant of the castle since the death of the Baron Frankenstein, and had been seen in the the village on rare occasions. They were a bit nervous around him as they were uncertain of his age and of his mortality. Some speculated he may be as old as 110, well over two life spans at the time.

The first sign of any strange happenings occurred about a month after the castle was restored, when a villager disappeared. Bonnie, a young, pretty maiden, had gone through the gate late one afternoon to pick berries and hadn't returned. Afraid to open the gate at night, the search had begun the following morning, and there was no trace of Bonnie. Ruling out the possibility of a wild animal, they were all focusing on the castle above, but were loath to go there. They decided to return to the village and let the authorities handle the matter.

The Baroness, Lisa, as had her grandfather, had a burning desire to create eternal life, and she had known his work was incomplete, She had contracted with and gotten the famous Surgeon, Lena, to come to the castle and work with her in the laboratory there. Almost daily, equipment and supplies and a few people had arrived and been trundled up the winding rocky road to the castle. Everything was almost in place.

It had been forty-five years since the fearful villagers had finally stormed the castle to destroy the monster created by the mad Doctor Frankenstein. Having accomplished this, they fled the dreaded castle and never returned. Baron Mike Frankenstein was never seen again and was presumed to have either fled or perished.

To their knowledge, Pup, the faithful lab assistant to the Doctor, was the only known occupant of the castle for all those years.

Lisa had become frustrated. Her intense desire to create eternal life was progressing too slowly. She had finally gotten in contact with a villager named Lilly, who had informed her of the lone occupant of the deserted castle. Lisa had been at the castle as a child, and she remembered the gruesome creature as her grandfather's assistant. She had no idea what to expect to find at the old castle, but somehow she felt a visit there just might uncover some of Baron Mike's old journals, speeding her research immensely.

Lisa's crew was almost assembled. Dr. Lena, the surgeon, had written repeatedly on the subject of immortality, and many articles on the aging process. Dr. Chrissie, the newly-arrived neurosurgeon, had eagerly accepted the offer to come. Bill and Karen, two retired police inspectors, from New York City and Scotland Yard respectively, had joined in the venture. The roomy old castle would be searched very thoroughly. Ros, from Stuttgart, was probably the world's foremost expert in the field of old European castles, and was eager to study the old structure. Dan, Lisa's valet and bodyguard, and Dawn, head of household at the castle, rounded out her staff for the time being. The only other ocupant of the castle at this time was Gaet, the carriageman.

The cavernous castle had revealed very few secrets during the first months of search. Ros had noticed many similarities between this castle and many others she had researched, but only one sliding panel had been found so far, and the passage was short, leading only to another room on the same floor. Due to the sheer size of the castle, it could be a long time before they found Mike's laboratory, assuming there was one.

Finally, a day at the castle proved eventful in that they finally "found" Pup, and Bonnie, the adventurous village maiden arrived at the castle. Bill and Karen, the analytical policemen, were certain that if there were a large laboratory on the grounds, it would be underground, and were searching the ground floor for a hollow wall, or some clue as to how to get under the castle. Ros had assured them that there was almost certain to be an access to some type of staircase or tunnel leading underground.

Lisa and Dan had taken a bright sunlit stroll around the old castle, and suddenly, nearing some overgrown bushes where the west wall joined the mountain, they "flushed" what they thought was a deer at first, scurrying for cover. The alert Dan grabbed the fleeing Pup and held on to him. When Lisa saw what Dan had caught, she couldn't believe her eyes. It was Igor, her grandfather's loyal assistant, and he hadn't aged a day as far as she could tell.

Lisa was ecstatic. Igor would know where the access to the lab was, and could also give her much information. It was almost impossible he could be still alive. She remembered him well. She remembered he was mute, but somewhat literate. She also knew he knew more about her grandfather, Mike, than anyone. Pup's only sound was a sort of gutteral growl, "Ahhh-goor," hence his nickname.

Lena had also taken advantage of the beautiful late afternoon, and had strolled almost to he village wall, where she came upon a very comely maiden picking wild plums. Exchanging greetings, they began conversing. Bonnie seemed surprised that Lena lived at the castle, and was a bit alarmed at first. Lena told her how the castle had all been redone, how beautiful it was, and very comfortable. Bonnie already really liked Dr. Lena, and hesitatingly agreed to come up with her and see the castle. Lena assured her they would have Dan or Gaet take her back to the village before nightfall.

Igor had settled down some and had apparently lost some of his fear of the newcomers. He seemed to faintly remember Lisa, and stayed near her. He had been hiding nearby for months, but where? Lisa didn't want to pressure him prematurely. She knew they needed his confidence.

Lena arrived at the castle with Bonnie, where Bonnie was welcomed and given a tour of the huge, beautiful castle. It was nearing nightfall when Dan and Bonnie left for the village. Arriving, the gate was already closed. Bonnie knew the villagers wouldn't open the gate after dusk, and resigned herself to a night at the dreaded castle. Somehow it seemed ominous again. She shivered.

CHAPTER II

The Lost Laboratory

The trip back to the castle was slow. Dan was an expert carriageman, but the tortuous, dark, narrow road was barely illuminated by the carriage lights, and he proceeded slowly, Bonnie was terrified and kept inching closer and closer to Dan. She was somehow attracted to the big, handsome bodyguard. Rounding the last bend, she was relieved to see the porte-cochere was well-lit and inviting.

Gaet was waiting for the carriage and horses, and they had arrived just in time for dinner. Igor, as he was called at the castle, had disappeared. Bonnie had a sumptuous dinner and her first glass of wine ever, listening to a lot of talk she barely understood. She did ascertain that they were examining the old castle very closely, but why? The gracious Baroness assigned her to spend the night with Lena. Lena's cavernous bedroom had a second smaller, comfortable bed, and Bonnie, surprisingly, had a good night.

The following day Lisa decided to make her first trip to the village when they returned Bonnie. She needed to employ three or four good groundskeepers, a gameskeeper and hunter to keep the castle supplied with fowl and game, and some household personnel. Ros was occupied mapping and studying some of the artifacts found in the old castle. Drs. Lena and Chrissie were busy setting up a laboratory in a large room on the ground floor, where they could experiment with lab animals, and Karen and Bill were methodically searching yet another area of the ground floor.

The carriage arrived in Adlerdorf shortly after lunch, and Dawn set out to purchase a few supplies. Villagers were watching with awe as Bonnie exited the carriage, waved to them, hugged Lisa and Dawn, and went home. Inquiring, Lisa was able to find her correspondent, Lilly, present herself, and explain why she was in the village.
Lilly, a confident, attractive, blond lady, was more than willing to help.

They decided to operate out of Lilly's neat, clean cottage, a good central location. Lilly paid several of the neighborhood children to inform the villagers the Baroness was here and hiring, and the wages were excellent.

Bonnie was the first applicant, and the first one hired. She opted to serve full-time and live at the castle. She would work under Dawn. Jojo, a willowy, attractive, young lady, the next hiree, was assigned to Dawn, and she would commute daily from the village. Georgia, a capable, attractive woman was hired as head groundskeeper, and she would hire her own staff. Temporarily, at least, Georgia would live in the village. Interviewing her, Lisa felt she had chosen well. She wanted the overgrown, stark castle grounds to be beautiful again, and felt Georgia could accomplish it. Lilly was curious about the castle, and agreed to "fill in" for Jojo or Bonnie if needed, and help out on special occasions. No more villagers appeared. Lisa thanked Lilly and was preparing to leave when a young, very pretty, athletic looking woman appeared, inquiring about the gameskeeper position. Her name was Doo, and she was a bowhunter. Doo was skilled at dressing animals, and was a journeyman butcher. Lisa hired her and Doo decided to reside at the castle. Gaet would return at midday tomorrow to pick up Bonnie and Doo and transport them along with their belongings to their new home.

Back at the castle, Igor had appeared out of nowhere, and was watching Bill, who wore a stethoscope and was tapping on walls and floors with a mallet. Igor appeared a bit worked up about this, and Bill was growing uneasy. Karen appeared and they finished "scoping" the area and decided to call it a day.

A week later, the first experiments were being performed in the still makeshift lab. Igor's apparent agelessness was discussed as being possibly related to the Baron Mike's work, and Lena wanted a blood sample, but Lisa wasn't ready to permit that yet. She needed Igor's confidence, and she was getting nowhere obtaining it.

No one could figure where Igor disappeared or reappeared from. Everyone was on the alert to keep their eyes open, even follow him if possible. The Baroness and Ros were sure he was hiding underneath the castle somewhere.

Doo was dressing a deer on the lawn near a wooded area just east of the castle when she spotted Igor. Not moving a muscle, she watched as the little hunchback disappeared into a small grove of bushes near the cliff. Grabbing her bow, she launched an arrow into the exact spot to mark it. Shouting at Georgia, working nearby, to join her, they raced toward the arrow.

Igor had indeed vanished. No trace could be found. Bill and Karen were summoned and began searching the area for a cave or a break in the cliff. Karen was making a drawing of the area in relation to the castle which she would present to Ros.

With the aid of the drawing and assuming Igor had gone underground, Ros now had a pretty good idea of what rooms needed to be sounded out. Bill and Karen diligently went to work, and several hours later, they had found a hollow-sounding interior wall. It was getting late and they decided to resume tomorrow.

Jojo and Georgia now lived in the castle. Dinner had become an adventure, as they all dined together. The servants quarters were a large part of the ground floor rear, and were spacious, cool and clean.

The Baroness was elated that they may have found a passage to the lower regions of the castle. She was excited and rose early, heading for the coffee. Almost everyone in the castle was already there. Ros had made a large diagram of the possibilities here, She suspected the wall would grant access to a stairway, as this particular castle wasn't laid out to accommodate many passageways.

Bill and Karen had studied the area thoroughly and no lever or anything that might attain access had been found. Lisa, somehow, was hesitant to tear part of the wall out, and she was thinking. Ros had exhausted her possibilities of what to look for.

Igor suddenly appeared in their midst, seemingly distraught, waving his arms and muttering. Approaching Lisa, he tugged her skirt and led her to the fireplace. Placing his thumb against a small indentation just to the left of the fireplace, he moved forward, placing both feet on the same tile. The wall behind Karen silently swung open on its pivot, revealing a wide staircase going downward.

Igor ran to the staircase and faced the group, as though he were defending it. He pointed down, then pointed to Lisa. He paused, then pointed to Chrissie, and beckoned, starting down. The stairway was lit by incandescents and went down maybe 25 feet, ending in a rather large tiled landing. The three were now facing a large double-door.

Igor went to the door, turned, and gave Lisa a rather long, pleading look. Then he opened the unlocked door.

It was obviously Mike's laboratory. Brightly iluminated, and large. White walls with electrical components and switches seemingly everywhere. Lab tables containing all kinds of jars and receptacles surrounded two gurney—type raised tables. One was empty, but the second supported a rectangular, coffin-shaped glass receptacle which they curiously approached.

Igor was getting pretty upset by now. He didn't seem to want them near the contents. Trying to protect the object on the table, Igor made a writing motion with his hands. Chrissie found and gave Igor paper and pencil. He scribbled on the paper for some time, finally handing the paper to Lisa. The Baroness looked puzzled for a few moments, then her face went white. She had to support herself from falling. Chrissie took the paper from her hand and read it. Igor had made a crude drawing of the table and the receptacle, and he had written one word on the receptacle —MASTER!

CHAPTER III

Preparing for the Resurrection

Igor was growling and muttering as Lisa and Dr. Chrissie peered into the liquid-filled receptacle. The almost clear, yellowish liquid was transparent enough that they could see the outline of what appeared to be a cadaver submerged in it. Igor was at their elbows watching closely, and muttering wildly. He threw a switch and a bright light above the table illuminated the contents. The Baroness gasped, clutching her throat. It was her grandfather, Mike, just as she remembered him from childhood! Igor excitedly handed her another scrap of paper. "MASTER LIVE." Lisa had to sit down and collect her thoughts. She dispatched Chrissie to the landing to summon Dr. Lena.

An hour or so later, despite Igor's not letting them touch or disturb anything, they were beginning to sort things out somewhat. A gruesome find, for sure. Mike was fully submerged in this liquid clad only in a loin-cloth type garment, and the back of his skull and his brain were missing. It was impossible that he could be alive, but Igor kept pointing and making motions that he was fine and they could somehow reassemble him.

Dr. Lena wanted a sample of the liquid to analyze, and Dr. Chrissie was wanting to examine the remains more closely, meaning she wanted a tissue sample. Igor would have none of this, and he was starting to get a bit violent.

Lisa was very observant. She had noticed a few relationships beginning to form among the castle personnel, primarily that between the maiden, Bonnie, and her trusted bodyguard, Dan, who were spending a lot of time together. She had noticed that whenever Igor appeared at the castle, he now seemed to gravitate to Dawn, and sort of hang out around her. Lisa sent for Dawn and Ros to come to the lab.

Ros knew there had to be an office somewhere adjoining the lab, as records must be kept, and as amazing as this lab was, some sort of trail of evidence as to what had happened here in years past might be found. Igor, always keeping an eye on the others, was hampering her search, and she was getting irritated.

Dawn, after her initial shock, was filled in on what had been discovered here. Igor was visibly happy to see her and had calmed down immeasurably.

If Mike had any other marks on his body, they were undetectable from this position. Dr. Lena borrowed

Igor's pencil and wrote," What happen master to die?" Igor went to the stairwell, pointed upwards, and then made a downward, tumbling motion. Had Mike fallen down the rocky stairs? Igor seemed to indicate that he had. They could assume he had fallen and probably hit his head, but why were part of his skull and his brain missing?

Many unanswered questions here. It seemed logical that whoever preserved the body had also preserved the brain. There were some organs and body parts pickled in jars on the tables, but no brains.

Dr. Lena had surreptititiously gotten a small vial of the liquid from the receptacle and she was eager to analyze it. Ros simply couldn't find any other openings off the lab, and they decided to leave, lay out a plan, and return later. Lisa didn't want to lose contact with Igor, as she knew they needed him at their beck and call. She had a few private words with Dawn, and they all left the lab.

Lisa immediately put Igor on the payroll. He showed her "his" room, on the second floor of the castle. He was assigned to Dawn, and moved his meager belongings into the castle.

Several uneventful days went by, and the lab below the castle was left undisturbed. Igor was almost always somewhere near Dawn, and had even gone to the village with her and Gaet. This shopping became one of his chores. Igor really liked Gaet and

Gaet would sometimes let him handle the carriage over the safer parts of the road.

The two physicians were a bit puzzled after attempting the analysis of the "embalming" fluid. Dr. Lena had determined it to be an enzyme of some sort, but couldn't categorize it. She had read a medical paper on longevity some years ago where the physician averred that enzymes would probably be involved in the "Fountain of Youth" were such a thing even possible. Medical science had been experimenting with enzymes for years, and there had been some small breakthroughs.

Igor was unique in that, if the Baroness were correct, he should be well over 100 years old, and, despite his genetic condition, still extremely spry. Was it possible that he ingested this stuff? Many possibilities here. An injection? Periodic doses? One dose for life? Dr. Lena was determined to find out.

Dr. Chrissy and Lisa had planned to sneak into the lab and get a tissue sample from Mike's cadaver when Dawn went to the village, taking Igor, but they couldn't get the wall panel to open. Ros was called and she, too, failed. Igor remained their only access to the lab, and it was a huge setback.

The Baroness and the two doctors had a conference and arrived upon a plan. They would put it into action the following morning.

Lilly, Lisa's friend from the village had now moved into the castle, joining the staff there. Her arrival had been a boon to Dawn, as Igor took an immediate liking to the pretty, blond lady, giving Dawn a respite.

The Baroness had summoned Igor to open the panel to the stairway and she, Ros, the two doctors, and Dawn had been anxiously waiting some time now. Finally, Lilly entered, followed by Igor. Igor was agitated over something, and refused to open the panel. Finally, he indicated he would, but only he and Lilly would go to the lab. Lisa was puzzled as to why Igor had suddenly acquired all this apparent affection for Lilly, but she trusted Lilly, and agreed. She knew she would get a full report from Lilly later. Dr. Chrissie got Liilly aside and said she desperately need a tissue sample from the remains, handing her some glass slides and a small scalpel.

Needless to say, Lilly was nervous as they entered the old laboratory. Igor made a quick check to make sure nothing had been disturbed, and motioned for her to approach the table with the glass "coffin" on it, proudly showing her the contents, and then tugging at her to see something else. He moved a table from against a wall, then moved to the wall, and it swung open, revealing yet another large room.

Motioning the half-frightened Lilly inside, he partly closed the door. The room, brightly lit, contained a large filing cabinet, an ancient roll-top desk completely covered with papers and junk, and a table against one wall on which were four large, round, glass jar-shaped containers. The containers appeared to contain human brains, each submerged in a bubbling liquid of some sort, and they had electric wiring coming out of them. The containers had an eerie glow to them, and all the frightened Lilly wanted to do was to leave and go back up to the castle.

Suddenly, Igor became alert, rushed to the door leading to the lab, and Lilly could now hear voices in the laboratory. Bill, Doo, and Karen had just entered the lab from yet another opening in the far wall, and were looking around in amazement. Igor was muttering and growling, running toward the table containing the old Baron. Doo, startled, had even drawn down on Igor with her bow.

When they saw Lilly, they relaxed, approaching the table. Trying to assure Igor they meant no harm, they studied the contents of the glass container. It was exactly as it had been described to them. Igor was really agitated now, and he hurriedly closed the panel to the adjoining room, sealing it off for now. Lilly seized the moment, and, reaching down inside the "casket", obtained a chunk of Mike's skin. Much to Igor's relief, they then left the lab, going up to the castle.

Lisa was elated to hear that Bill and Karen had found the tunnel entrance from the eastern grounds of the castle to the hidden lab. Now they had access at will. She knew they'd never go in without poor Igor, though. Somehow, she'd grown fond of the pathetic creature.

Both Chrissie and Lena had had extensive forensic experience, and when Lilly gave them the tissue sample, they rushed to their laboratory. Every test they ran indicated it to be live tissue, even though that was almost impossible. They finally concluded it was indeed live tissue. Therefore Baron Mike was, as Igor had stated, not medically dead!

A resurrection was possible, but not without his brain. Dr. Chrissie had always dreamed of performing a brain transplant, but this was an altogether different situation. It would be a brain replacement.

Dr. Lena, always analytical, posed her thoughts on what may have happened. The Baroness Lisa, having reassured Igor that things would be just fine, had joined them, followed by Ros. They conversed at length, with Lena giving input, then discussion, then more input.

When the villagers had stormed the castle many years ago, they had probably wanted to destroy the Baron, but somehow he had eluded them, made it into the stairwell, and, possibly due to haste, he had fallen down the rocky incline, fatally damaging himself.

Igor, his devoted servant and assistant, had dragged him to the table, and, surgically removing the damaged part of his skull, had preserved him in the liquid, to be "reassembled" at a future date. Igor knew a brain needed electrical stimulus, and had removed the Baron's brain and probably had preserved it. The Baron had experimented on cadavers for years, and, assisting him, Igor had probably acquired a good knowledge of the Barom's macabre work.

With Lilly's knowledge, they were now aware of the preserved brains in the Baron's "office" and could only hope that one of them was the one that been removed from his skull. They had a lot of work to do, Countless measurements to be made, personnel trained, and Dr. Chrissie, the famous brain surgeon, was to be in charge of the operation. Many old records to study, and the two physicians were eager to enter the room off the laboratory.

CHAPTER IV
What Hath God Wrought

By taking measurements of Mike's inner cranium, and studying the knife strokes made by Igor when removing Mike's brain, they had been able to determine which of the four brains had indeed been surgically removed from the Baron. The brain tissue was alive, and the brain appeared to be functioning. Dr. Chrissie was becoming optimistic that the operation could actually be performed. Things were progressing, but no date had been set for the operation. Still many things to do.

Igor had preserved the missing, fractured piece of Mike's skull and scalp between his feet and the end of the receptacle, and examination of it showed the fracture was healed and the bone was alive.

It was decided that both surgeons would perform the operation. Ros was being trained to be the anesthetist, and was getting efficient with the pentathol, as well as learning the medical language. Dr. Chrissie wanted as little pentathol used as possible. Jojo, sure-handed and quick, would be between the two surgeons with the trays of tools required.

Igor wanted to assist somehow, but was told he could only watch, and he was told not to cry out or interfere in any way, lest his Master perish.

A pair of oxygen tanks were put in place. Lighting was good, masks and surgical gowns ready, and preparations for the operation were nearly in place.

A final pre-operation conference was called for tomorrow morning, and then a date could be set for the operation. Chrissie and Lena were optimistic as to the outcome, as they had, technically, at least, such a healthy patient. Mike's vital signs seemed excellent in this hibernated state.

Mike's old records had yielded a mountain of information. He had gotten Pup, (as he was called in the village) at an early age, trained him somewhat in medicine, and they had become grave-robbers. The Baron had used fresh cadavers for his grisly experiments, and they would usually dig them up, if possible, the very night after they were buried. The Baron had kept good records, even to having purchased at least one still warm cadaver. There was no doubt that he was demented, and the two surgeons, discussing it, really didn't want to bring such a monster back into the world.

There was no evidence of the Baron "creating" his own cadavers, however it was a possibility. The enzyme he had formulated was a miracle drug indeed. Igor had inadvertently almost immortalized himself just by immersing his hands frequently in the oily liquid. No formula for this amazing discovery could be found in Mike's records and journals, to their disappointment. There was no doubt that Mike was a brilliant scientist, albeit a bit unscrupulous.

The villagers had begun locking the gate to the castle road at night again, as they were more and more concerned as to the what was going on there. Even the formerly popular Georgia and Doo were now being shunned in the village. Nothing was being delivered to the castle now, and Gaet and Dan were making almost daily trips to Adlerdorf for supplies.

Dr. Chrissie had formed a very close relationship with the Baroness, Lisa, and she knew Lisa desperately wanted her grandfather to be restored. Dr. Chrissie had arrived at a plan. She would first consult with Dr. Lena, and proceed from there.

Igor was no problem now that he knew they were trying to help him, and had actually become quite helpful. He spent a lot of time showing Ros the seldom frequented upper reaches of the old castle, and she had recovered, studied, and tagged many valuable artifacts. In addition, the personnel at the castle could now go to the old lab and do whatever was necessary without impediment.

Dr. Chrissie had told Dr. Lena what she planned to do, and Lena agreed it should work, but should they tell Lisa? Discussing it further, they decided not to, and they would proceed. They would inform no one.

That afternoon, the two surgeons went to the deserted laboratory office and performed a lobotomy on the brain of Dr. Frankenstein. Normally a prefrontal would surgically remove the section of the brain that causes violent or aberrant behavior in the patient. Rarely performed, it had proven effective in some cases. Dr. Chrissie, in this case had not done a radical, as the Baron wasn't actually homicidal to their knowledge, and too methodical to be manic. They hoped, for the Baroness' sake, it would work.

Their primary concerns with this procedure were that Mike might forget the formula to the mysterious enzyme, and the other being that they didn't want to turn him into a completely passive vegetable. Well, it was done now, and they left the lab, now eager to perform the surgery.

Mike's surgery was scheduled for tomorrow morning at 9AM. Everyone involved was to be in the laboratory at 8:AM for prepping, a partial rehearsa, and a briefing from the surgeons. Lisa was so excited at the possibility of her grandfather being really alive that she slept very little that night.

Everyone was assembled in the laboratory and both entrances were closed, with Bill and Doo guarding the outer entrance and Karen and Dan were in the castle at the other. An intrusion could be critical.

Lisa, Igor, Bonnie, Lilly, and Dawn were seated near the table with a good view of the operation. Dr. Chrissie would explain things pretty much as they unfolded, and the spectators were advised to make no noise at all and no sudden moves. The brain had been moved to the head of the table next to Jojo. Twelve minutes to go.

Dr. Lena had completed placing the IV for the pentathol in Mike's arm. She gave Ros a piercing "You're on, kid!" look, and assisted Chrissie blocking Mike into a sitting position. Mikes legs and arms were then strapped tightly to the table. Five minutes to go.

Both surgeons knew that the most delicate part of this operation was reconnecting the optic nerves. Once they were connected, the operation would be fully underway. The brain then could be partially inserted, the carotids sutured, and then the crucial final placement of the brain inside the cranium. The otic nerves would then be connected. Lastly, if all went as planned, the placement, stapling and suturing of the posterior skull plate. Probably at least a three-hour job, even for two skilled surgeons.

The operation was progressing well. the brain was now in the cavity, and blood was flowing. Ros was administering pentathol at Dr. Chrissie's command. Jojo was almost heroic. She was adept at quickly slamming the proper tool into the surgeons' outstretched gloved hands, Lilly, fascinated, had to refrain from cheering her on.

Mike's signs were still very good, and he was showing signs of life now. His chest was rising and falling slightly, and his body would occasionally twitch. Knowing they had gotten blood to the brain in time to prevent any atrophy, the two surgeons were relaxing somewhat. Satisfied that the brain was exactly where they wanted it, they leisurely, replaced the mssing skull place and secured it. The operation was technically over, the liquid was drained from the table, and Baron Mike Frankenstein was in post-op intensive care.

Surprisingly, Igor had behaved well. He had appeared a bit agitated when the brain was removed from the jar, but it was so carefully handled he had settled down. He had been told maybe one more day before he could approach and see Master up close. The two surgeons and Ros and Jojo spent the night in the lab monitoring and tending to their patient. The next morning Mike was fed via IV, and Dr. Chrissie felt they could probably allow him to regain consciousness around noon.

The word spread, and at noon the entire staff of the castle was in the lab. The pentathol IV tube had been removed. Mike had a healthy pallor to his cheeks. His chest was rising and falling steadily, and his breathing was regular and strong.

Everyone was seated and the anesthetic was wearing off. Only moments now and they would see one the oldest live men on earth, as Mike was approximately 125 years old, maybe more.

Mike stirred and groaned. His lips were moving, and his eyelids fluttered. Dr. Chrissie cautioned everyone that Mike was almost conscious now, and to remain silent, as Mike would be very weak for many days yet.

Mike stopped moaning and his eyes opened. Suddenly, with a curious jerky movement, he was in a sitting position. Mike had a smile on his face and his eyes were twinkling. He eyed the assembled people, and coming to rest on Igor, he said, in a loud, booming voice, "Hey, Igor! Fetch me my slippers and a dooby."

Mike then swung his legs over the side of the bed, scratched his hairy chest, smiled, studied his thighs for a moment, smiled again, then looked over the awe-stricken throng watching his every movement. Suddenly, he roared, "Anyone want to pair up for a few games of crib?"

THE END

A Few Limericks

There was a lady from the east side of Britain
Who was a flirt, and had some guys smitten.
'Til she ran into a guy,
Who remarked with a sigh,
"Nice act, but not my type of kitten."

There was a guy, all mouth in the lobby,
Said he was Brit, and also a bobby.
The Shrimp said with flair,
"You're so full of hot air
Muting your azz is becoming a hobby."

Pup bet on the old Detroit Tiggers
Who got beat by a team of big leaguers.
Pup said, "It's a shame
That a team of such fame
Should lose, but with my luck, it figures".

There was a lady who was expert at "fake-it".
She could, shudder, could moan, and could "shake-it".
'Til she got with a guy
Who was too young and too spry.
She thought," Lord, I'm gonna have to "make-it."

There was an old maid from the East Side of
Leeds,
Who rued her lost youth and her teens.
But she had had some chances;
Some at school dances,
And another once out in the weeds.

There was a lass from lower Manhattan
Who was a tease, and loved to go "cattin".
She went out with a beau
Who was soon ready to "go",
But she said, "Cool it. It ain't gonna happen."

Ode to the PITA

Chrissie was well-liked although a pain in the azz,
And when having a tantrum, could spout off real
fast.

There could be forty people patiently waiting to play
And she'd come into the lobby and spoil everyone's day.

She usually had a cold or some type of chit
Which she'd usually spread around for everyone to
get.

Never could figure why they liked her so well
'Cos whenever she showed, she'd raise Holy Hell.

I figured they'd ban her for all the ruckus she made
But God!, They loved her whenever she played.

Suddenly she changed, became quiet, demure,
What had made Chrissie so polite and so pure?

Had she gotten religion, had some type of attack?
Suddenly, everyone wanted the old Chrissie back.

Pup

People weren't playing much. Too quiet in Squares.
With Chrissie shut down, it was too much to bear.

We'll never know what happened. Maybe she had a relapse,
But she came in one day and was her old horse's azz.

She cussed and snorted, banged around on poor Dawn.
In no time at all they wished she'd be gone.

Then they all realized this was what they'd been missing,
This wild, noisy hoot they'd named PITA Chrissie.

Daring Rescue

They were lynching the Pup, his neck in the noose.
They'd caught him riding Mike's favorite cayuse.

The big oak tree had a wide-hanging limb
And if Pup had a future, 'twas getting pretty dim.

In the old Wild West, justice was swift and was sure
Making sure deeds like this did not reoccur.

Pup never asked for a smoke nor any last words;
Just looked at the sky, silently watching the birds.

A thunder of hooves, the bugles were blaring,
And onto the scene the Cavalry was tearing.

The Army Captain, Chrissie, with saber in hand,
Had surrounded this blood-thirsty mean lynching
band.

Monica and Lilly had drawn down on the blokes,
And they cut Pup loose from the wide spreading
oak.

Ken guarding the rear, they took him to Squares
And the little horse-thief was told to stay there.

His teamies needed him to play and win them some
games.
Not stealing people's horses and playing Jesse
James.

The Tombstone Saga

With the Clanton's in town, wasn't a soul to be seen.
The Clanton's were tough, and the Clantons were
mean.

Mike Earp, the deputy, and the dentist, Doc Pup
Had been drinking all night, and were just waking up.

Don Earp, the sheriff, was a lawman of renown,
And he had a reputation for cleaning up towns.

He was deadly with a shotgun and quick on the draw,
And had quickly made Tombstone a city of law.

The Clantons hated his guts and weren't leaving town

"Til this lawman they hated was somehow gunned down.

Tombstone had a corral at the west end of the street.
It was here the two clans were destined to meet.

Don handed Doc a shotgun and six or so rounds.
The three checked their weapons and were OK Corral bound

Another Earp joined in as they strode west on the street.
In just a few moments the two sides would meet.

The Clantons and McLaurys, they now numbered six.
But two were unarmed and stayed out of the mix.

The lawmen strode west, and at point-blank range
Guns were produced and shots were exchanged.

The gunfight was over in less than a minute
With several people hit, and two killed in it.

Over thirty shots fired, blue smoke clung in the air.
Only Ike Clanton and Don were still standing there.

Pup was wounded in the hip and Mike shot in the arm.
There were two dead Clantons, and Don was unharmed.

Many stories and legends from the wild, woolly west,
But this saga from Tombstone is always the best.

PUP

Surprise Party

Dawn's birthday was nearing and not a word for Pete's sake.
She wanted a big party with presents and cake.

She hmmm'ed and she hawed and had given out some clues,
But her efforts were failing and she was getting the blues.

One day to go, and everyone was still mum.
"Twas almost as though they all were struck dumb.

The dawn of her birthday she arose for the day.
She'd go into Squares, but wasn't going to play.

She had an E-Mail from Marie. No hint of a bash.
Dawn was now on the verge of a mental collapse.

An E-Mail from Bill! She could count on this guy!!
No mention of her birthday. Dawn was starting to cry.

"Twas time for the 4. Dawn was in disarray.
Not one Happy Birthday from anyone all day.

She went into Squares, her heart was now torn.
Her friends had left her so sad and forlorn.

The 4 was a bash!! Her name was in lights!
Presents and cake much to her delight.

Happy birthday to Dawn. Her friends were all cheering.
Dawn dug into the cake, her eyes happily tearing.

Good Book, Huh?

"Twas All-Hallows' Eve and Mike was tucked into bed.
His nightcap was was pulled way down on his head.

He picked up his book from the stand 'side his bed,
Which was written by Pup, and already half read.

A story of ghoulies and things of the night.
Mike loved anything that would give him a fright.

He read and he read 'til his eyes started to close.
His breathing grew shallow. He started to doze.

The book now lay on the bed by his side.
His eyes were closed and his breath came in sighs

Out from the book, like small puffs of steam,
Tiny ghosties and goblins got into his dreams.

Mike tossed and he turned. He screamed out in fright.
Never on earth had one had such a night.

Sweat poured from his body, as the ghosts, one by one,
Then returned to the book after having their fun.

Mike awoke with a start. He was covered with sweat,
His mind still reeling from the creatures he'd met.

He regained his senses, arose from his bed,
Had a big shot of whiskey, and to the door he did head.

He headed for Squares. His dander was up,
And when he got there he was gonna kill Pup.

Chrissie's Birthday

Another year had passed, and today was the day.
Chrissie was frantically checking for any more gray.

Enroute to her party, she was happy, yet grave,
Knowing, once arriving, she'd have to behave.

Dressed up real pretty, she was a sight to behold.
She was one of those people who never grew old.

She came into Squares amid a round of applause.
She stood in the doorway, bowing as she paused.

She greeted her friends, accepting some punch.
She was so happy today. She loved the whole
bunch.

You've heard of Dr. Jekyll and his alter-ego, Hyde?
What happened at the party will boggle your mind.

'Twas almost as though their guest had been purged.
Lady Chrissie disappeared and the PITA emerged.

She suddenly got loud, created a trerrible uproar,
Banging on peeps, spilling punch on the floor.

She then went over where her presents were piled.
Started ripping off wrappimgs like a three-year old child

Pup

She oohed and she aahed, made a few nasty faces,
Strewing ribbon and paper all over the place.

Then, clutching the gifts she wanted to keep
On her powerful legs she arose from the heap.

Grabbing the rest of the cake and going out the door,
She paused on the threshold and waved au revoir.

Watching her leave, her friends were all cheering,
Blowing her kisses and thanks for appearing.